PRAISE FOR

The Hive Mind at Work

"*The Hive Mind at Work* is a beacon of wisdom in navigating today's turbulent business landscape. McHale introduces a revolutionary model—Group Intelligence (GQ). Her insights are game-changing, offering a profound alternative to traditional change management. With a keen blend of teamwork, purpose, and resilience, the hive mindset captures the essence of what makes an organization thrive amid uncertainty." —Hubert Joly, former Best Buy CEO, senior lecturer Harvard Business School, and author of *The Heart of Business*

"*The Hive Mind at Work* disrupts the traditional approaches to workplace change management. Siobhán McHale challenges the limited perspectives of machine-like fixes or social network influencers. Her four-step method paired with real-world examples and action items provide a clear understanding of essential best practices we all can implement. A must-read for anyone interested in meaningful and lasting organizational change." —Matt Abrahams, lecturer at Stanford GSB, host of *Think Fast, Talk Smart: The Podcast*, and author of *Think Faster, Talk Smarter*

"Siobhán McHale unveils a pioneering model for organizational change, emphasizing the critical role of Group Intelligence (GQ) inspired by the collective and purposeful dynamics observed in beehives. McHale's insights provide a fresh perspective that challenges traditional approaches, offering a comprehensive solution to the complex challenges businesses face in today's ever-changing landscape."

—Dr. Ruth Gotian, Thinkers50 #1 emerging management thinker in the world and author of *The Success Factor* and *The Financial Times Guide to Mentoring*

"Siobhán McHale has developed a proven method to deliver change fast and with less noise. Essential reading for anyone tasked with making change happen."

—Gary Hamel, visiting professor, London Business School

"Siobhán McHale has been the executive in charge of change in a series of large organizations. From this 'insider' role, she displays a deep understanding of how people behave in groups (as bees do!) and uses this to show us different ways to make change happen. An essential guide for managers, HR professionals, and advisers."

—Carolyn Taylor, global culture change expert and author of *Walking the Talk: Building a Culture for Success*

"Siobhán McHale is the genuine article. *The Hive Mind at Work* is a timely guide for managers, HR professionals, and advisers who want to create real and lasting transformation."

—Dr. Tasha Eurich, organizational psychologist and *New York Times* bestselling author of *Insight* and *Bankable Leadership*

"In a sea of business books, Siobhán McHale's *The Hive Mind at Work* stands out as a game-changer, reshaping our approach to organizational change with a revolutionary model based on Group Intelligence (GQ). Drawing inspiration from the collective brilliance of beehives, McHale doesn't just theorize; she provides a practical four-step road map grounded in real-world experiences. As someone who values actionable insights, I appreciate McHale's insider stories and her unique perspective as a change expert who has navigated the complexities of large organizations. This book isn't just about understanding change; it's about making it happen. Embrace the hive mindset, unlock Group Intelligence, and transform your approach to change in the ever-evolving business landscape."

—Mihaly Nagy, founder and CEO, The HR Congress

"In *The Hive Mind at Work*, Siobhán McHale presents a powerful metaphor for implementing sustainable change in our workplaces, using insights from how bees operate in their communities and applying them to companies and work teams. A powerful resource for change agents and business leaders."

—S. Chris Edmonds, speaker, author, and executive consultant with The Purposeful Culture Group

"Siobhán McHale has developed a unique approach to creating meaningful and lasting change that addresses today's complex challenges. An insightful read for leaders seeking to elevate their skills and organizations seeking a competitive advantage."

—Dr. Kate Barker, global adviser and chief future of work officer, NEOM

"Efforts to bring about change in the workplace typically fail because they do not address underlying issues. This is a must-read book if you want to learn how to avoid these pitfalls to create meaningful and lasting change."

—Jonah Berger, marketing professor at the Wharton School and bestselling author of *Contagious*

"True leaders understand the need for group intelligence during potentially dangerous transitions. *The Hive Mind at Work* is an expert guide to developing group intelligence thinking. Excellent book!"

—Oleg Konovalov, the da Vinci of visionary leadership, author of *The Vision Code*

"Siobhán McHale is globally recognized for her expertise in change and leadership. This book is filled with her 'insider' stories and her disruptive four-step approach to change. This is a must-read book if you want to learn how to implement successful workplace change."

—Peter F. Gallagher, ranked #1 change management global thought leader 2020–2023 by Thinkers360

"Nature is our greatest teacher. Through the observation of nature and understanding that organizations are living, breathing organisms, Siobhán McHale has developed a proven method that delivers change faster and with less noise. If you want your change efforts to be successful, you must read this book."

—Dr. Terry Jackson, TEDx speaker, global transformation leader, and challenger of organizational performance paradigms

"This book posed a personal challenge to me: Am I really putting into practice the ecosystem ideas I believe in? Do my friends and colleagues really form a hive mind with group intelligence beyond each other? Do our interactions with our customers and allies generate the patterns of change we hope for? Or are we perhaps stuck in group dynamics that are well-meaning but ineffective? Siobhán's step-by-step process is helping me make change where I need it most."

—James F. Moore, author of *Death of Competition*, and business ecosystems pioneer

"What a joy to read. Great book, great insights, great examples, super useful and usable. None of us are as smart as all of us, and the organizations that can tap into their hive mind will maintain relevance in an increasingly chaotic world. Those who ignore the laws described in this book are destined to go the way of the dinosaur!"

—Tony O'Driscoll, professor of business administration and engineering, Duke University, Durham, North Carolina

"Packed with useful case studies, Siobhán McHale explains why most change initiatives fail and how the complex ecosystem of change requires a hive mind instead of a top-down or linear approach. If you're embarking on change, this book is essential reading to set your organization up for successful change."

—Jude Jennison, Leaders by Nature, author of *Leading Through Uncertainty* and *OPUS: The Hidden Dynamics of Team Performance*

THE HIVE MIND AT WORK

THE HIVE MIND AT WORK

HARNESSING THE POWER OF GROUP INTELLIGENCE TO CREATE MEANINGFUL AND LASTING CHANGE

SIOBHÁN McHALE

HarperCollins Leadership
An Imprint of HarperCollins

Design by Neuwirth & Associates

ISBN 978-1-4002-4623-6 (eBook)
ISBN 978-1-4002-4622-9 (HC)

Library of Congress Cataloging-in-Publication Data
Library of Congress Cataloging-in-Publication application has been submitted.

Printed in the United States of America
24 25 26 27 28 LSC 10 9 8 7 6 5 4 3 2 1

I dedicate this book to all those
who strive to create better workplaces.

CONTENTS

Prologue: Bees Do It and So Do We xiii

1: Exploring the Hive's Wisdom 1
Harness Group Intelligence in the Service of Change

2: Simplifying Complexity 21
Map the Basic Patterns That Govern Behavior

3: Creating a Compelling Case for Change 41
Complete the Essential Groundwork

4: Testing New Flight Patterns 59
Experiment Before Rolling Out the Change

5: Making the Critical Change Decisions 77
Tap into the Wisdom of the Hive

6: Emerging Hive-Wide Leadership 95
Avoid the Three Critical Mistakes Bees Never Make

7: Nudging the Hive Forward 115
Overcoming Obstacles and Objections

8: Reaching Critical Mass 135
Create a Powerful Swarm

9: Aligning Technology and Processes 153
Install the Right Hive Infrastructure

10: Making the Change Stick 173
Prepare for Distractions and Surprises

Conclusion: The Evolving Hive 193

Acknowledgments 199
Notes 201
Index 235
About the Author 245

PROLOGUE

BEES DO IT AND SO DO WE

For so work the honey bees,
Creatures that by a rule in nature teach
The act of order to a peopled kingdom.
—William Shakespeare (*Henry V*, act 1, scene 2)

Growing up on a farm in Finea, a small village in southern Ireland, I watched the bees move like a single organism as they swarmed in our orchard. This led me to investigate the intricacies of natural ecosystems.

As a young adult, I attended Sheffield University, gained my master's degree in organizational psychology, and went on to spend the next three decades studying groups in the workplace. This experience taught me about the power of harnessing the Hive Mind and the group intelligence needed to create meaningful and lasting change.

My childhood experience watching the bees in our family's orchard launched a lifetime of research into group intelligence in complex ecosystems.

As I worked toward my degree in psychology, I gravitated to the study of workplace change, first as a management consultant, then as a hands-on change leader in organizations.

As an executive in charge of change in a series of international firms, I rolled up my sleeves and set to work, helping leaders at all levels make change happen. One of the most successful transformational change programs took place at the Melbourne-based Australia and New Zealand Banking Group (commonly known as ANZ).

My work there was featured as a case study at Harvard University written by John Kotter, the renowned professor of leadership who was at that time the foremost authority on managing change.

After seven years of hard work, ANZ went from the lowest performing financial institution in the country to the number one bank globally on the Dow Jones Sustainability Index. We achieved that goal using many of the tools and techniques you will learn about in *The Hive Mind at Work.*

This is not some theoretical approach that comes from the ivory tower but from the trenches where change really matters.

Much of my thinking goes against the theories that have dominated the change management discipline for decades, and my ideas often shatter some prevailing myths about transformation.

I fervently believe that organizational leaders need a new approach in this era of relentless innovation, global crises, ferocious competition, and unstoppable disruption.

My case studies come from groups I've worked with, either as an external consultant or an "insider" and the executive in charge of transformation (sometimes with names and organizations disguised in pseudonyms to protect client confidentiality).

In this book I will discuss and help you implement the Nine Laws of Group Dynamics I developed over the years, drawing on my knowledge of how bees do it and my experience with how we can harness group intelligence in our human organizations to create meaningful and lasting change.

What does this have to do with bees? Throughout this book we will explore the relevance of the Nine Laws to businesses seeking change. But before we jump into that subject, I'd like to prepare you for the journey by explaining how the behavior of bees beautifully illustrates the Nine Laws of Group Dynamics in action.

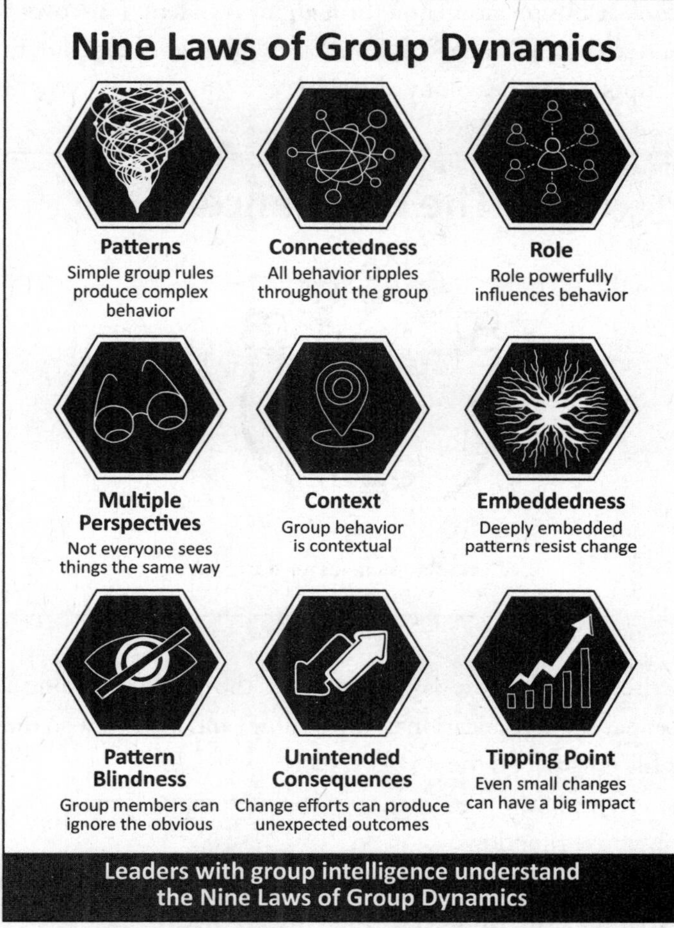

1. LAW OF PATTERNS: SIMPLE GROUP RULES PRODUCE COMPLEX BEHAVIOR.

The milling beehive may seem like a chaotic and disorganized throng, but certain patterns can explain the colony's behavior. The Austrian scientist Karl von Frisch uncovered this phenomenon when researching the way bees move. In a famous discovery, von Frisch found that bees performed a "waggle dance" to communicate the location of food supplies to fellow colony members.

As I look at this phenomenon through my own lens, I discover the Bee Dance Pattern where "finder" and "follower" bees work together to locate essential supplies for the colony's survival:

Von Frisch described the dance pattern as "the most astounding example of non-primate communication that we know" and in 1973 won the Nobel Prize for his research on the waggle dance.

Once you grasp the significance of the pattern, you can better understand how a hive functions.

Unlocking the secret to change in an organization means appreciating the power of the Hive Mind and group intelligence to make sense of what otherwise looks like a lot of chaotic milling about. When you carefully scrutinize the dancers, you can see the important patterns that influence organizational behavior.

2. LAW OF CONNECTEDNESS: ALL BEHAVIOR RIPPLES THROUGHOUT THE GROUP.

Imagine a flycatcher bird chasing after a honeybee as it forages among the lavender in a broad meadow. The frantic bee releases an alarm pheromone that smells like banana and signals "Danger!" to colony members, who fly to the location to defend their hive mate. One bee's behavior connects everyone to the situation with a ripple effect. Think of it as the ripples caused by dropping a pebble in a pond or the vibrations caused by pulling on a strand of a spider's web.

In organizations, one human being's behavior connects to all other workers, whether they realize it or not. An action by one affects the whole group and produces identifiable patterns. The whole is greater than the sum of the parts. If you want to change a pattern, you must deal with all those individual contributors.

3. LAW OF ROLE: ROLE POWERFULLY INFLUENCES BEHAVIOR.

Each bee steps into a specific role and takes up that role in harmony with bees who take on different roles. Some worker bees fly out to forage for food supplies that will turn golden nectar into honey. Others serve as nurses, caring for the young and feeding them royal jelly to insure successful growth. Cleaners remove debris, creating one of the cleanest and most sterile environments in nature.

Although born into a specific role, a honeybee may shift its responsibilities in response to the changing conditions in the hive. In peacetime and in episodes of danger, the collective hive operates as a well-functioning ecosystem. Astonishingly, their team efforts can produce more than three hundred pounds of honey each season! Organizations that obey the Law of Role can also achieve amazing results.

4. LAW OF MULTIPLE PERSPECTIVES: NOT EVERYONE SEES THINGS THE SAME WAY.

Without the hard work of the world's master pollinators, our pantry shelves would contain no blueberries, cherries, avocados, onions, grapefruit, apples, oranges, or pumpkins. They get the job done because they possess remarkable eyesight. But not all bees see things in the same way.

A drone's large eyes contain seven to eight thousand individual photoreceptors, allowing it to detect the queen in flight; the eye of a worker bee contains four to five thousand photoreceptors, enabling it to see the shorter ultraviolet wavelengths emitted by bright flowers.

The queen, the one responsible for laying eggs, does not need such acute vision. Her smaller eyes contain about thirty-five hundred photoreceptors.

Vision depends on role. In organizations, change depends not on forcing everyone to see things the same way but on uniting different perspectives behind the cause.

5. LAW OF CONTEXT: GROUP BEHAVIOR IS CONTEXTUAL.

Honey's color, texture, flavor, odor, and viscosity vary according to location and season. In Maine, honey tastes like wild blueberry; on Kangaroo Island in Australia, it tastes like sugar gum; and in Nagano, Japan, it tastes like apple blossom. Its aroma runs from a bright and citrusy smell to dusty and sweet.

Its texture can be thick if made from desert wildflowers, or it can turn crystalline if made from linden flowers. In any working group, context influences individual and group behaviors, good or bad.

6. LAW OF EMBEDDEDNESS: DEEPLY EMBEDDED PATTERNS RESIST CHANGE.

In his color vision experiments, researcher Karl von Frisch observed that bees could get stuck in old patterns. When he set out a glass dish of sugar solution over a piece of blue paper, he noticed how the bees drank the sugar solution, flew back to the hive, and repeated this behavior a few times. Then he used two pieces of paper—one red and one blue—and placed them each under dishes that contained no sugar water. The bees paid no attention to the red paper but continued to fly to the blue paper. They repeated that behavior over and over again despite the fact that it produced no results at all.

Groups of humans, just like the bees, can get stuck in patterns that no longer serve them well: "Since this has worked for us in the past, it will always work for us." This explains why it takes so much concentrated effort to effect successful organizational change.

7. LAW OF PATTERN BLINDNESS: GROUP MEMBERS CAN IGNORE THE OBVIOUS.

Bees see some things but not others. Able to detect light in wavelengths from approximately 300 to 650 nanometers, bees can easily see blue, purple, and ultraviolet light, which enables them to find the colorful flowers they need to make honey. But watch a red rosebush in full bloom, and you will probably not see one honeybee land on a blossom. Humans, able to detect wavelengths from 390 to 750 nanometers, can see the roses but become blind to certain aspects of their environment, including the patterns that govern group behavior.

In organizations, secrets and hidden agendas can sabotage change efforts, but the real change killers are the realities people cannot see. Change will never happen until people remove the blinders.

8. LAW OF UNINTENDED CONSEQUENCES: CHANGE EFFORTS CAN PRODUCE UNEXPECTED OUTCOMES.

In 2007, beekeepers across the United States began to report that bees were abandoning their nests for no apparent reason in a phenomenon that became known as Colony Collapse Disorder. The data from biologists confirmed a 60 percent reduction in hives, from about 6 million in 1947 to 2.4 million in 2008.

This collapse came about because of the unintended consequence of endeavors to feed a growing human population: agricultural land expansion, more limited floral resources, and the increased use of pesticides. Researchers found a "pesticide cocktail" of more than 150 chemical residues in bee pollen.

The reduction in industrious efforts of the planet's most prolific pollinators ended up threatening human food supplies. In organizations, a poke or prod in one area can produce a lot of surprises, some positive, some negative.

9. LAW OF THE TIPPING POINT: EVEN SMALL CHANGES CAN HAVE A BIG IMPACT.

During the warmer months in spring and summer, half the beehive's population, including the current queen, may swarm out of the hive in order to form a new colony. Overpopulation has triggered this change, thus ensuring the survival of the species.

The mathematical theory of tipping points suggests that small changes (or perturbations) in a complex dynamic system can trigger a large response. In organizations, a tipping point is a critical juncture when a dramatic change occurs. It can start with a small change that has a big impact on the organization.

In the pages ahead we will dive deeply into these laws and discover how to tap the power of the Hive Mind to make the changes your organization needs to thrive in an ever more challenging future. While other organizations are struggling to stay alive, you will be making the tastiest honey ever.

By the way, my fascination with bees continues today on my seven-and-a-half-acre farm overlooking Wombat Hill in the foothills of Australia's Great Dividing Range, where I love watching an abundance of bees feed on embankments of native flowers. And nothing delights me more than a spoonful of honey gathered from one of the hives.

THE HIVE MIND AT WORK

1 EXPLORING THE HIVE'S WISDOM

Harness Group Intelligence in the Service of Change

Scientists have traditionally worked in isolation, often competing with one another rather than cooperating to solve problems. But when the COVID pandemic swept the globe, members of the scientific community realized that they needed to join forces to get a quick and effective result.

Researchers in big pharmaceutical firms, university departments, hospital labs, and even in their kitchens with their laptops fully charged began sharing information and ideas.

As COVID patients poured into hospitals, doctors scrambled to gather information and post it in online repositories accessible to those working to solve the problem. Like bees banding together to protect their hive, researchers went from solitary workers to a swarm of cooperating individuals as they tapped the power of the Hive Mind.

As one scientist put it, "In the last eleven months, probably ten years' work has been done." Within one year of the outbreak, the united effort delivered three vaccines that curbed a devastating threat to the global hive.

This amazing accomplishment illustrates an inspired way to effect a major change. When it comes to organizational change, however, few leaders harness the power of group intelligence.

Over three decades I've observed countless leaders attempt to implement change strategies to transform their organizations. The case studies in this book show some of the companies I've watched try to transform, remake themselves, or become more competitive. They had one basic goal to make fundamental changes in how the business operated, often to help meet the demands of new, more challenging market conditions. Some of these corporate change efforts have been successful and others have been dismal failures. Many fell short of delivering the expected benefits of the change. Why?

Change failures usually stem from two conventional ways of thinking about transformation:

1. Organizations function like **machines**, where managers can "fix" problems with an engineer's mindset (intelligence quotient or IQ).
2. People form **social networks** wherein individual influencers can make change happen by developing effective interpersonal relationships (emotional quotient or EQ).

This book introduces a third option: organizations are **complex ecosystems** that require a Hive Mind or group intelligence (otherwise known as group intelligence quotient or GQ) to get optimal results.

Before we delve deeply into the ways leaders can use this option to create major, lasting change in their organizations, we must first examine the nature of change in the contemporary world. Grasping these underlying principles will require a little patience, but rest assured, you will find many specific ways to apply these principles in later chapters.

UNDERSTANDING WHY CHANGE EFFORTS FAIL

In our complex world, many well-intentioned change initiatives get off to a good start, pick up some steam, but then go off the rails, leading to an enormous waste of time, energy, money, and opportunity.

It was different in a simpler world, where a single individual could more easily create big changes. Take the discovery of penicillin or the invention of the polio vaccine. In both cases we know the name of the individual who led the work to make it happen.

Alexander Fleming, working alone in his lab at Saint Mary's hospital in London, discovered that bread mold could effectively kill bacteria. That insight led to a drug that saved millions of lives. A United States physician named Jonas Salk introduced the polio vaccine after testing it on himself and his family. The drug virtually wiped out a disease that was crippling children around the world.

Nowadays, as the world grows ever more challenging and unpredictable, it often takes more than a lone-wolf inventor to create meaningful change. Just look at the last few decades. Our organizations have faced increasingly volatile and explosive change: market disruptions, digital transformation, instantaneous global communication, the expansion of a powerful urban consumer class, more stringent regulations on corporate behavior, the COVID pandemic, war, homelessness, social inequality, racism, climate change, poverty, and hunger (to name a few).

A scary state of flux has replaced a slower and more comfortable rate of change, obliterating any sense of the certainty, stability, and familiarity that characterized earlier eras.

Yet these threats to organizational success serve as a mere wake-up call for what lies ahead. The future will bring even more complexity, instability, uncertainty, unpredictability, and unexpected consequences to our change efforts.

Are you prepared to deal with this new reality? If not, you will surely drown in this sea of change. If you feel confident that you can steer your ship through relatively calm waters and arrive safely in the future, think again.

Change comes in many shapes and sizes. Some involve relatively straightforward technical adjustments. Who can't easily change a light bulb, replace a flat tire, install a new software program, or add a new HR policy? It's a snap, really.

You see the problem, perhaps do a Google search, and know immediately how to solve it. Organizations encounter a lot of technical problems every day. When a new federal law extends rights to certain groups, you easily accommodate it with a new HR policy.

Such technical challenges lend themselves to a fairly straightforward, logical solution. Easy-peasy.

But a major organizational change gets a lot more complicated. It often requires groups of people to change: frontline employees, managers, executives, customers, potential customers, suppliers, investors, community members, and government bodies.

Get a lot of people involved, and you've exponentially increased the complexity of the situation. You're not changing a light bulb; you're challenged with changing a bunch of human minds as unlike one another as snowflakes. It will take a lot of work to change their thinking and the way they do their jobs.

Simple technical "fixes" will not get results. You'll need a new type of intelligence, one suited to today's organizational environment. Out with the old, in with the new.

THE OLD WAYS OF THINKING

Organizations as machines: This way of thinking views change as a mechanistic, linear process inside an organizational machine. You can manage it with an engineering mindset and a high technical IQ.

Sir Isaac Newton, born in 1642 in Lincolnshire, England, introduced the concept of a hierarchical, command-and-control organization: not surprising coming from the great mathematician and physicist who fathered much of modern science.

According to Newton's way of thinking, you can fix and tinker with organizations as if they are clock-like mechanisms. Replace this spring, oil this ratchet, tighten this screw, and voilà, you've accomplished the desired change.

This approach led to ever more specialization, the proliferation of rules and regulations, and military-like command-and-control management.

Processes such as planning, budgeting, organizing, communicating, delegating, decision-making, and measuring ruled the day. The machine metaphor with its emphasis on top-down control, efficient work processes, procedures, restructures, standards, and hierarchical control greatly influenced management throughout the twentieth century. Human beings? They were just cogs you could manipulate with logic and control.

Organizations as social networks: This way of thinking emphasizes the importance of relationships in the social network and values emotional intelligence (EQ) as the key to managing change.

The term *social network* was coined by anthropologist J. A. Barnes in 1954 when he studied the complex relationships in a Norwegian fishing village.

To understand an organization, you need merely analyze and map the number and strength of connections formed by individuals within the network. Human beings are simply "nodes" connected by straight lines.

Rutgers University psychologist Daniel Goleman stamped his mark on this movement with the 1998 publication of his book on the importance of emotional intelligence in business leadership.

Success depends on building strong relationships and a tight social network. Change "agents" or "influencers" skillful at doing that could easily persuade others to change. Goodbye clockwork, hello people skills.

Change management depends on understanding and influencing individual subjective motivation, mindsets, behaviors, and habits. This view of a hyperindividualized world produces an avalanche of self-help books on happiness, grit, psychological safety, growth mindset, trust, and personal styles, ad nauseam.

My education, research, and boots-on-the-ground experience led me to set aside these old ways of thinking about change in favor of a much more effective option: organizations are not just logical machines or social networks; they are living, breathing ecosystems.

EMBRACING THE THIRD OPTION

A third option, **organizations as ecosystems**, requires a thorough examination of how all parts of the collective hive operate together. Since this view assumes that organizations function as communities of interacting parts, you can't bring about change without understanding group dynamics and the nature of group intelligence. Note the key differences in the three views in figure 1.1

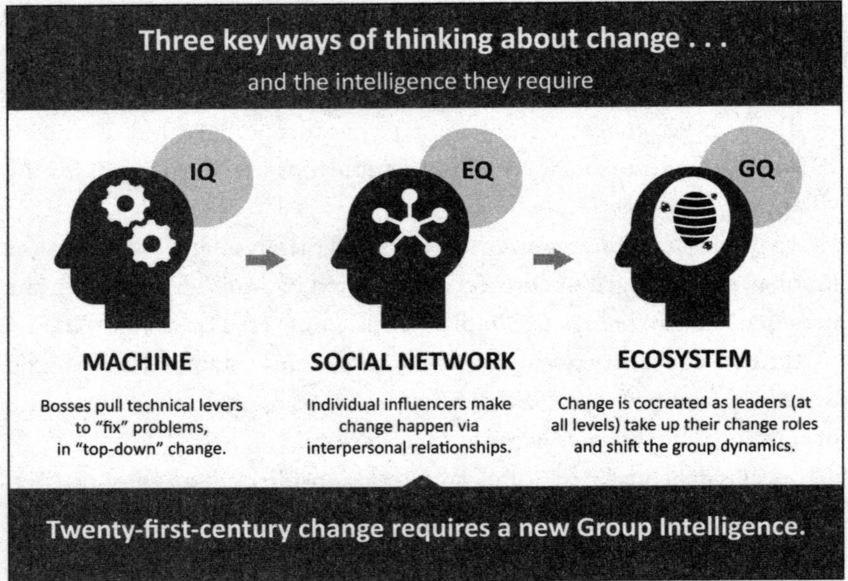

Figure 1.1

We can trace the idea of organizations as ecosystems back to 1951, when Ludwig von Bertalanffy proposed that living systems (or all life-forms) displayed common dynamics.

Organizations behave as living, adaptive systems where interconnected groups work together within their environment. To understand them you need to determine how the whole ecosystem functions and how all the various components relate to one another.

Ideally, you could create order out of potential chaos. This game-changing idea began to influence those who grapple with group change, including family therapists, system thinkers, and academics. To succeed in their jobs, these professionals needed to develop group intelligence.

The same holds true for anyone trying to effect organizational change. Leaders with group intelligence concentrate less on individual mindsets and behaviors and more on group behavior and the complex interactions among all the members of the group.

The bad news? It takes a lot of time and patience to rewire your brain to look at the world through an ecosystemic lens.

The good news? You can get quite good at it. Let's start by looking at the problems caused by the old mechanistic or relationship lens.

FAILING TO OBEY THE NINE LAWS OF THE HIVE

The multinational beverage corporation Coca-Cola, with a market share in more than two hundred countries, committed one of the biggest faux pas in marketing history when it launched Dasani in the UK in 2004. The water brand failed in this new market because it broke the Nine Laws of Group Dynamics (see figure 1.2).

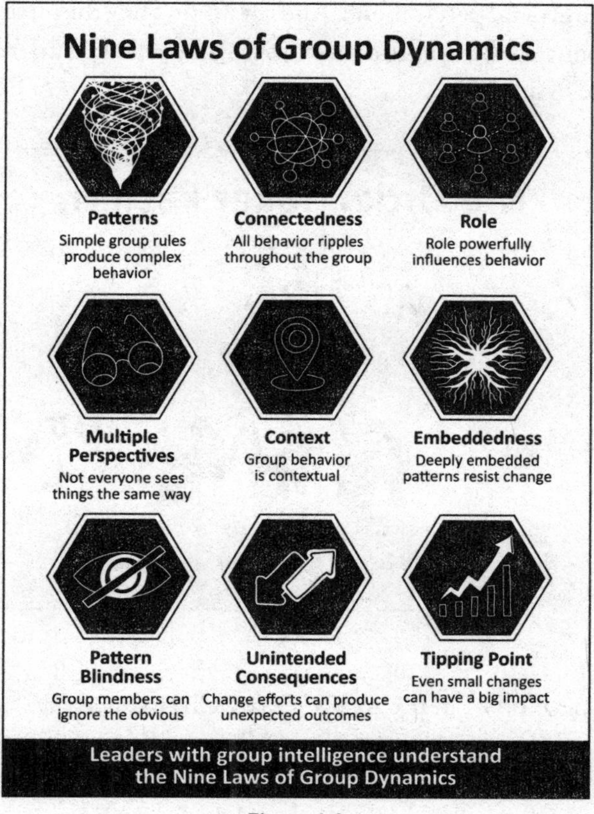

Figure 1.2

Let's consider how Coke failed to make change happen because it violated these laws.

1. Law of Patterns: Simple group rules produce complex behavior.

There was a storm of commentary on every media channel in the UK about the public's reaction to what they essentially saw as Coke selling a half liter of plain old tap water (worth about 0.03 pence) for 95 pence.

Nevertheless, Coke was extolling the virtues of its purification process that passed the water through three filters before a final stage known as reverse osmosis, a technique perfected by NASA to purify fluids on spacecraft. Who would not pay for such so-called "pure, still water"?

Well, the general public didn't. And they didn't buy the pitch for Dasani brought about by the simple pattern that Coke relied on to make change happen (see figure 1.3).

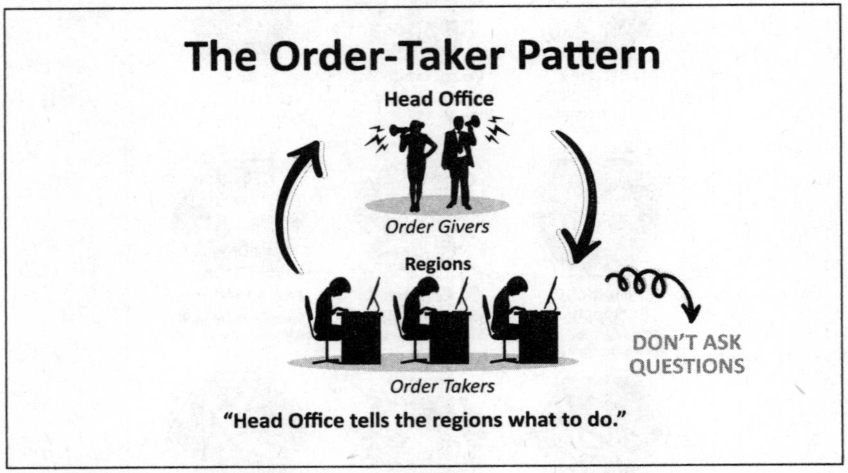

Figure 1.3

Coke's head office in the role of Order Giver issued orders, expecting everyone in the company and millions of thirsty Brits to follow them. The marketing team in Coca-Cola's headquarters in Atlanta, Georgia, thought they just needed to pull the right levers and the Order Takers in the machine would crank out profits. But those thirsty Brits, it turned out, were not good soldiers. They questioned the value and quality of the product.

The road to oblivion is paved with marketers who took their customers for granted. And the road to failed change initiatives is cluttered with leaders who could not see the patterns in group behavior.

2. Law of Connectedness: All behavior ripples throughout the group.

Coca-Cola's woes began when a journalist at *The Grocer* magazine mentioned that the advertising watchdog was looking into a complaint about Coke's use of the word *pure* in Dasani's marketing literature. That news swept like a ripple through the media and made everyone, including consumers, doubt the claims about the new product. Was it really "unique" and "specially formulated for the UK market"?

Judith Snyder, Dasani's PR manager, poured fuel on the fire when she insisted, "We would never say tap water isn't drinkable. It's just that Dasani is as pure as water can get. There are different levels of purity."

Snyder's comments offended Thames Water, which pointed out that its tap water already achieved a 99.92 percent rating in quality trials. A spokesman dismissed Snyder's claim: "If the water regulator thought any more treatment was needed, they would ask us to do so. Tap water is pure. People don't need to buy this stuff to get excellent quality water."

What began as a ripple turned into a tsunami that swept through the UK market.

3. The Law of Role: Role powerfully influences behavior.

Coke's marketing team in Atlanta had stepped into the role of Order Giver and was gearing up for a transatlantic assault on European water brands, including Perrier and Evian.

The Law of Role holds that individual and collective roles powerfully influence group dynamics. Since Coke's research indicated an unprecedented demand for bottled water, the Atlanta team foresaw huge profits for the Dasani brand in the UK market.

Individually and collectively, Coke's marketing team had developed a mental map of their role as Order Givers, asking the local team and the British public to pay big bucks for what was essentially tap water in a plastic bottle. They made one big, fat mistake, however, when they took the UK public for granted.

4. Law of Multiple Perspectives: Not everyone sees things the same way.

UK and US consumers saw bottled water quite differently. In the US, purified "tap water" sat side by side on the shelf with natural spring waters from the mountain peaks and still managed to win over customers. The American public did not fret about the water's origins as long as they believed it was safe to drink.

Coca-Cola never claimed that Dasani was a natural mineral water. On both the bottle's label and on its website, the company cited the manufacturing process. The response of US consumers: "No problem." The UK response: "Are you kidding me?" The Brits just didn't swallow the claim that the company was using a "highly sophisticated filtration process" developed by NASA engineers.

The Atlanta marketing team broke the Law of Multiple Perspectives again when it used the same online ad campaign that had run in the US without testing the tagline: "Water with spunk."

While in America "spunk" means courage and determination, in the UK it's slang for semen. Again, "Are you kidding me?"

5. Law of Context: Group behavior is contextual.

The Law of Context examines the environment and contextual cues that shape group behavior. Those factors vary from situation to situation.

In the case of Coca-Cola's Dasani product, the marketers made another mistake when they assumed the same context applied to the US and the UK: that, having struck gold in 1999, when it launched Dasani in the US, the company would automatically enjoy the same success elsewhere in the world.

Footnote: Most US consumers did not realize that most bottled water sold in the US comes from the same municipal sources that supply tap water. Coca-Cola made Dasani at the company's Detroit plant by purchasing, treating, and bottling municipal water, before selling it at a significant markup to consumers.

Pepsi does the same when it bottles its Aquafina water brand in Detroit. Despite that little known fact, by 2004 Dasani had become the second-biggest selling bottled water in the US, just behind Aquafina, and it seemed poised to generate more than $1 billion in revenue for the company within a decade of its launch.

Coca-Cola opened a production plant in London, spent £7 million on an ad campaign, and planned to roll out Dasani in nineteen other European markets following the UK launch.

Why mess with what works? Well, what works in New York does not always work in London.

6. Law of Embeddedness: Deeply embedded patterns resist change.

Groups tend to practice the same behaviors over and over until they become deeply ingrained habits. One of Coca-Cola's ill-fated habits contributed to Dasani's downfall—to win over customers they simply needed to educate their target audience with three proven steps:

1. We use a purification process perfected by NASA to purify fluids on spacecraft.
2. We add calcium, magnesium, and sodium bicarbonate to the purified water, making it even more tasty and healthful than natural spring water.
3. We mark up the product by a whopping 316,600+ percent, charging 95 pence for a half-liter bottle of Dasani water, while the same amount of tap water costs about 0.03 pence.

These steps have produced great results in the past. Of course they'll work in the UK. Big mistake. Those tried-and-true steps turned out to be a very bad habit indeed.

7. Law of Pattern Blindness: Group members can ignore the obvious.

Coke's introduction of Dasani to the British market failed miserably, to the gleeful pleasure of the British press, who made the product sound like nothing but a bad joke. This turn of events blindsided Coca-Cola. The marketers might have opened their eyes to the possibility of failure if they had just watched a classic television show.

In an hour-long episode of the popular British comedy show *Only Fools and Horses*, which aired on Christmas Day 1992, the two lead characters, Del Boy and Rodney, scheme to sell tap water as Peckham Spring.

A massive audience of 20.1 million people, or about a third of the British population at the time, glued their eyes to their TV sets that day.

In the episode, Del Boy tricks an old school mate of Rodney's into investing in his Peckham Spring water, which he claims comes from a spring on his grandad's old allotment. Ha! A decade later, Brits who loved that episode found it hilarious that Coke built its Dasani factory only nine miles from the very spot where Del Boy had bottled his own tap water and sold it for a pretty penny.

The media piled on with *Only Fools and Horses* jokes, comparing Coca-Cola to the fictional scam merchant Del Boy. Once formidable and clean-cut, Coca-Cola became a laughingstock almost overnight. Coke must have wondered, "Why didn't we see *that* coming?"

8. Law of Unintended Consequences: Change efforts can produce unexpected outcomes.

Just when the executives in Coke's head office in Atlanta thought the situation couldn't get much worse, it did. In the final stages of Dasani's purification process, when the purification protocol used ozone to sterilize the water, that chemical reacted with the small traces of bromide contained in ordinary tap water, producing bromate.

Bromide's okay; bromate's not. It's a potentially cancer-causing substance. Contaminated bottles of Dasani were shipped to stores with up to twice the legal limit for bromate.

The Law of Unintended Consequences states that a change in a complex, adaptive ecosystem can produce unexpected outcomes. In Dasani's case this was a ten-milligrams-per-liter threat to the health and well-being of those who drank the polluted water. Again, the Coca-Cola folks must have been shaking their heads, wondering, "How did *that* happen?"

9. Law of the Tipping Point: Even small changes can have a big impact.

The discovery of illegal levels of cancer-causing bromate chemicals in its bottled, filtered tap water served as the tipping point for Coke, which had no choice but to recall Dasani and abandon the drink's launch in the UK.

A mere five weeks after introducing the product to the market, the company withdrew five hundred thousand bottles and closed its UK plant for good. To this day you won't find any Dasani on Great Britain's grocery shelves.

The Dasani debacle left Coke with a £25 million loss from canceled production contracts and advertising deals. Analysts estimated the damage to the firm's reputation at twenty times that figure.

The company broke every Law of Group Dynamics. Leaders with group intelligence avoid similarly disastrous mistakes by viewing change through the Hive LENS.

FOLLOWING THE FOUR STEPS OF THE HIVE LENS

As a management consultant jetting in and out of hundreds of organizations across four continents, I learned to differentiate what distinguished successful change leaders from those who got less than desired results.

I noticed that many leaders felt comfortable with technical changes, such as designing a new store layout, sketching an arch bridge, drafting a schedule for data migration, or creating a plan for a product launch.

But these same leaders struggled when making changes that involved groups of people shifting their behavior. In most cases, they relied on tried-and-true IQ and EQ techniques rather than the group intelligence (GQ) required for ecosystem change.

The successful change leaders possessed a Hive Mind or group intelligence that allowed them to understand how groups functioned and to lead them toward meaningful and lasting change.

I discovered that those who harness the power of group intelligence follow a four-step process I call the Hive LENS (see figure 1.4). This simple but powerful model captures the essence of group intelligence practices deployed by extraordinarily successful change leaders. Adopting these steps will not only build your group intelligence but increase the likelihood that you will achieve the best possible results.

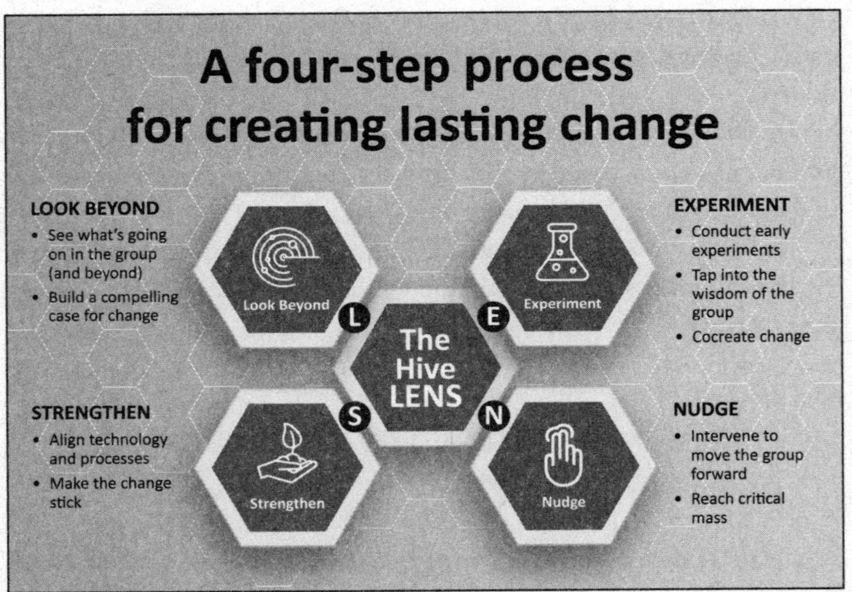

A four-step process
for creating lasting change
LOOK BEYOND
• See what's going on in the group (and beyond)
• Build a compelling case for change
EXPERIMENT
• Conduct early experiments
• Tap into the wisdom of the group
• Cocreate change
STRENGTHEN
• Align technology and processes
• Make the change stick
NUDGE
• Intervene to move the group forward
• Reach critical mass
Look Beyond
Experiment
Strengthen
Nudge
L
E
S
N
The Hive LENS

Figure 1.4

In a nutshell, you must:

- *Look Beyond* to examine how the ecosystem currently functions and what changes need to be made.
- *Experiment* to figure out the best way forward.

- *Nudge* the group to move in the right direction.
- *Strengthen* the new ways and bring them to life every day.

Note that the Hive LENS is a circular rather than a linear model because change never follows a straight line.

We will explore the model in detail throughout the book, but let's take a quick look at how the Hive LENS was applied to the pharmaceutical company Pfizer in one of the most significant change efforts in recent times.

Look Beyond (L) to examine how the ecosystem currently functions and what changes need to be made.

In March 2019, as COVID-19 swept around the world, Pfizer CEO Albert Bourla began challenging everyone in his company to "make the impossible possible," developing a vaccine more quickly than anyone had ever done before.

Bourla knew he had set a very high bar. The mumps vaccine, heralded as one of the fastest ever previously developed, had taken *four years* to move from the lab to distribution.

Bourla, who had trained as a veterinarian in Greece, had taken the helm as Pfizer's CEO that year and had never envisioned how daunting the job of running the world's largest pharmaceutical company would become. On March 13, Bourla released a five-point plan to guide Pfizer employees and its Big Pharma peers in a joint effort to defeat the coronavirus.

The newly installed CEO recognized the old, siloed pattern that had been embedded in the scientific community for decades. Researchers at Big Pharma A and B worked in their labs in almost complete isolation from one another.

Bourla understood that he would need to break this pattern (see figure 1.5) and forge a new one that embraced collaborative working, not only within the walls of Pfizer but throughout the industry. The fate of the

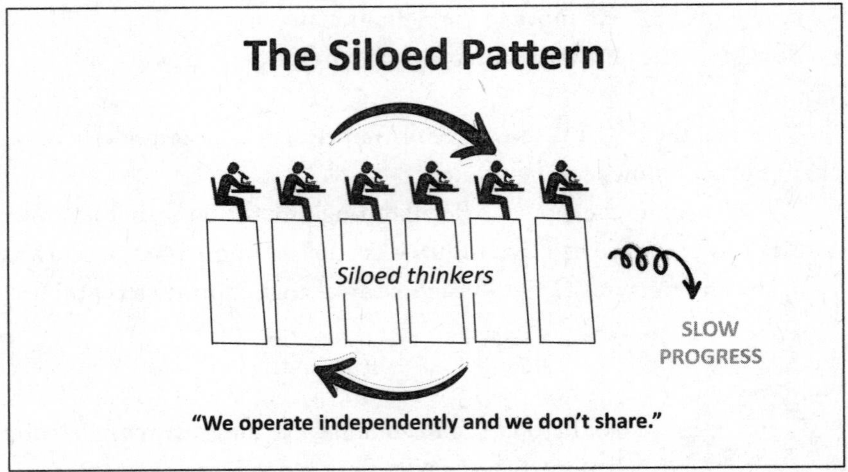

Figure 1.5

world rested on a new way of doing things around here (a fair definition of "culture").

Bourla's five-point plan enshrined collaboration as the optimum way to marshal a rapid response to the virus. Researchers would now share insights, tools, data, expertise, and capability with the collective goal of saving millions of lives by getting a vaccine to market as soon as possible. Speed would trump individual glory, but not at the expense of scientific rigor.

Bourla's commitment ran into its first major test later that month when Kathrin Jansen, his chief of vaccine research, spoke with the folks at BioNTech, a small biotech company based in Germany, about their unproven gene-based mRNA technology.

Many in the pharmaceutical industry doubted the efficacy of mRNA, which had not yet been used in an approved product. After Jansen's chat with BioNTech, Bourla gave Jansen the go-ahead to collaborate with them to employ the mRNA molecule (a messenger that carries genetic instructions to tell cells to produce an immune response) to take a giant step toward an effective vaccine.

I think Bourla and bee researcher Karl von Frisch would have become fast friends. Both appreciated the value of stepping back and figuring out exactly how a group functions. That awareness, Bourla understood, precedes any meaningful, lasting change.

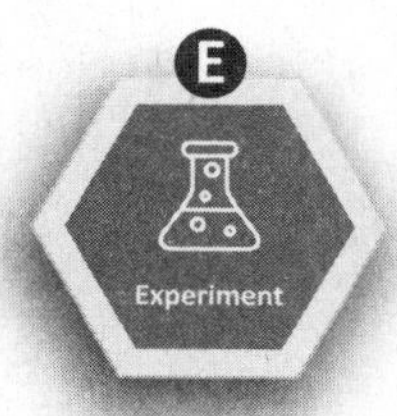

Experiment (E) to figure out the best way forward.

Experimenting and opening yourself up to novel ideas spark creativity. Pfizer's Kathrin Jansen implemented this step when she led a team of 650 scientists who would narrow down vaccine options, collaborating all the while via videoconference with BioNTech researchers.

The scientists shared everything they discovered in their test tube experiments, testing twenty potential vaccine candidates, examining various doses, and looking for molecular signs that proved the vaccine both safe and effective. It was a tough job because they needed to amass massive amounts of data on the previously untested mRNA vaccines.

In the case of the vaccine hunt, the researchers came up with unorthodox ways to fast-track the testing process. As Jansen observed, "We needed speed, and with speed, you have to rethink how you normally go."

Instead of following three separate and sequential test stages, they combined the second and third trials, began testing multiple versions of the vaccine to see which one performed best, and sent almost daily batches of test data to the US Food and Drug Administration rather than waiting until the tests had concluded.

By April 12, the scientists had eliminated sixteen candidates, whittling the selection down to just four. The team pressed full speed ahead, testing the four remaining possibilities on volunteers in Germany and quickly eliminating two more when they gave test subjects fevers and chills.

The final two experimental vaccines underwent thorough testing in the US. On July 24, Jansen decided that Pfizer would take one of the vaccines into the large, final trial that regulators would use to determine whether to authorize its distribution.

But Bourla knew that all this progress would not get the desired result unless he kept nudging the team in the right direction.

Nudge (N) the group to move in the right direction.

Leaders cannot ignite a change then sit back and watch it succeed. They need to keep a wary eye on what's happening and intervene when necessary.

Albert Bourla did just that, instigating a twice-weekly gathering of his leadership team to make sure they were collaborating and making the right choices for Pfizer's vaccine program.

The meeting lacked a formal agenda because the CEO wanted to encourage free-flowing discussion among its two dozen attendees, all of whom had grown accustomed to Bourla's tough questions and requests for ever-faster progress.

When, in mid-March, Jansen forecast a vaccine by the middle of 2021, the CEO spoke up. "Sorry, this will not work," he insisted, reminding his team that people were dying from COVID-19.

In June, Bourla also kept pressing the manufacturing team to ramp up production, urging Mark McDermott, his manufacturing chief, to increase commercial production at least tenfold: "Why can't we make more and why can't we make it sooner?"

Bourla was a first-class Nudger. "I always try to shoot for the stars, because I know that even if you miss it, you will land somewhere in the moon."

But just nudging the ecosystem won't get you to the moon if you do not strengthen the new ways of doing things around here.

Strengthen (S) the news ways and bring them to life every day.

It's so easy to fall back into bad habits. To ensure long-term change you must strengthen the new ways of doing things until they become part of the group's lifeblood.

When the scientists searching for a vaccine determined the best candidate, Mark McDermott's manufacturing team at Pfizer was already gearing up to produce fifty million vaccine doses in 2020 and up to 1.3 billion doses in 2021.

One big problem: Pfizer didn't possess the equipment to make an mRNA vaccine, which required a new and different manufacturing process. Bourla stepped in and committed more than $2 billion to build a global manufacturing network for a radical new vaccine based on a technology that had never been approved before.

The CEO allocated $500 million on the design and purchase of equipment to make the vaccine and retrofitted its plant in Andover, Massachusetts, to make mRNA. The company also dedicated its Saint Louis factory to the production of raw materials for the shots.

In early April, Bourla signed off on seven mRNA vaccine formulation machines, each costing $200 million, and ordered them installed in plants in Kalamazoo, Michigan, and Puurs, Belgium.

Later that month, McDermott and his team started working on how they would transport the fragile vaccine at subzero temperatures. By July they had designed a suitcase-sized box that could hold nearly five thousand doses, complete with a GPS tracker.

Although the contraptions worked well during hundreds of test trips around the world, when McDermott showed one to Bourla, the CEO balked, pointing out that pharmacies and doctor's offices would need fewer doses. He sent the team back to the drawing board to design packages that could hold 25 or 125 doses of the vaccine.

By mid-August the manufacturing team was building up vaccine supplies in its Belgium factory that they could deliver to any country that approved its use. By the end of September, 1.5 million doses were ready to ship. Meanwhile, other Pfizer manufacturing sites were gearing up to manufacture shots by installing, testing, and certifying new machines.

Less than eight months after Pfizer began working with its partner BioNTech, their vaccine trials racked up a 95 percent efficacy rate. On December 2, the Pfizer vaccine became the first fully tested COVID-19 vaccine approved for emergency use.

Pfizer successfully delivered an approved vaccine faster than outside experts and even its own employees thought possible.

Albert Bourla had enabled a Hive Mind: Pfizer's seventy-nine thousand employees in more than 125 countries had relied on what he called "inter-company cooperation, liberation from bureaucracy, and most of all, hard work." The effort produced one honey of a success.

If Albert Bourla could do it on such a grand scale, you can do it, too, no matter how big or small or scattered your group. Just make sure you obey the Nine Laws of Group Dynamics and follow the four steps of the Hive LENS.

Change has become a tsunami. You can either surf the waves by co-creating meaningful change, or you can remain complacent and get swept to oblivion.

POINTS TO REMEMBER

- Workplace change efforts fail to deliver desired results because leaders rely on the wrong skill sets to manage change (IQ and EQ).
- The best results come when you cocreate change with a new way of thinking (group intelligence or a high GQ).
- Failure usually stems from a failure to obey the Nine Laws of Group Dynamics.
- The four-step Hive LENS model will help you create meaningful and lasting change.

2

SIMPLIFYING COMPLEXITY

Map the Basic Patterns That Govern Behavior

In late spring, the bees have been feeding hungrily on the local native flowers and the colony has doubled in size from twenty to forty thousand. Space has become so crowded in the hive that the queen's pheromones cannot reach the entire colony, disrupting the hive's customary order.

Having outgrown their home, the honey gatherers know that they will not be able to produce enough honey to see the colony through the tough winter months ahead. Bees Look Beyond their current circumstances before taking the steps necessary to ensure a lasting and successful colony.

The Hive Mind examines the milling community for signs of overcrowding, determines that they cannot collect enough supplies to feed the entire group during the winter, and decides to initiate a major change by splitting the hive into two populations. That's a daunting change, but long-term survival depends on it.

Sadly, too many business leaders fail to look beyond pressing day-to-day matters to see crucial patterns or underlying problems that might threaten their survival.

Take the New York–based investment bank Lehman Brothers, for example. The firm came to a grinding halt on September 15, 2008, triggering the subprime mortgage crisis that cost an estimated $10 trillion in lost economic output.

The financial experts swooped in to pick apart the Lehman Brothers catastrophic failure, blaming everyone from the CEO, Richard Fuld Jr., and the company's auditors to over-leveraging assets, making poor investments, relying on shaky funding, and paying executive incentives that rewarded problematic behavior.

But the commentators missed a crucial dynamic at Lehman that was sowing the seeds of its downfall. Stay tuned for the details.

Effective leaders who understand the power of group intelligence avoid Lehman's fate by taking the first step on the Hive LENS model: Look Beyond to determine how the ecosystem is functioning, searching carefully for the underlying patterns that indicate the time has come to initiate some major changes.

LEARNING TO SEE THE PATTERNS THAT GOVERN BEHAVIOR

If you want to grasp how an ecosystem is functioning, you don't call a technician or a social networker; you call a biologist. You could, of course, call bee expert Karl von Frisch. Or you call D'Arcy Wentworth Thompson.

In 1917 the Scottish mathematical biologist used a simple equation to describe the complex spiral patterns displayed by animal horns, pine cones, and mollusk shells. These incredibly intricate and beautiful structures adhered to the Fibonacci sequence or "golden spiral" ratio, where every quarter turn lies farther from the origin by a set factor.

Amazing fractal patterns could be found everywhere in nature. You just had to look closely enough at such natural phenomena, from tiny, microscopic organisms to gigantic galactic superclusters.

Add physicists and mathematicians to your call list. Scientists studying complexity theory and nonlinear dynamics have also contributed to our understanding of patterns and ways of relating.

Edward Lorenz, the American mathematician, meteorologist, and father of chaos theory, proposed what he called the "butterfly effect" to describe how something as small and seemingly insignificant as a butterfly flapping its wings in Brazil could set off a series of chain reactions that could eventually produce a tornado in Texas.

Such seemingly random events, Lorenz claimed, follow a set of distinct and predictable rules.

A paradox emerges in complex ecosystems such as climate, cities, industries, financial markets, governments, and cultures: On the one hand, complex ecosystems seem volatile and hard to predict.

On the other hand, even the most complex systems obey certain basic rules and patterns.

While you may never be able to predict exactly what will happen in complex ecosystems, as the Law of Patterns states, you can identify the patterns and rules that provide the keys to unlocking meaningful and lasting change.

Back to the beehive. All those milling bees may seem like pure chaos, but a closer look at a simple pattern such as the waggle dance makes all that buzzing around quite clear: the bees are performing complex and intricate behaviors that turn individual localized jostling into majestic cohesive action.

When a bee waggles, she's telling her mates, "Hey, guys, I've found a wonderful source of nectar. Let's go make some honey!"

Look for the waggle dances in your group. Leaders who understand the power of group intelligence know that all the rules and patterns people follow reveal a Hive Mind that tells people how to think and move.

Of course, groups can act collectively in both positive and negative ways. Managed effectively, the Hive Mind can bring about increased energy, vitality, creativity, and a thirst for learning and growth.

Left to run amok, however, it can also lead to dangerous dysfunction such as overcompetitiveness, greed, disrespect, and bullying.

Patterns spread silently throughout the workplace, shaping the behavior of long-standing employees as well as capturing new ones soon after they walk through the door. Individuals may come and go from the group, but the patterns, or agreements between the parts, tend to remain the same.

Culture persists. But the "way we do things around here" that worked wonders in the past may, as the environment changes over time, ends up causing more harm than good in the future. Clearly, an organization intent on long-term success must change its outdated rules and patterns to establish a *new* way of doing things around here.

Obviously, you can't change patterns if you do not see them. If you close your eyes and hold an elephant's foot, you might imagine you're touching a tree. Grasp its trunk, and it feels like a big snake. The ears? Must be a beach umbrella.

To see the whole animal, you must open your eyes and step back to see all the connections that create the whole animal.

To see any organizational pattern clearly, you must do the same, stepping back and looking for the connections before jumping to any conclusions.

Some years ago, I was consulting to "Jack Hammond," an ex-army sergeant and the CEO at "TopChoice Maintenance (TCM)," a Washington, DC–based provider of maintenance services to infrastructure and government clients. (Note: this is a real case study with pseudonyms in quote marks to protect client confidentiality.)

Hammond desperately needed to do something about the firm's poor financial performance. When I met with him to discuss his concerns, he insisted that he had identified the root cause of the problem: two hundred contract managers who lacked sufficient financial acumen to manage their budgets effectively. "Over 60 percent of TCM's contracts are losing money! I've got to get them trained up, and I need to do it fast. My job depends on it."

The board had already warned him that he needed to turn things around or start looking for a job that better suited his abilities. "I've already set up a financial training program we can launch next week."

I nodded. "Okay. But could we hit the pause button for a minute here?" I could see that Jack believed he had a handle on the problem, but I thought he might be holding the proverbial elephant's foot. He was not seeing the whole picture. Given the cost of the new finance program, he agreed to step back before marching his troops off to training school.

The following week I visited a TCM road maintenance project at the mud-frozen side of a busy Washington highway where I met with contract manager "Diego Gonzalez." We shook hands amid a swirling snow shower before stepping into the first of a series of gray prefabs.

Comfortably ensconced in the warm trailer, Diego spoke quite frankly. "My job is keeping our customers happy, Siobhán, but the finance team only counts pennies. They don't get the fact that if we don't make our customers happy, they won't have any pennies to count."

When the road crew arrived for morning coffee, Diego told them the customer wanted additional work done before an expected snowstorm that evening. The team shuffled out into the drifting snowfall.

I thanked Diego for his insights and continued my whirlwind tour of TopChoice Maintenance sites before concluding the day with finance manager "Emma McQueen."

Emma was practically climbing the walls. "The contract managers don't care two hoots about working within their budgets and expect the finance manager to clean up any messes they make. All I hear is 'The customer says this, the customer wants that, blah, blah, blah.' They don't realize that all their little favors for customers end up costing us a pretty penny."

The more I chatted with people, the clearer the pattern became. A few days later, I caught up with Jack Hammond and sketched the pattern on his office whiteboard (see figure 2.1).

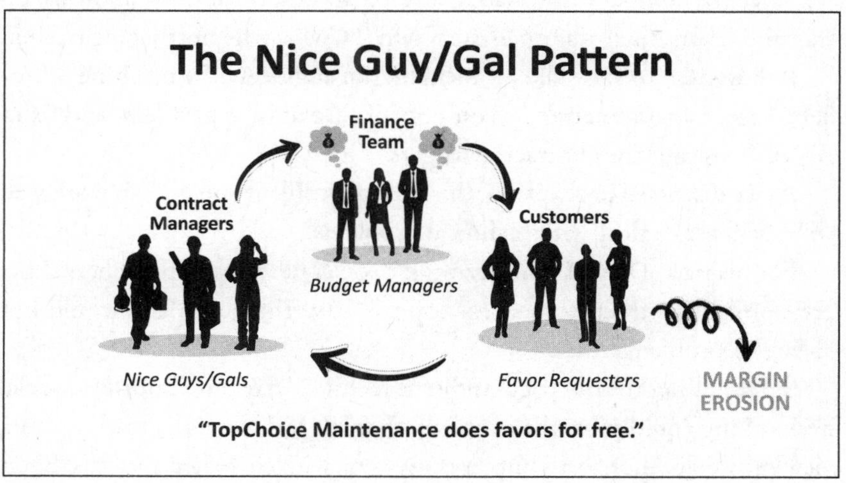

Figure 2.1

The pattern or rule that was causing the issue: "TCM does favors for free," and each part of the ecosystem had stepped into a role to cocreate it:

- **Customers:** in role of Favor Requestors who expected contract managers to provide extras and small jobs for free
- **Contract Managers:** in role of Nice Guys/Gals who provided favors to keep customers happy
- **Finance Team:** in role of Budget Managers responsible for dealing with the company's increasingly dire financial position

In the past, TCM signed "cost-plus" contracts that would add any extra work charges to the agreed price.

But the market shifted, and clients, wanting to have cost certainty, introduced "hard contracts" with a set price, period.

Now the contract managers needed to manage tighter budgets. New business model plus old pattern equals disaster.

- "Clear unexpected snow from the driveway!" "Sure!"
- "Spread a second layer of salt and sand on the roads!" "Of course!"
- "Fill the potholes on the highway ramp!" "Right away!"

Since the company now had to absorb the cost of all those add-ons, extras, and favors, there was no mystery why TCM was hemorrhaging red ink.

Jack wanted to solve the problem like an engineer. The machine is broken. Take it apart, analyze its components, isolate the problem, and fix it. By "it" he meant the contract managers.

As we discussed in chapter 1, this type of problem-solving can work well when you are dealing with technical problems.

For his part, Diego Gonzalez took a social network approach, making relationships with customers his top priority. That approach would not solve this problem either.

Since neither the old tried-and-true technical fixes and improved social networking could solve the problem, that left Jack with the third option, viewing the situation as a complex ecosystem, with cocreated patterns. Enter the Hive Mind and group intelligence.

Jack got it. "Sending contract managers to finance training is not going to fix the problem because they will walk right back into the same pattern once they leave the course." I nodded in agreement. "Let's talk about the next step."

For his next step Hammond called a meeting with his contract managers and finance team to present the old pattern and explore a new one. "Can we figure out a way to manage customer relationships *and* bottom-line performance?" He drew a possible new pattern (see figure 2.2) alongside the old one on his whiteboard:

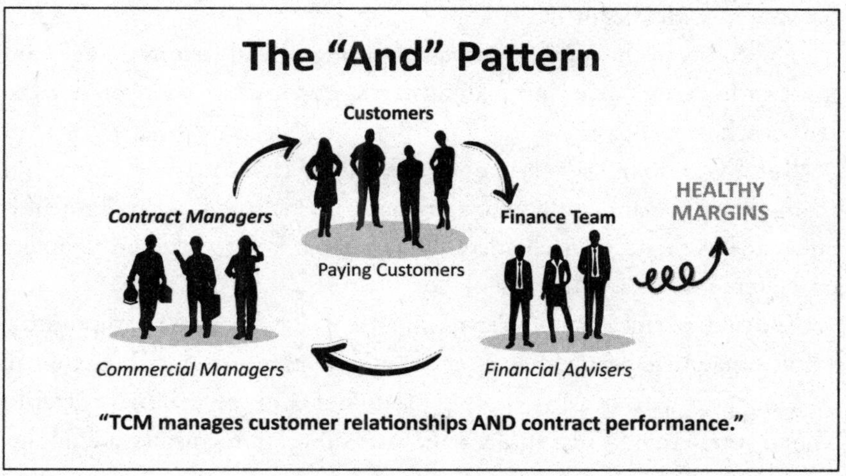

Figure 2.2

Jack framed a new role for the contract managers. "You are not Nice Guys/Gals, just here to please the customer. You need to take up your Commercial Manager role to make sure your contract meets the needs of our multiple stakeholders, including our shareholders. The finance team can advise you on ways to meet budget expectations."

After both teams stepped into their new roles, Hammond coached his contract managers to take up their commercial role, including explaining to customers that they need to pay for big and small add-on jobs.

The CEO reinforced the change with monthly meetings to track progress toward agreed financial goals. Word soon got around that Jack Hammond was serious about transforming TCM.

And became a mantra in all of Hammond's interactions with TCM's people: "Our job is to ensure that the firm's finances remain healthy *and* our customers stay happy."

Finance managers stopped compensating for the contract managers and took care to emphasize that everyone's future depended on meeting budget expectations. Those who delivered won rewards; those who didn't moved to other roles or to jobs at other companies.

By the end of the fiscal year Hammond happily reported to the board that the firm had met its budget forecast for the first time in several years. This news gave shareholders confidence that they would get a good return on their investments in TCM.

As you begin the journey toward meaningful and lasting change, you must gather all the relevant qualitative and quantitative data you need to see the whole elephant.

But if you do it, as Jack Hammond did, by isolating root causes and fixing them, you are jumping to a premature conclusion. Such cause-and-effect analysis reflects mechanistic thinking that fails to take the complete ecosystem into account.

The data (red ink) may offer some important clues but does not capture the whole situation any more than an elephant's ear represents the whole animal.

Change is hard because ecosystems do not easily reveal their patterns. When you're caught in a spiderweb, your situation seems like a complex and tangled web.

On your left you see a dysfunctional culture; on your right you see a disengaged workforce; above your head you see a performance dip, corruption allegations, an inability to grow, and a quality issue; and below your feet you see a spike in customer complaints.

Which thread should you pull to get out of this mess? Go ahead, pull one. Pull another and another and another. You're still trapped. The more you pull on the threads, the more tangled you seem to get.

Leaders with group intelligence avoid pulling threads but step back to observe the whole web. Look closely. It's not a mess, it's a perfectly cocreated pattern.

How can you rewire the web and create a different pattern? Not by pulling strands willy-nilly, but with very intentional interventions.

It's all about seeing the *relatedness* between the strands, or the connectedness between the parts.

Like Karl von Frisch studying a beehive, you must examine how the group functions and distinguish the dancers from the dance, the individual behaviors from the patterns.

Successful change leaders know that you do not get where you want to go by changing people. You get there by changing patterns. And you can't change patterns if you do not map the ecosystem.

MAPPING KEY PATTERNS

When the New York–based investment bank Lehman Brothers came to a grinding halt on September 15, 2008, the collapse left twenty-five thousand people unemployed globally and triggered the subprime crisis that cost an estimated $10 trillion in lost economic output. The catastrophe almost took down the global financial system and catapulted the world into what became known as the Great Recession.

Could the company have done something to avoid its downfall? Yes, but it would have taken a lot more foresight than Lehman's leaders possessed. They simply failed to Look Beyond.

The financial experts looking for a root cause blamed CEO Richard Fuld Jr. A *Time* magazine write-up added to the finger-pointing in its article "25 People to Blame for the Financial Crisis."

Harold James, a professor of history and international affairs at Princeton University, offered another perspective. "The crisis was the product of escalating short-termism in financial markets."

Others chalked up the Lehman Brothers failure to a flawed reward system for traders. As Eric Dash at the *New York Times* concluded, "The open secret on Wall Street was that traders did not risk losing their own money, just the chance of receiving an enormous payout."

Economists call this a moral hazard problem and, in banker speak, it's known as the IBG YBG issue—as in "I'll be gone. You'll be gone if the trade goes south." It went further than south; it went to hell.

The blame game went viral, with fingers pointing at greedy and overly trusting investors, dodgy accounting, over-leveraging, poor long-term investments, shaky funding, the auditors, and everyone but the janitor's dog.

But I'd like to share a systemic explanation, an opinion based on a map of the Lehman ecosystem (see figure 2.3).

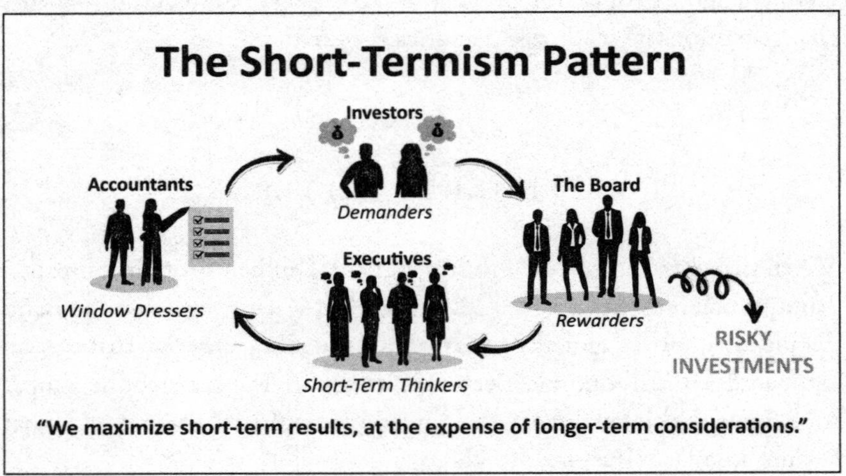

Figure 2.3

The Short-Termism Pattern at Lehman Brothers boiled down to a simple agreement: "We maximize short-term results at the expense of longer-term considerations." Key players cocreated this pattern:

- **The investors** were in the role of Demanders, expecting short-term and ever-growing profits.
- **The board** took up the role of Rewarder, gearing executive compensation to current-year performance with little regard to the future.
- **The executive team** stepped into the role of Short-Term Thinkers, taking ever-higher risks to fuel the moneymaking machine.
- **The auditor** accepted the role of Window Dresser for Lehman's risky financial structures, revealed in the US Government's Financial Crisis Inquiry Report.

Big-league banking is one of the most complicated organizational ecosystems in the world, with tens of thousands of employees performing both simple and intricate transactions, millions of customers depositing and withdrawing money, specialists creating complicated loan instruments, and investors acquiring stocks and moving money around, all plugged into the Federal Reserve System.

But if you step back to consider the whole elephant, you can see the pattern that governed everyone's behavior.

Can you map your own ecosystem? Use the one I created for Lehman Brothers as a guide. Can you pinpoint the key parts and draw the connection between them? Can you define each of their roles?

Asking these questions will help simplify the mapping process. The aim of all mapping is to translate visible complexity into the simplicity of (often) invisible patterns.

You can sit alone in your office asking these questions and sketching your map, but I have found that leaders get the best results when they involve key parts of the ecosystem in the exercise. At the very least, you need to interview enough people to form a clear picture of the roles and relatedness between the parts.

A word of caution: Do not assume you hold the cut-and-dried truth about roles and connectedness between the parts. Don't impose your view on others. Encourage them to open up and talk freely about their own perspectives. This will help you see what's really going on around here and what, if anything, must change.

LISTENING TO DIFFERENT VIEWS ABOUT WHAT NEEDS TO CHANGE

A bee colony may look like nothing but a lot of chaotic movement, with each bee buzzing around according to its own wishes; yet, somehow, thousands of the little critters can pool their intelligence to make a collective decision about the colony's need to change.

Their behavior epitomizes the power of group intelligence. A lot of individual experiences go into the decision to create another home.

Bees do it. So did Hubert Joly when he took the helm at Best Buy, one of the US's last surviving national electronics chains.

Back in 2012, Joly needed to reverse a trend toward languishing sales and poor customer satisfaction ratings. As he later said in a *Harvard Business Review* interview, "Back in 2012, everybody thought we were going to die. There were zero buy recommendations on the stock."

Facing a dire situation, Joly did not mandate immediate changes. No, he stepped back, and he listened to different views about the company, including those held by Best Buy's all-important customers.

Despite steady sales and revenue growth during the 1990s and 2000s, the company had earned a reputation for caring little about customers who began flocking to discount websites such as Amazon and even electronics manufacturers.

By 2012 its share price plunged to twelve dollars (the lowest in a decade), and the company lost $1.7 billion in Q4 of 2012. Bankruptcy lurked just around the corner.

As the new CEO began listening to how customers felt about Best Buy, he discovered they saw the company's thousand-plus stores as showrooms where they could browse electronic gear before buying what they wanted somewhere else.

On the other hand, they admitted, "We love your well-mannered, highly trained Geek Squad when we need something fixed or installed. And, wow, they do it for free!"

- "Need help installing your security camera? No problem!"
- "Connect your sound system? Absolutely!"
- "Unsure how to use your new Amazon Echo? Let me show you!"

How, Joly wondered, could he counter the negative and leverage the positive?

The Geek Squad became ambassadors of goodwill, helping customers see new possibilities and increase their purchases at Best Buy.

Joly went a step further, rewarding customers with points toward future purchases whenever they shared their views about the company's products and services. He even provided an app that enabled employees to gather customer feedback in real time.

Joly also collected employee views. One common perspective about the value of the Geek Squad led to the creation of "Geek Squad Lounges," where customers could obtain one-on-one assistance with purchases before leaving the store. The CEO then empowered his people to take swift action to resolve any customer issues from product availability and price matching to deliveries and returns.

Fast-forward to 2015. The changes implemented by the Best Buy Hive Mind boosted the company from a multibillion-dollar loss generator to a billion-dollar profit machine.

That's one honey of a turnaround! It started because a leader sought multiple perspectives about what needed to change.

As for Hubert Joly, in 2018 he won acclamation as one of the World's Best CEOs from *Barron's* magazine and as one of the Best-Performing CEOs in the World from the *Harvard Business Review*.

Gathering multiple perspectives may seem like an easy task, but it takes more humility and empathy than you might imagine.

A company's stakeholders, from the most junior employees to the angriest customers, not to mention the least accommodating suppliers and the most suspicious government officials, seldom feel comfortable telling you the bald truth about your organization.

NASA learned this the hard way during the early stages of its investigation into the *Challenger* catastrophe.

On the morning of Tuesday, January 28, 1986, the space shuttle *Challenger* exploded in the sky, killing all seven astronauts on board. In the aftermath, NASA investigators asked, "How can we prevent this type of disaster from ever occurring again?" They put Roger Feynman, the Nobel Prize–winning physicist, in charge of the inquiry.

As Feynman asked a broad range of people at NASA headquarters about the catastrophe, including astronauts, engineers, and physicists, he made a rather astonishing discovery: little ninety-nine-cent O-ring seals on the rocket's boosters had frozen before takeoff, igniting a chain reaction that ended up in a fireball over the Atlantic Ocean.

Shockingly, NASA executives knew about the risks posed by the O-rings but ignored them.

The day before the space shuttle launch, the Morton Thiokol contract engineers who were working on the rocket booster organized an emergency teleconference with NASA executives to sound the alarm about the O-rings, but their worries fell on deaf ears. NASA would not delay the launch over such a trivial flaw.

The countdown began: ten, nine, eight, seven, six, five, four, three, two, one, liftoff! Then *boom*!

Let's look at the pattern that led to such a devastatingly bad decision (see figure 2.4). In this case, NASA officials, pressured to push ahead with the mission, suppressed the bad news; Morton Thiokol engineers, wanting to retain the lucrative contract, fell silent.

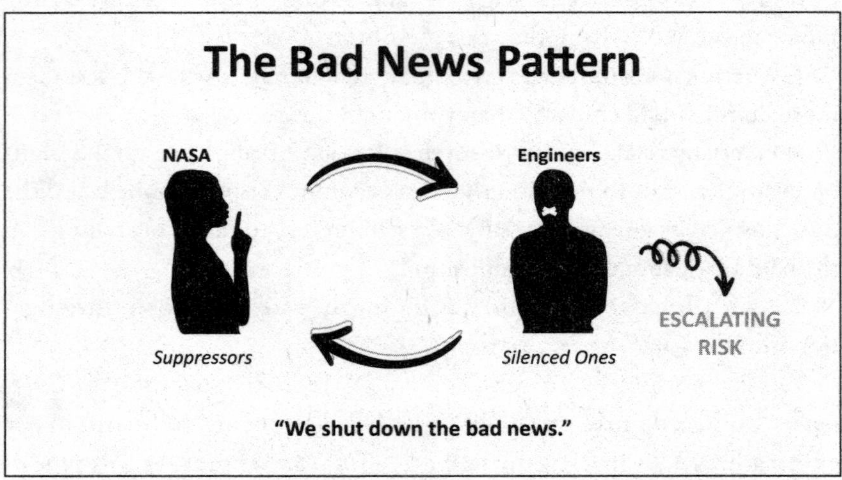

Figure 2.4

When, at a famous news conference months later, Feynman dropped an O-ring into a glass of liquid nitrogen, both NASA officials and Morton Thiokol engineers saw dramatic proof of their dangerous pattern as the O-ring shattered into a thousand pieces. That's what allowed hot gas to pour into the fuel chamber and ignite the fireball. Such a disaster could happen again unless NASA executives created a new pattern (see figure 2.5).

Figure 2.5

This new pattern would require NASA executives to step into the role of Listeners, open to hearing good and bad news and encouraging team members to take up the role of Sharers who could safely tell the truth.

You can imagine what would happen if bees ignored the bad news that their hive has become life-threateningly overcrowded. Eventually, the colony would suffer irreparable damage. Humans, too, can ignore bad news for only so long before it causes great harm.

Don't suppress bad news; welcome it. Make sure people who deliver bad news do so without fear of punishment or the sort of silencing that prevents a much-needed change.

Encourage people to speak up, listen to what they say with empathy, and gather a wide range of perspectives. Only then can you discover patterns that must change before your team or organization achieves the results it needs. It all comes down to seeing the true reality of your current situation.

SEEING THE TRUE REALITY OF THE CURRENT SITUATION

When my former colleague "Kate Rowland" and her husband, "Bob," set up sportswear company "A1ActiveWear," they could not foresee the damage the coronavirus pandemic would inflict on their business in the United States.

The San Francisco–based firm had grown rapidly to include twenty boutiques across the country before it ran into trouble. As my friends explained in a Zoom meeting, "Good day, Siobhán. We need help. Profits nose-dived in the first half of 2020 when the pandemic drastically reduced foot traffic to our stores. If we don't find a way to turn the ship around, we might be facing the end of the road for our business."

"That's serious," I responded. "Have you thought of opportunities to grow revenue at this critical time?"

Bob responded, "To be frank, Siobhán, our current cash crisis and the safety of our employees have been our main focus during the pandemic. Maybe we just need to tighten our belts and wait for the crisis to end."

I agreed to help. I began by interviewing members of the A1ActiveWear executive team to discern a pattern the company might need to change.

The pandemic was turning much of the planet into sweatpants-wearing remote workers busily converting garages into home gyms and avoiding trips to physical stores. Experts were seeing US customers spend in the neighborhood of $791.70 billion on e-commerce in 2020, up 32.4 percent from the year prior to the pandemic.

While experts agreed that the activewear market was set to boom globally, A1ActiveWear's leaders and executives had gotten stuck in a Shortsighted Pattern (see figure 2.6). The Shortsighted Pattern was the agreement at A1ActiveWear that "we are in the stores business, not the online business."

Cofounders Kate and Bob had pretty much buried their heads in the sand, restricting their thinking to their original business plan; their senior managers had accepted the view that the company was in the business of selling garments in beautiful boutique stores and had failed to appreciate the opportunities offered by the world of online business.

Once the Rowlands saw the Shortsighted Pattern, they reoriented the firm from a "stores business" to an "activewear business" with multiple channels that included internet shopping (see figure 2.7). The founders, reframing their role as owners of an activewear business, assembled a team that confirmed the potential of A1ActiveWear's move to online shopping.

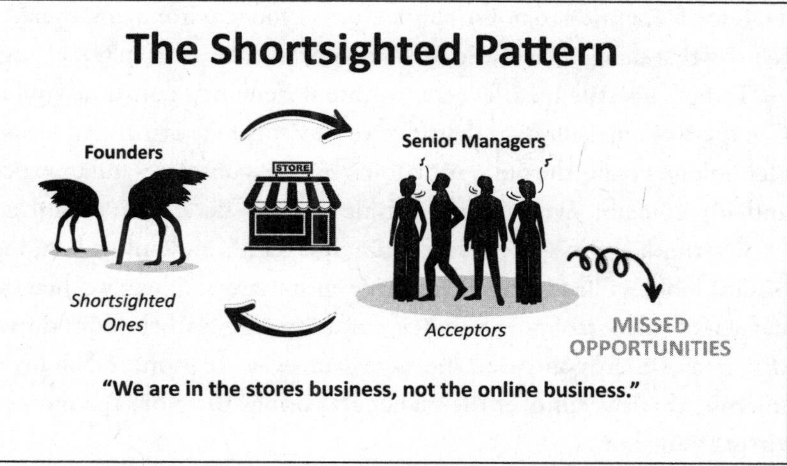

Figure 2.6

Figure 2.7

Senior managers took up their role as Channels Managers—who would use whatever means necessary (app, online, or in store) to deliver products to customers. In nine months, an online marketing campaign and a high-traffic, eye-catching website boosted revenues a full 20 percent over the prior year.

It's not always easy to see or, more importantly, accept reality. It's only natural to keep doing things the way you have always done them because you fear the discomfort change might cause.

Look for subtle and not so subtle clues in your environment, signals that tell you that danger lies ahead if you do not initiate some major changes.

Today's volatile business environment demands constant vigilance. Competitors make moves that take you by surprise, disruptive ideas and technologies make the old way of doing business obsolete, and unexpected and unpredictable events may blindside and even derail your organization.

Just think about some recent examples: ATMs and online banking replacing lobbies filled with tellers, movie enthusiasts unplugging their cables in favor of video streaming, a military invasion on the other side of the world that creates energy and food shortages, runaway inflation, and an invisible microbe that sweeps over the planet and brings the global economy to a virtual standstill.

Toy maker Hasbro's COO, Brian Goldner, foresaw big changes in his industry. When he joined Hasbro in 2000, the company had built a strong market share with such well-known brands as My Little Pony, Monopoly, Dungeons & Dragons, Power Rangers, and Nerf.

At the time the company's executives thought of themselves as "toy makers." Goldner, however, saw an opportunity to transform the company into something much more in tune with the changing times.

Kids, he thought, didn't just play with toys, they used them to act out parts in *stories*. But Hasbro wasn't in the storytelling business. It relied on the bright ideas of others to fuel their growth, such as licensing the wildly popular Pokémon to bolster revenues.

Every year management held its collective breath, hoping that the pre-Thanksgiving shopping spree would help end the year with substantial profits.

Brian did not hold his breath. He began work on Transformers, the miniature cars that can shape-shift into robots. Kids already loved Transformers, the key characters in a popular television cartoon. Why not take a big, if risky, leap into the future and turn toys into feature-length-movie heroes?

When Goldner pitched that idea to Hollywood executives, he caught the attention of the movie mogul Steven Spielberg, who agreed to coproduce a film that became a Hollywood blockbuster, raking in $710 million at the box office and increasing toy sales fivefold.

A year after the first *Transformers* hit the market, Goldner became CEO. Under his reign, six big-budget *Transformers* movies grossed about $5 billion worldwide.

The new CEO sold off Hasbro's factories to give the job of toy manufacturing to third parties. Hasbro had fully transformed itself from Toy Maker to Star Maker.

In 2018, while Toys "R" Us was filing for bankruptcy, Hasbro's revenue hit a record $5.2 billion and continued to do big business, including a 17 percent revenue spike in 2021 to $6.42 billion.

In 2021 Brian Goldner succumbed to cancer having made an enduring mark not only on his company but on the whole world of children's entertainment. His ability to see reality created the largest toy company in the US and earned him the ninety-sixth spot on the *Forbes* 2019 list of America's most innovative leaders.

A rather small percentage of today's leaders possess the sort of foresight that enables them to initiate and embrace transformative change. A higher percentage take their organizations down a path to a graveyard, including Nokia, Blockbuster, JCPenney, Kodak, BlackBerry, MySpace, Sears, Polaroid, Borders, and Pan Am, to name a few.

Effective change leaders don't just sit in their offices in the C-suite figuring out how to keep the board happy. They get out into the field, walk around their organization, talking to lots of people, from the janitor who vacuums the carpet in the CEO's office to the people who maintain the supply chain, listening carefully to what they have to say about the way we do things around here.

These leaders keep a keen eye on the ecosystem in which they operate, not just their competitive environment but the world at large. Then they put it all together in their minds. In a nutshell, they Look Beyond where they are to see where they need to be.

In order to initiate change, smart leaders tap the power of group intelligence. Change, after all, does not work when it comes from the top. It works when the whole Hive Mind gets involved in the process.

Mother Future, like Mother Nature, may hold her secrets tight, but if you take the time to understand her, she will reveal the changes your group needs to make in order to thrive in the coming years.

POINTS TO REMEMBER

- Simple patterns govern behavior in every ecosystem/organization.
- Mapping the ecosystem can help reveal the hidden patterns.
- An accurate picture of the ecosystem depends on taking multiple perspectives into account.
- An understanding of the true reality of a situation must precede any change initiative.

3

CREATING A COMPELLING CASE FOR CHANGE

Complete the Essential Groundwork

Bees know how to orchestrate change that benefits the whole group. When they sense overcrowding in the hive, they begin devising a plan to solve the problem.

The queen must leave, taking about half the colony with her in search of a new home. Worker bees pave the way for a successor by building cup cells where new queens will hatch, with one eventually taking over the current hive.

The old queen stops laying eggs, reduces her food intake, and becomes lighter. The worker bees stop foraging and gorge themselves with honey, readying themselves for an arduous journey.

Corporate leaders do not always prepare themselves and their people for a major change. Take, for example, Apple's launch of Apple Maps in 2012.

In the company's rush to counterattack in its escalating rivalry with Google Maps, Apple overlooked the complexity of this market niche: businesses opening and shutting down, locations changing, new roads and highways being built, customers' impatience and addiction to instant results.

This was not an environment in which you should even toy with the idea of releasing a product with dodgy software. It was a failure of blockbuster proportions (pun intended) that seriously tarnished Apple's hard-earned reputation for reliable products.

Failing to prepare yourself and your people for something as tricky as entering a new market can end up costing a lot of wasted time, energy, and money, not to mention putting a dent in your reputation.

Nothing will doom any change effort more quickly than the absence of a well-thought-out case for going where you want the group to go.

Why do so many leaders shy away from creating a compelling case for change?

Quite often it comes down to the fact that they feel more confident working on day-to-day challenges than on the complicated task of envisioning the future and contemplating all the relevant details involved in making the change to where the group needs to go.

You can't just wish for a brighter future; you must think through the important steps on the journey.

Leading meaningful and lasting change requires both an understanding of group dynamics and the skills needed to harness the power of the Hive Mind. Change leaders don't do what Apple did, reacting to a competitor's threat without taking the time to consider all the variables that could spell the difference between success and failure.

AVOIDING THE REACTIVE RESPONSE

My client "Aisha Sultan," a newly appointed general manager at the international construction company "Clancy Builders," had set her sights on creating a top-notch division. She faced some serious challenges.

As Sultan told me when we met in her office overlooking a tree-lined Melbourne boulevard, a recent survey had revealed a lot of unhappy customers. "Our customer satisfaction scores are in the bottom quartile, and I need to get to the crux of the issues fast. There's a lot resting on my shoulders. Our CEO, 'Noah Akira,' expects me to turn the division around. Pronto!"

"What's the problem with your customers?" I asked.

"Not sure. That's why I need your help, Siobhán. My best guess? Outdated equipment. I'm investing heavily in updating everything."

We agreed that Sultan should delay ordering the expensive new construction fleet until I'd checked out what was really happening on the front lines.

The following week, I trekked to one of the division's latest projects in the Goldfields region of North-Central Victoria where Clancy Builders was installing fiber-optic cables to deliver faster internet access to local residents. Customers were already complaining about delays.

The temperature showed 32 degrees Celsius (90 degrees Fahrenheit) as I turned off the ignition and went to meet project manager "Mike Beaumont," a tall fellow wiping sweat from his brow as we stepped under the shade of a eucalyptus tree to look out over the cable-laying site below.

Beaumont explained the project delay. "We've had issues getting through the white quartz rock in this region and are waiting for an order of jumbo drills to claw back lost time."

"Did this problem come as a surprise?" I asked.

Beaumont hesitated. "Um, we really didn't see that coming and put nothing in the budget to pay for it."

Later that morning, site manager "Adam Schmidt" explained that they had called in additional workers to help until the jumbo drills arrived. "But we're just falling further and further behind."

After visiting several other Clancy Builder sites later that week, I met with Sultan to review my findings: "Your poor client satisfaction scores result from the pattern governing work on your sites, not from outdated equipment." I sketched it on her office whiteboard (see figure 3.1).

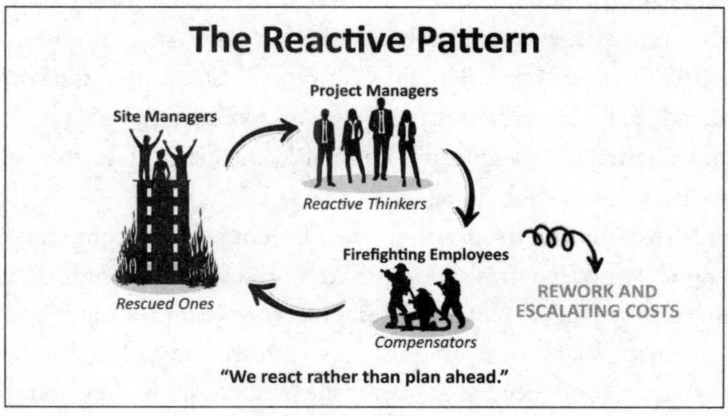

Figure 3.1

Sultan saw it immediately. "Ah, we react rather than plan ahead."

"Yup. Mike Beaumont and other project managers take up the role of Reactive Thinkers who wait for problems rather anticipate them.

"Site managers, including Adam Schmidt, step into the role of Rescued Ones who need saving when problems crop up. That's when you rush in organizational firefighters to compensate for the lack of planning.

"Your whole division is whirling around in circles dealing with urgent fires. Proper planning would stop the tornado. Can you see this pattern?"

Sultan frowned. "It's an epidemic throughout Clancy Builders. Folks here love playing the hero, riding in on white chargers to save the day."

I laughed. "But your customers *hate* it."

The sort of Reactive Pattern at work in the Clancy Builders culture often shows up at the beginning of change efforts when managers feel tremendous pressure to deliver quick results. They swiftly go into action mode without taking time to consider *all* the consequences of their actions, especially ones it's hard for them to foresee.

Fires break out. The best way to stop the fires? Anticipate them. Plan to keep them from breaking out in the first place.

Before we look at Sultan's decision to make some changes at Clancy Builders, let's pause to consider the folly of reacting too hastily to the need for change.

Aisha Sultan joins a rather long list of leaders beset by the Reactive Pattern. That list would include those responsible for the fall of the Knight Capital Group, a global financial services firm based in Jersey City, New Jersey, once the largest trader in US equities.

In 2012, Thomas Joyce, Knight Capital's CEO, decided the company needed to install new software to comply with recently imposed regulations. Underestimating the complexity of the task, the firm's IT team was given one month to get the job done.

In the rush to meet the deadline, the IT team failed to copy an updated program to one of the firm's eight production servers. The result? At 9:45 a.m. on August 1, 2012, Knight Capital's servers went on a rogue one-hour spending spree, snapping up 150 stocks worth around $7 billion.

Lacking the funds needed to pay for the purchases, Knight Capital could do nothing but quickly resell the stocks at a staggering loss of $460 million.

With his company teetering on the brink of bankruptcy, Thomas Joyce found himself battling not only the financial disaster but a sudden lack of confidence among investors.

By December 2012, Knight Capital had been acquired by rival Getco.

It had taken seventeen years of hard work to build Knight Capital Group into one of the leading trading houses on Wall Street and less than an hour for it to come tumbling down. It all started with a decision to react to the need for new software with an order to make it happen faster than humanly possible.

In the early stages of change, when you may not possess all the information you need to make wise decisions, you can often find yourself under considerable pressure to move faster than you should.

If a chorus of voices are demanding decisive action, you naturally worry that a delay will cost the vital support of your board, your boss, customers, employees, suppliers, and the public.

It's a tired old cliché, but haste does make waste. Sometimes, when the world demands, "We need it; and we need it *now*!" you should pause and say, "No! We're not ready yet."

Taking a step back enables you to do the change groundwork that will increase your chances of success. That's exactly what Aisha Sultan at Clancy Builders did.

Rather than buying new trucks that year, Sultan decided to establish a team of experts from across the division to review client proposals before submitting bids, a simple way to sniff out problems that might cause increased costs and delays.

A new Forward-Thinking Pattern began to emerge at Clancy Builders (see figure 3.2). Now project managers in the role of Forward Thinkers would put more thought into their proposals, and site managers, in the role of Prepared Ones, would develop better plans.

Nine months later Sultan called me with some good news. "Customers are noticing our more thorough project planning and are giving us higher marks for our performance. Our satisfaction score has moved into the top quartile for the first time in years. Plus, we've been awarded an extension to the broadband contract, boosting revenues by 20 percent this year. You can imagine the smile on my boss Noah Akira's face!"

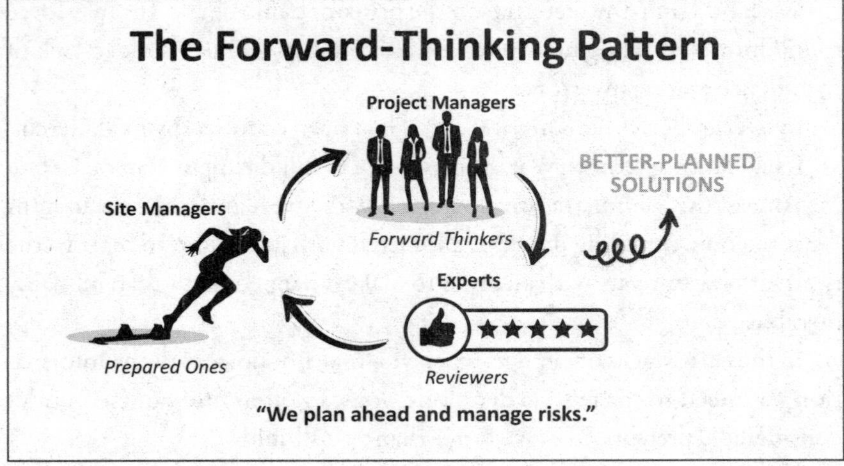

Figure 3.2

Of course, you might think you've done the necessary groundwork only to find that your ultimate decision does not work out as well as you'd planned.

Curveballs in the competitive environment may take you by surprise. Nevertheless, I recommend you never forget one cold, hard fact of ecosystem life that every bee knows—the flight plan is not the flight path.

The bee's waggle dance has shown the hive members the location of a new flower source, but as a busy worker bee leaves the hive, she spots a predatory dragonfly and takes a detour. She knows that the dragonfly is a powerful predator who can pounce on a bee and kill it in seconds by drawing juices from its body. One dragonfly can kill many bees in a day.

Plans are great until they encounter reality. You must alert group members to prepare themselves for the dragonflies that they may encounter along the way.

Leaders who rely on group intelligence don't apply Band-Aid solutions that address symptoms; they develop plans for curing the causes of those symptoms. They work on shifting the ecosystem's underlying patterns, a shift that is accelerated with inspiring a vision of a better future.

ENVISIONING A BETTER FUTURE

Let's assume you've hit upon a new idea for a business or have come up with a miracle cure for what ails your organization.

You know that both undertakings depend on making some major changes. You see a brighter future right around the corner.

But wait. Will people automatically help you make it happen? Not unless you persevere with your inspiration and keep building a compelling case for why people should fly in that direction.

Every movement, from a radical new business idea to a change in an existing brand identity or a corporate restructuring, requires a mobilizing idea that galvanizes people to rally behind the cause. It must be so clear, concise, and compelling that people grasp it, believe in it, and support it.

Take Frederick "Fred" Wallace Smith who created the $56 billion FedEx empire. In 1971, Yale University student Smith came up with the idea for air freighting packages overnight. Though legend has it that the case study earned him a C on his student paper, the ex-Marine persevered with his idea, keeping in mind the Marine Corps' motto: "Make the mission clear." That led him to his own motto: "People, Service, Profit":

PSP

People: Value your people so highly that potential employees in the company's headquarters in Memphis, Tennessee, would rather work there than anywhere else. Even when money was tight, FedEx offered generous wages, overtime pay, and medical coverage.

Service: Smith devised a well-thought-out plan for using a fleet of planes to pick up packages, fly them to Memphis, then reroute them to their destinations. It was a costly proposition. Smith made such a compelling case for the plan that he convinced skeptical investors to buy into his vision. With $91 million from venture capitalists, in addition to his own $4 million inheritance, he launched the business on June 18, 1971. Within a few short years FedEx became a household name.

Profit: Although FedEx lost $29 million in its first two years, it began to show a profit in 1976. The vision of a better future had become a reality.

At the time of this writing, FedEx had grown to become the biggest cargo airline in the world, with 681 aircraft, more than 200,000 vehicles, and 570,000 employees worldwide handling an average of 15 million packages a day.

Fred Smith changed the way people send and receive merchandise and how time-sensitive packages were tracked. If you want to change your own little corner of the world, you must do what Smith did, casting your eyes to the future and reimagining what's possible.

But just *seeing* the future won't get you there. You must inspire others to join the odyssey. It's harder than it seems at first blush. You've got to think about a lot of complex elements and pesky details. When you're looking for or proposing a significant change, you might try what I call Fast-Forward Thinking.

FAST-FORWARD THINKING

You are sitting alone at your desk, thinking about persuading others to follow you to a reimagined future. Ask yourself: *Can I paint a clear picture of the reimagined future? What must it include to inspire and motivate people? What roles must they step into to get the desired results? What solutions will it provide? What benefits will it deliver? How will it change people's lives for the better?*

As well as helping people see the "city on the hill," the case for change must stack up commercially. It must not strike people as an add-on or a nice-to-have new feature but as a must-have step toward the future. Otherwise, they may not enroll in the cause.

Fast-Forward Thinking may seem like a simple assignment. It's not. Since making any major change will most likely require a tremendous amount of thought, time, energy, and money, it's not for the fainthearted.

Jørgen Vig Knudstorp, appointed CEO of Lego in 2004, was not fainthearted. Soon after he took the job, the ex-McKinsey consultant assembled a team to reimagine a company that had fallen on hard times. Nothing, he told his team, was off limits. They were facing a rather dire situation, with sales 30 percent below the prior year, losses in excess of $400 million, and a crippling debt of $800 million.

How had it happened? The team made the startling discovery that Lego managers had lost track of which products were actually making money. In its R&D lab (known as the "Kitchen") designers were cooking up futuristic toy ideas without taking the production costs into account. All this dreaming had contributed nothing to the business since no value-adding products had come from the Lego Kitchen in more than a decade.

Part of the problem was the company's lack of focus. It had become a sprawling giant with too many irons in the fire.

From the mid-1990s to 2004, Lego had moved into TV programs, video games, clothes, jewelry, theme parks, and retail stores, many of them bleeding red ink onto the balance sheet.

Envisioning a different and better future, Vig Knudstorp and his team began formulating a clear case for change: "Lego cannot do everything." It was a simple message, something everyone could grasp, and it paved the way for selling the company's video games arm and theme parks and putting the iconic Lego brick back at the core of the business.

Embracing the need for *profitable* innovation, Lego's people accomplished a remarkable turnaround, producing revenues of $4.5 billion and profits of $1.5 billion in 2013. It happened because they saw their present predicament, imagined a better future, planned for it, and *did* it.

The case for change must specify the outcomes you wish to achieve. The best ones are succinct, memorable, and doable, like a strong mission statement. A robust case for change does not just describe what people will do to achieve desired outcomes; it also tells them what they should not do. In other words, describe missteps and risks that (like a dragonfly) might beset them.

Effective change leaders contemplate the consequences of the roles they want people to step into and the actions they want them to take.

In any meaningful and lasting change effort, some people win, some lose. If your plan calls for elimination of a historical process or the cancellation of a pet project that conflicts with the change goals, prepare yourself to say no to people who resist the decision. Making exceptions will cloud your focus and detour you from the path to better results.

Make it crystal clear! Julie Sweet did a terrific job doing just that when she took the reins at professional services giant Accenture in 2019.

Casting her eyes over a time of profound digital transformation in the business world, she spearheaded Accenture's most ambitious brand relaunch in a decade with a simple slogan: "Let there be change."

The firm's clients and its 720,000 employees got the message. The simplicity of this message helped Sweet advance Accenture into the digital age within three short years. By 2021, in the most uncertain period the tech market had ever faced, the firm delivered a record $50.5 billion in revenue, up 14 percent over the prior year.

Beware of the temptation to overwhelm the group with too many change initiatives. When you try to do everything all at once, you usually end up doing nothing but creating a lot of confusion. Progress slows down or grinds to a halt.

Too many small initiatives threaten concentration on the big prize. When people lose focus, they tend to wander off course or, worse, begin to doubt the validity of the change strategy. One big priority should always trump a bunch of little ones. Remind yourself that when everything is a priority, nothing gets done.

Complexity is the assassin of change because it kills decision-making and stops forward momentum. In my experience, you should focus on no more than three top priorities. Limiting roles and actions to the top three helps create the laser-like focus needed to keep the group inspired and moving steadily toward the results you need.

An inspiring mission captures the Hive Mind and motivates people to embrace and strive toward change, but it can also cause the sort of overzealousness that can damage some elements of the ecosystem. People must know they are doing good not just for themselves and the organization but for the world at large.

DOING WHAT'S BEST FOR THE ECOSYSTEM

Change leaders consider what's best for all parts of the ecosystem, including investors, employees, competitors, governments, and communities.

Bees have always done what's right for their ecosystem, fulfilling their role as Superpollinators who deliver a staggering $14.6 billion worth of crop production to the US economy annually.

A worker bee can visit over a thousand flowers in a single day to collect supplies for the hive, and in her lifetime, will fly the equivalent of one and a half times the circumference of the earth to make less than one teaspoonful of honey.

Bees work both for the welfare of the hive and the ecosystem on which the hive's very existence depends. Today's organizations must do the same.

Unfortunately, the demands to grow and increase profits can cause some organizations to overlook the needs of the environment in which they function, a trap that snared Amazon during the COVID pandemic.

The unexpected crisis caught the tech giant off guard as panicked customers ransacked supermarket shelves and turned to online shopping to fulfill their needs.

When corporate management scrutinized product flow charts, they awarded preference to high-demand products—such as hand sanitizer, face masks, toilet paper, office supplies, and gym equipment. If only Amazon had treated their own employees as well as they did their customers.

The increased demand for products taxed Amazon's vast technology-enabled warehouses and made life there as bleak as a Dickensian workhouse. In England the *Guardian* newspaper described a day in the life of a frontline worker responsible for picking, packaging, and shipping products.

"Anna," working in a fulfillment center in South-East England, sat in a metal enclosure, peering at a screen from 7:15 a.m. to 5:45 p.m., four to five days a week, for £10.50 an hour. Her job required her to assign products to storage containers at the near impossible rate of 360 items an hour or around 3,800 a day (or one every 6.7 seconds).

It took a toll on Anna. "When I get home it's about 6:30 p.m., and I just go in, take a shower, and go to bed. I'm always exhausted."

This bad press ignited intense scrutiny of the working conditions at Amazon, with lawmakers, regulators, and unions demanding changes. During the pandemic, Amazon had proven that it could quickly change to keep its business growing, but it was slow to respect the needs of its own worker bees.

A hive must pay attention not only to the process of producing honey but to the needs of all the hive's stakeholders. Focused on the common good, the hive maintains collective productivity by helping a bee that falls behind.

Yes, the hive needs to grow and even split in two when it becomes overcrowded, but it never makes growth a priority over stakeholder needs. The Hive Mind knows that growth at all costs can lead to no growth at all.

A change in an ecosystem affects all its stakeholders. Improving the well-being of one part enhances all others; harming one part harms the whole. Employees at the Nestlé Carnation factory in Modesto, California, respected this Law of Connectedness when they embarked on a change that would end up benefiting the planet.

During a severe drought in the region, Nestlé factory manager Omar Askar began looking for ways to use water more efficiently during the manufacturing of the canned Carnation milk products used by bakers across the United States and beyond.

Askar discovered that one part of the factory was processing milk to remove 60 percent of its water content, generating about 200 gallons of evaporated milk per day and then paying to dispose of the removed water. Another part of the plant was purchasing 250 gallons of water per day for production and cleaning processes.

In 2018 Askar and his colleagues began to explore how both parts of the factory could work together to use all the water involved, maintaining quality while reducing costs. It didn't take long to install a new water recycling system that accomplished that goal, and then some.

By 2020 the factory was returning more than seventy million gallons of water to local Modesto farmers (enough to fill a hundred Olympic-sized swimming pools).

Omar Askar proudly summed up the success: "Above and beyond our investments, I am most proud of the fact that we have embedded caring for water into our employee culture." Nestlé's Carnation factory became the first dairy-processing facility in the United States to earn certification under the Alliance for Water Stewardship (AWS) standard.

The Nestlé team's actions to benefit the planet mimic the behavior bees have displayed for millennia. And who benefits the planet more than nature's Superpollinators? Unexposed to moisture, honey encased in wax lasts forever. Remarkably, archaeologists found three-thousand-year-old edible honey in King Tutankhamun's tomb in Egypt.

Just as bees serve a purpose, so should every organization and every member of that organization. McKinsey research reveals that 70 percent of employees define their sense of purpose from their work.

Without an overriding purpose, you're just going through the motions; with one, you can not only accomplish great feats, but you can also survive most any hardship.

Make sure the changes you make are purposeful. Ask not just *how* you will make the change but *why* you are making it. Does it energize your people? Does it serve the ecosystem's stakeholders? Will changing a widget enhance the customer experience?

The Hive Mind thrives on purpose. Fulfilling that purpose should benefit everyone and harm no one. A strong purpose, one that delivers results to all stakeholders, will align everyone around a change vision.

CREATING ALIGNMENT AROUND THE CHANGE VISION

Berlin's leaders intended to make the new Brandenburg Airport a bustling center of international commerce, but that purpose became a faint dream due to a lack of stakeholder alignment. Extended delays caused by that lack of alignment propelled the project to the land of stratospheric costs, billions of euros over budget.

Airport construction began on schedule in 2006, but the original 2011 opening date came and went, with the airport finally commencing operations in October 2020, just as the coronavirus pandemic was throwing the whole airline industry into disarray.

The signs of trouble appeared early on. Multiple stakeholders bickered about the airport's location: national government leaders, Brandenburg state leaders, city mayor, airlines, passengers, workers, citizens, safety authorities, and two other Berlin airports.

It took six years to agree on a site. But lack of alignment continued to plague the project, with a constant stream of requests for modifications that drove the architects nuts.

The project became a revolving door for executives, who could not cope with all the issues that cropped up with the terminal's construction, improper fire safety systems, and allegations of corruption.

Despite the German public's uproar over the state-funded debacle, the project kept limping along. It took thirty years from concept to operation, with seven missed opening dates. Rather than standing as a shining symbol of a revitalized German capital, the new airport became an embarrassing public scandal that drew the attention of parliamentary committee investigators.

How do you get a dozen horses to pull in the same direction? Not with a whip. Not only is it cruel, but you'll end up with a resentful herd that will bite the hand that feeds it when given a chance. No, you use carrots. If all stakeholders appreciate the benefits offered, they will be more likely to pull toward the envisioned future.

Competing interests can quickly derail change plans, as the Scotland police force discovered in 2013 when they implemented a new computer system that would supposedly enable police officers to spend more time on frontline operations.

Police Scotland and the Scottish Police Authority (SPA) awarded a ten-year, $72.1 million contract to global professional services company Accenture, expecting them to provide a new computer system for recording crime and missing persons. This would, police leaders hoped, release police officers from back-office duties to frontline operations and deliver £200 million in savings.

Accenture brought an impressive track record to the project, including the system it implemented for Spain's Guardia Civil police service, but weeks into the engagement cracks appeared as questions arose about the system's search function.

An argument broke out. While Police Scotland insisted that Accenture's search solution did not meet contract requirements, Accenture maintained that Police Scotland's search functionality requirements fell outside the contract's specifications and would require more time and money.

The dispute so deeply eroded trust that the project ended acrimoniously in July 2016 when the sides agreed to cancel the contract in a settlement that had Accenture pay Police Scotland £24.65 million for its part in the conflict.

A subsequent review of the project by Audit Scotland concluded that the project "ultimately collapsed due to a damaging loss of trust between those involved and fundamental disagreements about what the program needed to deliver."

It was, in other words, a clear case of stakeholder misalignment. Unhappy stakeholders can slow down or even shut down a change initiative. Without alignment you face the risk of ongoing disagreements, damaged relationships, and an erosion of trust that can turn an otherwise sound plan into a shouting match that can waste years of hard work.

When everyone is expressing conflicting opinions about problems with a change effort, you hit the pause button and start rebuilding alignment around the initiative's scope and requirements.

Keep an eye peeled for early warning signs of misalignment. Even tiny signals, such as jokes about the initiative by middle managers, can escalate into big headaches down the line.

The changemakers at European aircraft maker Airbus wish they had kept their eyes peeled back in 2004 when they began building the world's largest and most complex jetliner, which was delayed by years because of crossed wires between its French and German teams.

The project required the joint efforts of two teams, one in Toulouse, France, charged with assembling the 555-seat A380 superjumbo jet, and one in Hamburg, Germany, assigned the task of producing the 530 kilometers of copper and aluminum wiring that would be threaded through each plane in bundles as thick as a human leg.

The French knew the project was in trouble when the wiring they received from the German team didn't fit properly into the aircraft. It turned out that incompatible software had given the two teams quite different versions of the plane's 3D digital mock-up.

If only someone had detected this discrepancy before the teams discovered that the bundles of a hundred thousand wires needed to perform 1,150 different functions in the plane just didn't fit. As one employee exclaimed, "Everything had to be ripped out and replaced from scratch."

The whole Airbus project ground to a halt, with seven double-decker aircraft carcasses waiting to be assembled. The electrical wiring mishap began with a simple, easily fixed mistake that resulted in a massive $6 billion loss in company value and dealt a severe blow to shares in Airbus's parent company, EADS. A stock price plunge of 26 percent in one day eventually led to the resignation of the EADS chief and cochief.

You're ten miles into a hundred-mile trip across the desert, singing along to your road-trip playlist, when you see the check engine light blinking on the dashboard. *It's no big deal,* you think. *I'll have someone look at it when I reach my destination.*

You keep speeding along, but fifty miles later you hear a rattling sound and smell smoke. Suddenly the car grinds to a halt.

There you sit, stuck in the sand, facing thirst and starvation unless someone comes along to rescue you. If only you had taken that little warning light seriously and turned back when you had the chance.

Don't let that happen to you. Before you start your change journey, make sure you have outlined a high-level plan that will help you navigate the potential perils along the way.

DEVELOPING A HIGH-LEVEL PLAN

I often ask leaders embarking on a change initiative this innocent question: "What's your change plan?"

The question usually elicits an uncomfortable silence.

Not so my friends the bees. They always follow a plan. In the case of the overcrowded hive, they begin to organize themselves for the coming change.

Yet managers trained as marketers, accountants, engineers, or technologists often feel uncomfortable planning for group change. Why? Because they are much more confident dealing with black-and-white technical matters than with the complex gray of ecosystem change.

A finance executive can formulate a budget forecast, an R&D manager can whip up a new paint formula, and an engineer can sketch plans for a bridge that spans a broad river.

Ask these highly competent managers to develop a plan that accounts for the components of a group's change journey, however, and they draw a blank. "That's not my area of expertise."

Ask me why I wrote this book, and I could offer a simple answer: to help leaders overcome that perplexity and gain the expertise to create meaningful and lasting change.

Group change is a complicated, often messy, always frustrating, and seldom easy undertaking. Every unique situation resists easy answers or ready-made solutions. Group change requires leaders who can plan a course of action and make critical decisions amid uncertainty and ambiguity, something that the producers of the 1995 science fiction film *Waterworld* failed to do.

The movie starring Kevin Costner, promoted as a "Mad Max on water" adventure, became one of the biggest flops in cinema history. Even as shooting started, the director didn't have a finalized script.

Multiple rewrites and reshoots extended a ninety-six-day shooting schedule to 150 days, with costs escalating to $175 million ($75 million over budget). Not only did the movie blow the budget, but it left audiences disappointed with a long, tedious, disjointed postapocalyptic adventure.

It was, by all accounts, one of the most ill-planned feature films of all time. It took a decade for Costner's career to recover from the debacle.

If you want to make a big splash with a much-desired change, you must avoid the *Waterworld* syndrome and make sure you have concocted a thorough, well-thought-out plan.

If you don't plan before you shoot, you'll probably end up shooting yourself in the foot. No matter the nature of your business, your stakeholders expect you to put your best thinking and planning into any dramatic change.

Sadly, leaders at the cosmetics giant Revlon didn't put on their best thinking caps when they acquired Elizabeth Arden Inc., in 2018. Despite a major restructuring to accommodate the acquisition, Revlon executives were seeing early cracks in the relationship between the two companies.

What to do? React to the problem with a technical "fix," installing a new SAP (systems applications and products in data processing) across a huge portion of the company's North American business. It sounds rather complicated, and it was. It didn't take long for integration problems and weak controls to turn a well-intentioned but ill-planned fix into a problem as big as the ones it was supposed to fix.

Almost immediately after the SAP launch, COO Christopher Peterson, noticing emerging problems with the system, reported a slowdown in his manufacturing facility in Oxford, North Carolina. The system changeover had made it impossible to record and account for inventory.

By year-end Revlon had failed to deliver $64 million worth of cosmetic orders to US customers, and by March 2019 the company announced a delay in filing its annual financial report, blaming the new system for the tardiness.

Headline news in the business press prompted a disastrous 6.9 percent drop in the company's stock. Eventually, Revlon reported a $294.2 million loss, joining *Waterworld* in the Poor Planning Hall of Fame.

"The devil is in the details." It's the little devils that can blow up your change efforts. Remember that little blinking light? Successful change leaders look for the little signals that may be warning them about trouble ahead. They never rush blindly forward. They exercise great patience, keenly observe what's happening in the ecosystem, and identify the patterns that may help or hinder progress. A compelling case for change depends on it.

POINTS TO REMEMBER

- A reactive response to the need for change can take you down the wrong track.
- A vision for a better future can inspire and motivate people.
- The best change initiatives take the views of all stakeholders into account.
- Successful change depends on aligning all stakeholders with the mission.
- A high-level plan outlines how you will navigate the change journey and tackle the risks that may affect progress.

4

TESTING NEW FLIGHT PATTERNS

Experiment Before Rolling Out the Change

In the afternoon sunlight the hive's colony splits as thousands of bees take flight and settle on a nearby tree branch. They will need to find a new home within a couple of days or face the real risk that the colony will perish, as predators lurk and night temperatures plummet.

Scouts will fly from this temporary staging area, seeking ideal locations for the new hive. Seldom do the bees choose the first one they see but collect data from the hundreds of scouts who bring back information gleaned from their home inspections. You must take great care when you're doing something as important to the group as finding a new home.

Amazon founder Jeff Bezos navigates change by constantly experimenting and learning. Amazon spent four years (and more than $100 million) on the Fire Phone it released in 2014. It was a complete flop.

Bezos's response to his employees following the failure? "You can't, for one minute, feel bad about the Fire Phone. Promise me you won't lose a minute of sleep."

As it turned out, a good, sound sleep after the failure spawned a dream come true: the voice recognition software that eventually resulted in Echo, that digital assistant who answers such questions as "Alexa, who won the 2024 women's championship at the Australian Open?"

Over the years, I've asked many managers to describe a change they've undertaken. Invariably, they describe a rather logical, step-by-step process whereby they went from point A to point B to point C until they reached their desired destination.

It never happens that way, which brings us to the second step and the E on the Hive LENS: Experiment.

Traversing uncharted ground, you always find yourself skirting unexpected swamps, scaling boulders you had not foreseen, and dashing sideways to avoid a charging predator. It is, after all, a jungle out there.

Bees get that. So should you. Which brings us to one of the most important steps on the journey: redesigning your operating model in a way that facilitates change.

REDESIGNING YOUR OPERATING MODEL

The new home-seeking bees know that successfully navigating through the jungle of change requires a new operating model. Success will depend on replacing a Production Operating Model with a Change Operating Model (see figure 4.1).

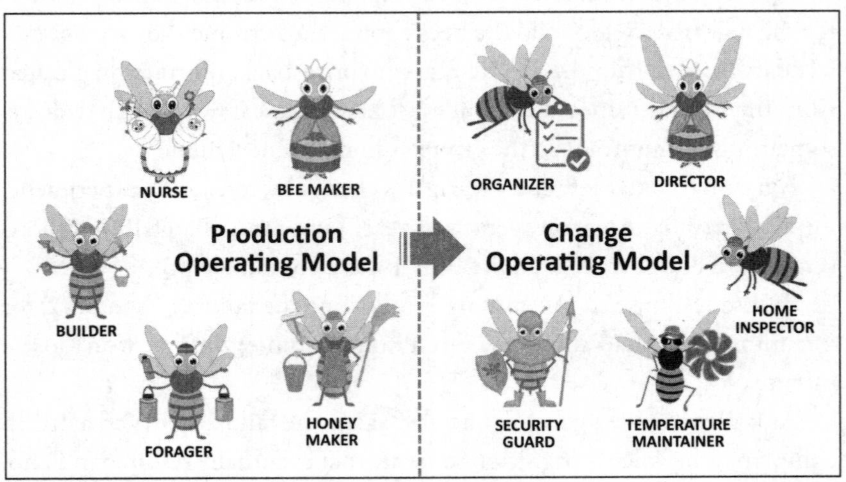

Figure 4.1

Each operating model requires that members of the group take up key roles. The hive's Production Operating Model includes the following roles:

- **Nurse:** newly born bees who take care of babies, feed the queen, and distribute medicinal honey to the sick
- **Bee Maker:** the queen and drones who produce up to two thousand eggs per day during a queen's two- to three-year lifespan
- **Honey Maker:** bees who break down the pollen and nectar into a simple syrup before storing it in honeycomb cells
- **Forager:** mature bees who leave the hive to procure nectar and pollen
- **Builder:** twelve-day-old bees who have developed the wax glands needed to construct honeycomb

The Change Operating Model requires a different set of roles:

- **Organizer:** bees who arrange for the queen's successor, then push the current queen to the entrance of the hive to lead the split
- **Director:** the queen who leaves the nest followed by a massive cloud of twenty thousand bees and sends out signals that call everyone to settle on a nearby tree
- **Home Inspector:** several hundred bees who carry out home inspections in hollow trees, old barns, and abandoned buildings and return to perform dances to share information about what they have found
- **Temperature Maintainer:** bees who keep the cluster's core temperature at 35°C/95°F by creating ventilation channels in the heat of the day and shivering to keep warm when temperatures drop at night
- **Security Guard:** older bees with well-developed stingers who remain on high alert for threats on the temporary perch

What does this tell us about change in today's business jungle? If you adopt the conventional mechanistic approach to change, you wait for instructions to come down from the executive suite.

If you use the old social network model, you rely on "champions" or "agents" to influence change.

In the new ecosystem change model, you begin your journey by reframing roles and designing the operating model that will facilitate your unique change initiative.

Let's take a look at how three well-known organizations did it.

Amazon's "Two Pizza" Operating Model

When Jeff Bezos founded Amazon in 1994, consumers did not immediately flock to the idea of buying books online. Bezos knew it would take a highly adaptive and responsive organization to turn Amazon into a household name. His "Two Pizza" Operating Model stipulated that teams, small enough to be fed by two pizzas, take up the role of customer-obsessed Entrepreneurs.

The founder intuitively knew that an organization with smaller teams and fewer management layers could more easily work on offerings that would win the trust of the book-buying public.

At first glance Amazon's structure appears highly centralized, with a group of senior executives (the S Team) reporting to the CEO. But if you peer beneath this hierarchical structure, you will find thousands of project teams governed by the "Two Pizza" Operating Model.

These small, hive-like teams obsess with delighting customers. For example, employees in the Devices Division spend less time navigating the hierarchy and more time meeting customer needs, to amass a string of successes that included Kindle, Alexa, Fire tablets, Fire TV, Echo, Astro, Ring, Blink, and Luna. "Customers would love a new gadget. Let's take up our role as Entrepreneurs to make it happen." Well, the results speak for themselves. Amazon became a dominant force in every industry it entered.

Apple's "Experts Rule" Operating Model

Apple's operating model saved the company from disaster and set it on a trajectory for a $1 trillion valuation. Steve Jobs used the "Experts Rule" Operating Model to banish organizational infighting and bestow decision-making on functional experts.

When Jobs returned to Apple in 1996, after a decade away from the organization, he found the firm he had cofounded in dire straits. Business unit general managers competed with one another, constantly fighting over transfer costs to their P&Ls.

This bickering had driven the company to the brink of bankruptcy. In a single day, Jobs laid off *all* the general managers and reframed employees as Functional Experts charged with bringing their deep expertise to projects.

In the case of camera technology, for example, when Jobs unveiled the iPhone on the Macworld Expo stage in 2007, he spent only six seconds describing its camera.

Enter Apple's Functional Experts, who began working on a string of astounding innovations that changed the shape of the industry, including high dynamic range imaging (2010), panorama photos (2012), optical stabilization (2014), live photo technology (2015), dual-lens camera (2016), portrait lighting (2017), night mode (2019), ultrawide-angle lenses (2020), and next-level hardware and a dramatically more powerful camera system (2022).

While all of Apple's functional areas reported to Jobs, in reality the "Experts Rule" Operating Model drove the culture. "You need the best camera in the world? Stand back and watch the Experts deliver!" No wonder Apple was voted by its peers as the Most Admired Company sixteen years in a row.

Microsoft's "Partnering" Operating Model

When Satya Nadella joined Microsoft in 2014 as the new CEO, the company teetered on the brink of irrelevancy and desperately needed to shift its dependence on Office and Windows licenses to the brave new world of cloud computing.

Before Nadella was hired, a cartoonist had depicted Microsoft as a jumble of warring factions: a leader perching atop a pyramid overseeing several gangs pointing guns at one another. This climate had armored itself against change.

Four years after taking over as CEO, Nadella installed a new operating model that split the Windows department into two separate groups: Experiences + Devices and Cloud + AI Platform.

Each part took up a clear role and was allocated the resources needed to accomplish their missions. A mandate to cooperate set the stage for the "Partnering" Operating Model.

That attitude cascaded to the four hundred thousand companies that sold Microsoft products. "You want to succeed in the world of cloud computing? Come partner with us!" As a result, Microsoft achieved an increase in market capitalization from roughly $300 billion in 2014 to about $2.32 trillion by 2023, becoming the second most valuable company in the world (behind Apple).

What do all three organizations (Amazon, Apple, Microsoft) have in common? They fashioned their own unique, changeable operating models.

The new models fueled change and the new way of doing things that produced positive outcomes for customers and shareholders alike. Their leaders knew that you don't innovate and grow by tinkering with the same old machine or getting your people to jump up and down like cheerleaders. You do it with a Hive Mind. You unleash the power of group intelligence. And you create new patterns and roles.

Stay with me while I delve deeper into the subject of roles. When you drill down to the heart of the matter, meaningful and lasting change is all about reframing the roles we all take up at work on a daily basis.

Kate Rowland, cofounder at A1ActiveWear, steps into many roles every day: mother, wife, daughter, sister, entrepreneur, executive team member, basketball coach, community member, neighbor, holiday planner, friend, to name a few. She finds stepping from one role to another as easy as changing from a business suit to a running outfit.

Take this Monday morning, when she arrives at her company's main warehouse in the San Francisco Bay Area only to discover that overnight storms have flooded the facility.

The normally introverted cofounder of A1ActiveWear immediately steps into the role of Crisis Manager, overseeing cleanup efforts and issuing orders. "Turn off the building's electricity; call the insurance carrier; clear out these water-damaged products; wash and sanitize those floors!"

By the end of day, Kate and her team have gotten the warehouse up and running again. Driving home after a long day, she thinks, *Can't believe how easily I went from shy, quiet-spoken executive to field marshal. Thank goodness Siobhán taught me that personality does not have to dictate behavior. But role can!*

There's a crucial lesson here relating to the Law of Role: the ability to shift mental maps works at both an individual and group level. With group intelligence you can reframe both, to harness the Hive Mind and bring about faster, more effective, and more widespread change.

In Kate Rowland's case, she not only reframed her role from business-as-usual executive to Crisis Manager, she inspired her people to do likewise, replacing their usual daily activities with the new role of Crisis Responder.

Kate did not need to change individual and collective roles permanently. But if she needed to do that, transforming her company in a major way to propel it toward a more successful future, she would have experimented with ideas for changing roles and patterns before she rolled out the full initiative. She'd take up the role of Research Scientist, devising and testing ideas by trial and error until she hit upon one to which she could fully commit time, people, and resources.

CONDUCTING RESEARCH EXPERIMENTS

In 2006, Alan Mulally, an aeronautical engineer by training, left his position as an executive vice president at aircraft manufacturer Boeing to become CEO of Ford Motor Company.

It was a very bad year for American automakers, who were suffering through the second-worst auto depression in history. Ford had recently posted its biggest annual loss in its 103-year history, a whopping $12.7 billion.

How do you cope with such a disaster? Do you curl up in a ball and wait for better times to come along? No, in Mulally's opinion; you tell your 205,000 employees to treat failure as an opportunity to learn, to have some fun, to experiment with new ideas. What have we got to lose?

Ford faced a monumental challenge. Japanese carmakers, especially Toyota and Honda, were making more reliable cars than Ford, at a lower cost, and their American counterparts seemed incapable of competing in the global marketplace. Mulally knew that this change needed to start at the top, and to make that happen he commenced weekly review meetings with his executive team in the Thunderbird Room at Ford's Dearborn, Michigan, headquarters.

Sitting in the "pilot's seat" at a dark, circular wooden table in a room fitted with three video screens, Mulally beamed at his team as he asked them to create a color-coded weekly progress report: green for good, yellow for caution, and red for problems.

During the first few follow-up meetings, every executive presented all-green reports that proved how well they were doing. Mulally called them on it. "You guys, you know we lost a few billion dollars last year. . . . Is there *anything* that's not going well?"

That's when the truth-telling began. Mark Fields piped up. Yes, there was a serious problem with the lift gate actuator on the Ford Edge tailgate that had stalled production.

The room grew so quiet, you could have heard a bee land on the table. Then Mulally began to clap, acknowledging Fields's courage in admitting failure: "Mark, I really appreciate that clear visibility." In the following weeks, the reports looked like colorful rainbows.

Mulally had seen the Punishment Pattern that was thwarting experimentation and learning at Ford (see figure 4.2). The hidden agreement at Ford was, "We punish those who make mistakes."

Managers in the role of Punishers who would not tolerate failure turned their people into Fearful Ones. Nothing paralyzes innovation more than the fear of failure. Exit experimentation, learning, and growth.

Let's pause for a moment before we get to the punch line at Ford. The pattern at the music-streaming platform Spotify offers a stark contrast to the one that was stalling Ford's turnaround.

In 2018, Daniel Ek and Martin Lorentzon announced that the world's largest music streamer planned to move into podcasting.

Within three years the company had not only made the move, but it had also accomplished the remarkable feat of toppling Apple from its number one spot in the market. How had they achieved such rapid progress? You guessed it. Experiments.

Figure 4.2

When Apple's Steve Jobs introduced the world to podcasts in 2005, Ek watched the medium skyrocket, fueled in large part by Apple's commitment to the continuous product development that kept its app fresh.

Ek decided to play the Research Scientist and launch a series of experiments, investing $500 million in a string of podcast companies including Gimlet Media, Anchor, Parcast, The Ringer, and The Joe Rogan Experience.

With the mandate to come up with something amazing, Spotify's small product teams, consisting of no more than eight people and working in far-flung regions of the globe, felt free to run their own little labs.

While Apple was focusing on distribution, Spotify's teams concentrated on creating new offerings across the whole ecosystem of users, creators, and advertisers. It became a circus of product updates, interactive tools, polls, Q&As, and other features at a velocity never seen in the podcasting space.

The Spotify Hive Mind flew fast, shipped software quickly, and performed their work with minimum overhead. Apple simply could not match this unprecedented string of innovations. They paid off big-time.

By 2021 the company had surpassed $1.2 billion in yearly ad revenue and had shot past Apple in terms of the number of users who listened to its podcasts on a monthly basis.

As Daniel Ek explained, "So why did we succeed this fast? . . . Our success is not attributable to just one thing but literally hundreds, if not thousands, of improvements that we're working on in parallel for the benefit of creators, users, and advertisers alike."

When Thomas Edison was asked how he came up with some of the most important inventions in history, the so-called Wizard of Menlo Park admitted that along the way his experiments had failed more often than they succeeded. But he waved all his stumbles away by purportedly saying, "I have not failed ten thousand times. I've successfully found ten thousand ways that will not work."

In other words, you've got to be willing to proceed by trial and error until you hit upon the right solution. That's what Daniel Ek understood. And that's what Doug Evans, founder of juice maker Juicero, should have known.

Launched in 2013 with the mission to help people get healthier by consuming fresh raw foods, the company initially seemed like a smart investment, but it ended up closing its doors just three years later.

The good news? Evans had spent three years working on a home cold-pressed juicing system. The bad news? He did not run the trial-and-error experiments that would have proven his device more or less useless. That's a big gap between a good idea and stark reality.

The idea: Juicero would collect and prepare fresh organic fruit and vegetables and put them in special single-serve packets that the juice press would squeeze into a glass, producing cold fresh juice, with no cleanup, hassle, or waste. Sounds perfect!

The reality: The Juicero Press cost an eye-boggling $699 but did not outperform a pair of human hands. At no cost to the squeezer.

Eager investors had injected $120 million into the company, enabling Evans to recruit a team of elite designers to create a machine that looked like a gizmo right out of *Star Wars*.

Its doom began the day a video appeared, showing a *Bloomberg* reporter hand squeezing a fruit packet to obtain a full glass of juice. The $699 Juicero contraption joined the discontinued Ford Edsel in the museum of ideas that should have been tested before they were inflicted on the world.

Getting back to the Ford saga, CEO Alan Mulally was stressing the need to conduct experiments and to learn from the ten thousand mistakes a company might make before they find the formula for a brighter future. Consider the new pattern at Ford (see figure 4.3). This pattern emphasized a new agreement: "We use experiments as learning opportunities." Managers stepped into the role of Encouragers who embraced the learning that comes from failure; employees took up the role of Experimenters who tested new ideas and approaches.

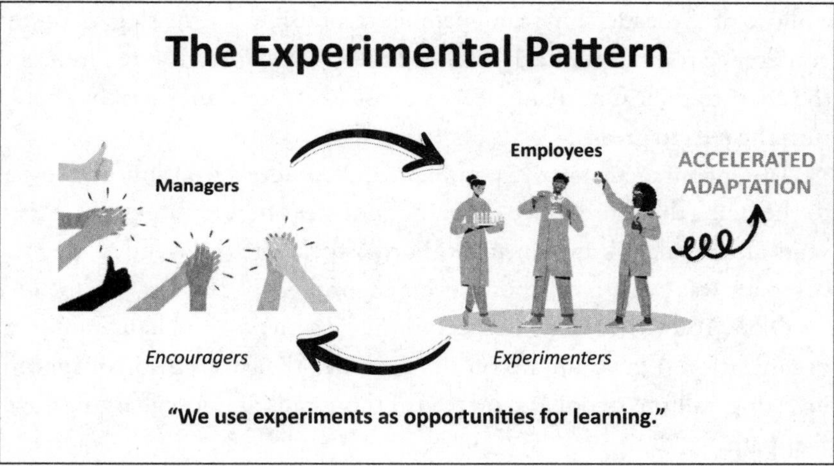

Figure 4.3

One experiment aimed to evolve in-car technology at Ford. Just four months after Mulally took over as CEO he appeared onstage with Microsoft's Bill Gates at the North American International Auto Show to announce SNYC, the "computer in a car" technology that would revolutionize the industry.

This moment signaled a huge step forward for the company and a radical reshaping of Ford from "just another car company" into an automotive tech pioneer.

Mulally supported experimentation across the entire company by setting a simple goal to create "an exciting, viable Ford delivering profitable growth for all." This would require a set of new behaviors and the knowledge that honesty would not be penalized.

This simple plan fit on the two sides of a single card given to every employee and to everyone doing business with the company. Ford would simplify its product line, reinvigorate its portfolio of brands, and introduce a One Team Operating Model.

Under Mulally's watch the company undertook many major experiments, including rebooting two of its most iconic cars, the Mustang and F-Series, which became leaner and lighter. Ford also brought back the Taurus, a car that had revolutionized the automobile design process in the late 1980s.

Mulally insisted on accountability and hung color-coded charts, with a photo of the leadership team member responsible for the targets, on the conference room wall. Each week executives explained the red items on the chart to their One Team peers and asked for ideas on ways they could turn the reds to greens.

The encouragement to experiment rippled out to frontline employees to the point that Ford, once again, became a profitable automaker. Seven years after Mulally's appointment, Ford's stock price rebounded, and the company was consistently posting annual profits.

Okay. You've decided you need to make some major changes in your organization. Do you jump on the first idea that pops into your mind, investing millions of dollars and tens of thousands of hours charging down that path?

Or do you isolate a half dozen possibilities, test them with intense mental scrutiny, and pick the best one before you lead the charge to the future? Seems like a no-brainer to me. Successful change leaders think deeply about each option, including identifying any hidden assumptions that might derail the change.

DEBUNKING FALSE ASSUMPTIONS

In January 2015, Target's new CEO, Brian Cornell, pulled the plug only two years into the retailer's disastrous foray into Canada. Subsequent investigations revealed a damaging hidden assumption behind the Minneapolis-based firm's failed first attempt at international expansion.

Initially Target's Canadian president, Tony Fisher, was promising investors that within two years of a rapid ramp-up to one hundred–plus stores, the Canadian operation would be producing huge profits. Although Fisher began hearing about supply chain problems that were delaying shipments from distribution centers to store shelves, he pressed ahead, promising, "If anyone can do this, we can!"

Despite reports about empty shelves, unexciting merchandise, and unattractive locations that should have alarmed Fisher, he proclaimed, "If there's any team in retail that can turn this thing around, it's us."

Fisher's steadfast proclamations may sound like a reasonable rallying cry, but it was a flawed assumption. Working long hours to overcome a seemingly endless series of hurdles could not, as it turned out, fulfill Fisher's promise of a shining success. As one former employee later said, "That was the biggest mistake we could have made."

In retrospect, the company should have focused on ironing out the kinks in its supply chain, ensuring that products would flow smoothly onto store shelves. Without a well-oiled delivery process, new stores would open faster than the company could stock the shelves.

Unfortunately, Target's work on its supply chain was not keeping pace with new store openings, leaving customers with a poor shopping experience. Why come back to a store with disorganized and often empty shelves? Had Fisher's team abandoned the hidden assumption about its invincibility, the Canadian venture would have achieved much better results.

In a last-ditch attempt to get the right results, CEO Cornell replaced Tony Fisher with a new Canadian CEO, but it was like placing a sterile pad on a gaping wound. The red ink continued to flow until, in January 2015, Target announced that it would exit the Canadian market, close all 133 stores, and refocus its attention on the US market.

The hidden assumption behind its expansion into Canada ended up costing the company a $5.4 billion write-down and a total net loss of $2 billion.

Confidence can carry you forward. Overconfidence can crash your hopes. In the case of Target's hope to conquer Canada, the "we can do anything because we believe in ourselves" mantra slammed into a brick wall.

Fisher assumed a false level of competence among his troops.

Sometimes you just don't know enough to know what you don't know. And what you don't know can send you speeding into a brick wall. Knowledgeable yet humble leaders never assume a false level of competence but make sure their assumptions sync with reality.

Samsung should have paid more attention to matching their assumptions with reality when the company released the Galaxy Fold, its first folding phone. Users, Samsung assumed, would love the product's doubled screen capacity and small size.

DJ Koh, Samsung Electronics' CEO, climbed onto the stage at the company's Unpacked event in February 2019 to announce the new device: "To those who say they've seen it all, I say, buckle your seat belt, the future is about to begin."

Despite a price tag of $1,980, potential buyers applauded an advancement that seemed straight out of a *Star Trek* movie. Tech reviewers disagreed, disparaging the phone's frustrating level of glitches, flickering screens, and sticky hinges.

DJ Koh initially pooh-poohed the criticism until, in a brutal admission, he conceded that Samsung's most exciting development in years was a car wreck. If only he had questioned Samsung's dangerously false assumption that in the smartphone race, "We need to be first."

Samsung's profits had traditionally come from its aggressive strategy to develop cutting-edge technology that would establish new benchmarks in the marketplace. A string of impressive successes justified its confidence, but it also created a false sense of infallibility.

In its race with Chinese vendor Huawei Technologies Co., which was also building a foldable phone called Mate X, Samsung spent years working on the Galaxy Fold and had filed more patents for foldable smartphones than its competitor. Samsung simply had to cross the finish line ahead of its archrival.

First with a clunker, however, does not win the race or the hearts of customers. As DJ Koh later admitted, "I pushed it through before it was ready." Less than a year after launching the Galaxy Fold, Samsung announced that it would be canceling orders, a move that dealt a severe blow to the company's reputation.

You need to debunk false assumptions before they sneak up and bite you, as Tarsus Distribution, the South African IT supplier, experienced when it tried to overcome problems with staffing.

Well, if you can't find enough good people, why not hire some good robots? The firm's management decided to solve its problem with Robotic

Process Automation (RPA), adding four robots named Betsy 1, Betsy 2, Betsy 3, and Betsy 4 to the workforce.

Uh-oh. They should have realized that this move might not sit well with human employees, who viewed the Betsys as a threat to their jobs and their families' welfare. Tim Proome, manager of Tarsus Distribution's supply chain, recalls the reaction: "We were talking about robots, and it started to freak people out."

A blind man could see the gap between management's assumption that "robots will help you" and an employee's reaction that "robots will take our jobs."

To resolve the conflict, Proome engaged in one-on-one conversations with employees, explaining how the Betsys could ease their workload but would never eliminate the need for human workers. "It was an uphill struggle, and it took constant reassurance," he admitted.

But imagine their reaction when employees returned to the office after the festive holiday season to find that the Betsys had processed fourteen hundred shipments in their absence. No one lost their job, and the Betsys went from Beasties to Besties overnight.

As this story illustrates, group assumptions shape how people react to change. Smart leaders constantly examine the assumptions in different parts of the ecosystem, looking for any misalignments or perceptions that spell danger. When they spot threats to successful change, they take corrective action. Effective corrective action depends on using the right yardstick to measure exactly where you are at every point along your journey to the future.

MEASURING WITH THE RIGHT YARDSTICK

Researchers in Microsoft's Human Factors Lab were studying the impact of new work habits during the COVID-19 pandemic. They systematically analyzed more than a trillion data points, including data from almost 250 million active Teams videoconference users.

Their probing discovered that a lot of consecutive video meetings could stress a human brain. As Jared Spataro, the company's VP of Modern Work, explained, "We started to see trends and patterns that we'd never seen before." Some of these patterns raised serious concerns about the impact of back-to-back virtual meetings on a participant's mental health.

So, should organizations abandon the practice? Not at all. They should just tweak it a little, allowing ample break time between virtual meetings. The researchers had discovered that a certain amount of downtime helped ameliorate the potentially harmful effects of the pandemic-induced practice of sitting at home in your bunny slippers while interacting with images on a computer screen.

Data. Like fresh air and sunshine, you can't get enough of it when you're contemplating the impact of change on an organization. Although you may not be able to access data from 250 million users, you can still establish important data points during the early stages of change.

Without the yardstick to measure impacts, you will never know whether you are moving forward, backward, or sideways. A twelve-man drilling crew at Texaco could have used a better yardstick when they went in search of oil on Louisiana's Lake Peigneur.

On the morning of November 21, 1980, the Texaco team began drilling for oil on the thousand-acre lake, a much-loved haven for fishermen in southern Louisiana. When a fourteen-inch drill bit got stuck just below the shallow lake's surface, causing the rig to tilt, the work crew abandoned it.

Ninety minutes later, safely onshore, they watched in horror as their 150-foot derrick vanished into a lake they assumed was less than eleven-feet deep.

It turned out that the Texaco crew had punched a hole in a subterranean salt dome that Diamond Crystal Salt workers were busily mining. That operation had created many crisscrossing tunnels under the lake's rocky bottom.

Punching through it created a whirlpool on the water's surface that eventually engulfed eleven barges, four trucks, countless 150-foot trees, and even a sixty-five-acre chunk of nearby Jefferson Island.

Amazingly, all fifty-five workers in the salt mine managed to escape unhurt, as the largest artificial whirlpool in history emptied the lake and sucked in salt water from the Gulf of Mexico to flood the lake's deeper bed.

A miscalculation by the Texaco drillers permanently transformed an eleven-foot-deep freshwater lake full of largemouth bass into a two-hundred-foot-deep saltwater sinkhole.

Could Texaco have avoided the mishap? Yes. The drillers could have obeyed the old maxim "Measure twice, drill once." Correct measurement would have saved the company from later lawsuits and an out-of-court settlement of $45 million in damages to local businesses.

Move without measurement, and you risk catastrophe; measure twice and proceed with a much better chance of success.

Bees do it. When searching for a new home, a scout spends nearly an hour closely examining each potential homesite, performing slow hovering flights around the location and a few dozen trips inside the cavity, buzzing over all inner surfaces to judge its roominess. Don't be a Texaco driller. Be a bee.

NASA learned this lesson the hard way when it lost the $125 million Mars Climate Orbiter (MCO) due to a measurement error. The agency launched the MCO on a two-year mission to explore the planet's water history and its potential for life. It would also provide a communications relay for future missions to Mars.

After a 286-day journey, the orbiter fired its engine to push itself into the planet's orbit, then disappeared. And went silent. NASA engineers scrambled to uncover how this mega disaster had happened.

It turned out that Lockheed Martin engineers in Denver were basing navigation commands for the spacecraft on English measurements (inches, feet, and so on), while the NASA team in the Jet Propulsion Laboratory in Pasadena, California, was using metric calculations (centimeters, meters, and so on). Since no one thought to convert the commands from English to metric units, the orbiter strayed off course and eventually disintegrated under atmospheric stress. Give those NASA folks a solid gold two-and-a-half-foot yardstick.

Measuring correctly is not rocket science. You may not hold a PhD in aeronautics, but you should know your business well enough to use a three-foot-long yardstick when you try to capture essential data that will help your transformation effort stay on track. You don't do it for your own enlightenment; you do it so your people will know where they are and where they're going.

At Amazon, Jeff Bezos measured everything. Each team, business unit, region, and warehouse relies on its own artificial intelligence systems to gather the data they need to stay on track and correct course when necessary. Bezos believes in the power of good data to keep transforming Amazon. He's fostered a true Hive Mind.

Amazon's people buzz around and into every nook and cranny of customer data models in order to keep satisfying customers and to move into new ventures that might delight customers even more. Such services as swift Prime delivery, one-click product and audiobook ordering, customer reviews and recommendations, special deals, and real-time assistance all result from constant investigation into the data. Busy bees, indeed!

It takes a certain amount of navigational skill to fly successfully from Tallahassee to Timbuktu. You need a good pilot who follows an accurate map, who knows the aircraft's capabilities, and who keeps track of progress every mile of the journey.

Organizational change is a flight from point A to point Z, with a lot of intermediate points along the way. Where are you now?

If you can't measure your position, you don't know where you are. You're plunging through the Martian atmosphere on your way to a disastrous smashup.

Hope is not a strategy. The road to ruin is paved with guesses and opinions that turn out to be wrong. Rip a page from the Book of Bees, experimenting and testing until you feel confident your flight to the future will begin and stay on course.

POINTS TO REMEMBER

- The right Change Operating Model reframes and redesigns the roles needed to achieve meaningful and lasting change.
- Experiments and test-drives result in the best final decisions.
- False assumptions can send the organization down the wrong path.
- Measuring with the right yardstick ensures that the change effort remains or gets back on track.

5

MAKING THE CRITICAL CHANGE DECISIONS

Tap into the Wisdom of the Hive

When the colony becomes overcrowded, those who will populate the new hive fly to a nearby branch. Scout bees leave the staging area to search for promising real estate. Once a scout finds a potential new home, she returns to the branch to deliver her report in the form of a highly animated dance. A favorable report will convince her companions to follow her to the site to conduct a group inspection.

The convocation buzzes with agreements and vetoes. While an excited dance prompts action, a more sedate one suggests the bees look elsewhere for a new home.

From all this hectic dancing, one choice emerges as the best possibility. As daylight wanes, roughly 80 percent of the scouts have voted for the new home in an oak tree cavity next to a grassy knoll at the edge of Wombat Forest.

David Novak, Pepsi's former head of marketing, could have saved a lot of time and embarrassment if he had orchestrated a more effective dance when he launched Crystal Pepsi, a change initiative that turned into the biggest mistake of his career. Although the debacle happened more than thirty years ago it still holds a spot on *Time* magazine's list of the top ten marketing failures of the twentieth century.

Novak thought he had hit upon a brilliant idea: creating a clear soda by removing the dye that gives Pepsi its brown hue. That should compete with other clear soft drinks, like ginger ale.

But wait. Some of the bottlers in the company who tasted the new drink didn't much care for it: "It doesn't taste enough like Pepsi!" Novak ignored the feedback, believing the product would quickly grow to become a billion-dollar brand: "I figured I was the marketing expert, and they just didn't get it."

Crystal Pepsi launched in a splashy ad during the 1993 Super Bowl with the tagline "You've never seen a taste like this."

A lot of customers bought the new product but didn't like its aftertaste. Novak regretted not listening more carefully to all the feedback, but he did learn a valuable lesson: "the importance of letting go of my confident position momentarily so I could actively listen to the wisdom offered by those around me."

When he had danced to the tune of the new idea, the other bees voted against it. Had he let the Hive Mind emerge the change solution, we all might be drinking see-through Pepsi today.

EMERGING CHANGE SOLUTIONS FROM THE HIVE MIND

The bees' house hunt involves hundreds of individuals, each one capable of influencing the final decision. Having pondered ten alternatives, the Hive Mind has selected the spacious tree cavity on the edge of Wombat Forest. The bees do not get bogged down in the past or make a hasty decision.

James Dyson, founder of the British technology firm Dyson Group, paid attention to his "scouts" when he decided to build a better hair dryer. Dyson had become a household name with its vacuums, hand dryers, fans, and air purifiers. Why not redesign the bulky hair dryer that had not changed since the 1960s?

Dyson's Hive Mind included a hundred engineers, scientists, and trichologists (hair and scalp experts), who worked alongside British Hairdresser of the Year Akin Konzi at the firm's R&D facility in Malmesbury, England. It was a state-of-the-art $53 million hair laboratory.

The design team ransacked every possibility. They even bought $60,000 worth of natural tresses to test their dryer on real hair, a purchase that led to a global shortage of wig-quality hair.

Four years and $71 million later, the company announced the Dyson Supersonic, a high-end handheld dryer packed with such technology as the Air Multiplier, a digital motor, and heat sensors.

By 2017 the product had become a bestseller in the UK, and by 2021 it had won numerous awards for its design, quality, and effectiveness. James Dyson's ability to activate the Hive Mind to emerge solutions during change has made him one of the wealthiest businessmen in Britain, with a net worth of $23 billion.

You may not be familiar with the word *emergence*, a term I have borrowed from the vocabulary of evolutionary theory. It expresses the idea that you cannot rely on existing conditions to fully predict or explain changes in an ecosystem.

In other words, successful change does not result from the actions of individual components of an ecosystem but from the interaction of all its parts. The group, not the leader, makes it happen.

Ask any bee. She knows all about emergence. While each scout contributes vital information, it takes a whole hive to find the right solution.

Despite this rule, some managers act as if they can force change by controlling each part of the organizational ecosystem. Fix Finance, fix Human Resources, fix Marketing, fix Manufacturing, and, voilà, the whole organization starts humming like a well-oiled machine. That approach almost always backfires because it ignores how systems function and the interaction between the parts of the group.

Let's suppose you want to build the world's best smartphone. To ensure success, you mix and match product features from Samsung, Apple, Google, iQOO, and OnePlus, choosing your favorite design, processor, screen size, display, operating system, RAM, camera, storage, and battery.

But when you assemble all these features and switch on the device, it vibrates and hums and lights up, but it doesn't work as well as its competitors. Why? It's the way that the components work together that makes a phone great.

Any sports coach will tell you that simply improving individual skills will not put a championship team on the field. The magic happens when the players' efforts harmonize in a way that makes the whole greater than the sum of its parts. Leaders with group intelligence focus on both the dancers and the dance to get the Hive Mind buzzing as a whole.

Going it alone, on the other hand, can lead to disaster, as Alitalia Airlines discovered in 2006, when, rather than seeking group advice, an employee at the Italian carrier made one of the most expensive typos ever. It involved two little zeros.

The staff member mistakenly priced a new deal on a business-class flight from Toronto to Cyprus at $39, rather than $3,900.

By the time the company discovered the error, more than two thousand passengers had already booked flights at the impossibly low rate. Alitalia Airlines decided to honor the fare rather than incur the wrath of travelers and an explosion of bad press.

The bargain basement price ended up costing the company $7 million, all for want of two zeros. It would not have happened if the typist had followed the old adage, "Many pairs of eyeballs are better than one."

During a change initiative, it pays to get lots of eyeballs and hands and brains involved. Different people bring different perspectives to the undertaking, the accumulation of which leads to the best decisions.

It takes a village. Smart leaders welcome all perspectives and take them seriously. By harvesting all views and opinions, they overcome the silo effect where those working in one part of the organization know little about the effects of their work on other parts.

Here's another word I suggest you add to your vocabulary: *humility*. A successful change leader knows that she does not know it all, does not possess the one right answer, and must invite and respect opinions that may radically differ from her own. She feels perfectly comfortable with the fact that she is not perfect and cannot just tell the hive what to do. She must remain humble as she helps the Hive Mind emerge the best solutions. She never dictates; she facilitates. And she never falls victim to flawed top-down decision-making.

ABANDONING TOP-DOWN DECISION-MAKING

Before he became prime minister, London's mayor Boris Johnson made the Garden Bridge his pet project. Wouldn't it be lovely to stroll along a pedestrian pathway across the river Thames among more than 270 trees and two thousand shrubs?

Well, a 2019 Transport for London (TfL) inquiry revealed that Johnson's lovely little dream had squandered millions of pounds of public money, largely because he ignored the advice of senior civil servants who warned about the cost of the complex endeavor.

Johnson blindly forged ahead. It didn't take long for costs to begin piling up. Caroline Pidgeon, chair of the London Assembly Transport Committee, lamented Johnson's single-minded approach. As she told the *Architects' Journal*, "During his last hours in office, Boris Johnson was desperately trying to force through his beloved Garden Bridge when officers at City Hall had serious concerns." It was "utter folly."

On August 14, 2017, after months of uncertainty, the Garden Bridge Trust abandoned the project at a total cost to taxpayers of $68 million. It was the epitome of falling victim to flawed top-down decision-making.

Every hive has its queen, but the queen knows she exists to serve the hive, a fact Mayor Johnson might have heeded before he kept hurtling down the primrose path to a botched initiative. "Scouts" in the form of advisers with different perspectives might have warned him about the folly of pursuing a pet project Londoners didn't really need. Deaf ears, vanity, and a lack of humility made him the poster boy for political and economic recklessness.

There's another word for your change vocabulary: *need*. All too often, leaders, especially those newly appointed to their positions, want to put their personal stamp on the organization. When tempted to do that, you should stop, look, and listen.

Stop trying to force the change, *look* for what the organization really needs, and *listen* to everyone's opinion about the matter. Ambition fuels success. But ambition uncoupled from the wisdom of the Hive Mind will never get you from where you are to where you want to be.

Top-down decision-making can trip up the leaders of the world's biggest cities, largest corporations, and wealthiest individuals, as Elon Musk learned in August 2021 when he botched the announcement that Tesla would be developing a humanoid robot dubbed Optimus.

The entrepreneur's plan to build a robot to carry out dull, risky, or repetitive activities made front-page news. But it turned out that the robot wasn't ready for prime time.

Unwilling to delay the announcement, Musk spoke while a guy in a black-and-white spandex jumpsuit did a funky little dance onstage. At the end of his talk, Musk proclaimed, "Obviously that was not real . . . the Tesla bot *will* be real."

The media shredded the performance. Usually a master of public relations who can keep himself and his company's products in the news, Musk stumbled with this stunt. It was one small dance for robotkind, a big blunder for the stuntman. A quick preview with trusted advisers could have prevented the debacle. Note to Mr. Musk: test your thinking before you put your reputation at risk.

An even bigger blunder occurred when the UK's 2002 National Health Service (NHS) IT project performed in a way that earned it a top spot on my personal list of mismanaged projects. The NHS responded to the UK cabinet's request to improve the health system by setting up a centralized electronic records system.

Unfortunately, decisions were left in the hands of cabinet ministers, civil servants, and project managers who lacked any deep knowledge of health care. As a result, the project turned out to be one of the most ineffective and expensive contracting fiascos in public sector history.

A public spending watchdog issued a damning report. "The Department could have avoided some of the pitfalls and waste if they had consulted at the start of the process with health professionals."

Finally abandoned in 2010, the NHS patient record system had frittered away nearly $15.5 billion of hard-earned taxpayer money.

End users and the workers who serve them always know more about the nitty-gritty inner workings of an ecosystem. Those who live in the C-suite should never make important change decisions without consulting the folks who put their boots on the ground every day.

When they don't consult their most trusted advisers, those who actually do the work, they create an army of Order Takers who simply wait for instructions to come down from "those who know best." Employees turn off their creativity, their problem-solving skills, and their initiative, the opposite of what any good leader wants to accomplish.

TURNING WORKER BEES INTO CREATIVE PROBLEM-SOLVERS

Patrick Houlihan, CEO of the Melbourne-based paint company DuluxGroup, along with his executive team, wanted to take the firm's capabilities into international markets. I know the story firsthand because I had worked with Houlihan as executive general manager of People, Culture & Change since 2016.

We had defined our purpose in 2007 as helping consumers "imagine a better place." In 2019, Nippon Paint swooped in to buy the company, a turn of events that handed Houlihan the key to going global.

Shortly after the fourth-biggest paint company in the world purchased DuluxGroup for $3.8 billion, Houlihan flew to Singapore to meet Nippon's chairman and majority shareholder, Goh Hup Jin.

Goh asked the DuluxGroup leader a pointed question: "What do you want to do, and why?" When Houlihan described his desire to both grow domestically and penetrate the global marketplace, Goh simply replied, "My job as the shareholder is to help you do what you want to do."

Houlihan, a thirty-four-year Dulux veteran, immediately recognized the opportunity offered by the new alliance. Rather than serving as a subservient acquiree, DuluxGroup would operate as a partner company, free to implement change with total autonomy and accountability. Of course, Nippon could also play the role of an enabler with access to low-cost financial capital.

Three years later, Nippon reported that DuluxGroup had doubled in size with two acquisitions: French paint producer Cromology including its Tollens brand for about $1.8 billion and Slovenia-based JUB for about $200 million.

While DuluxGroup continued to grow its Australian and New Zealand base, it not only forged a path in Europe, but also leveraged the Nippon distribution centers throughout Asia to lift sales of the company's Selleys adhesive products.

The new owner never dictated solutions to its recent acquisition but let its people unleash their ambition and creative talent.

Bees know all about creative problem-solving on the front lines. They constantly figure out the best sources of needed supplies, choose the right flowers to visit, and make a beeline to fetch the nectar.

When it comes to creative problem-solving in human organizations, it always pays to appoint those closest to the problem to the role of Problem-Solvers. Incyte, a Delaware-based global biopharmaceutical company, offers a good example of this approach.

Recognized for its innovative approach to finding solutions for serious medical problems, Incyte unleashes the problem-solving talent of workers who have experienced the effects of the medical problem in their own lives. As Paula Swain, executive vice president of Human Resources, explains, "We have a lot of stories of our staff working on disease areas that they are impacted by.

"One of our scientists had the opportunity to work on the program for life-threatening GVHD (graft-versus-host-disease, which can occur after stem cell or bone marrow transplants), and he had a relative die from this disease. Another person on our team has a daughter with a very rare blood cancer, and the drug she worked on at Incyte helped her daughter to manage this terrible disease."

Incyte goes a step further, holding regular town hall meetings with patients to help medical researchers appreciate the impact of their work on real human beings. Putting a face to an abstract problem makes finding a solution a personal cause.

With only two thousand employees globally, Incyte has become a biopharmaceutical powerhouse, winning recognition as one of the world's most innovative companies by *Forbes* magazine four years in a row (2015–18).

This story would baffle Frederick Taylor, the father of scientific management. Taylor strove to make organizations more efficient by removing the need for frontline workers to use their heads. Smart managers, not worker bees, could best solve whatever problems cropped up. As Incyte's leaders demonstrated, such an approach ignores a vast reservoir of untapped creativity and talent in our workplaces.

In today's fast-changing environments, leaders who know that they cannot possibly solve every problem by themselves tap the power of collective intelligence. They respect the Hive Mind. After all, who knows more about a problem than the folks who deal with it every day? Surely more than executives in pin-striped suits scanning balance sheets in the C-suite.

AmorePacific, the Korean beauty products company, engineered a revolution in the beauty industry by unleashing the power of its people to solve a frustrating problem. In the early 2000s, women who began to worry about damage from the sun's UV rays could not apply an effective layer of sunblock on top of makeup without turning their faces into gloppy-looking messes. Enter the Hive Mind.

The AmorePacific research team began its quest for a solution to this problem by rethinking the way women applied sunscreen. Why not borrow a technique used by Korean parking attendants to apply a parking stamp without leaving a smudge on the paper? Hmm. "We just need to find the right material to use as a stamp."

This question spurred a team dubbed "The Cushionists" to visit factories that made sponge material, including doll makers, mattress manufacturers, and pillow producers.

They conducted thirty-six hundred tests on two hundred different types of sponges over three years, until they found a foam with eight hundred thousand pores that had never been used in the cosmetics industry before. Its use in the Cushion Compact ignited a beauty revolution.

A woman could use the expandable foam sponge, housed in an airtight container, to stamp a liquid product on the face, ensuring an even application. As an added bonus, the liquid in the sponge offered an "all-in-one" sun protection, moisturizer, and foundation, a perfect solution for busy professionals on the go.

The time savings, coupled with fewer base makeup ingredients, fueled one of the bestselling beauty products of all time. By 2015 a user was buying a Cushion Compact every second around the world.

That same year, AmorePacific debuted at number twenty-eight on *Forbes*'s annual list of the World's Most Innovative Companies. At that point the firm's revenue had increased 20 percent over the previous year to $4 billion, with the price of company shares surging more than 250 percent. Give "The Cushionists," those intrepid worker bees, a big round of applause.

But hold your applause whenever bureaucracy takes the stage. The number one producer of wasted time and red tape in organizations could not solve a shop-floor problem if its life depended on it. And it often does.

That's why effective change leaders place a stick of dynamite under the archaic structures that slow down worker bees and prevent them from fulfilling their role as creative Problem-Solvers.

BLOWING UP THE BUREAUCRACY

CEO Nick Grayston of The Warehouse Group (TWG), one of New Zealand's largest retailers, was facing increased global competition, a decline in earnings, and changing customer expectations. As he scanned the organization, he saw employees navigating a preposterous chain of twelve management layers.

Grayston concluded that streamlining decision-making by eliminating most of these layers and the organization's functional silos could greatly improve the company's competitiveness and levels of customer satisfaction, not to mention the bottom line.

Every New Zealander knows The Warehouse, a retail outlet nicknamed "The Red Shed," where most Kiwis shop for everyday goods such as food, household cleaning essentials, health and beauty products, and pet supplies.

When Grayson took stock of the organization's structure, he found such overly complex processes as three separate call center teams and five different systems for managing customer engagement. It was a cumbersome pattern (see figure 5.1). The Bureaucracy Pattern immobilizes workers by tying them up in red tape. This not only thwarts decision-making at the front lines, but it also saps people of the energy they will need to change the ways they serve the company's customers.

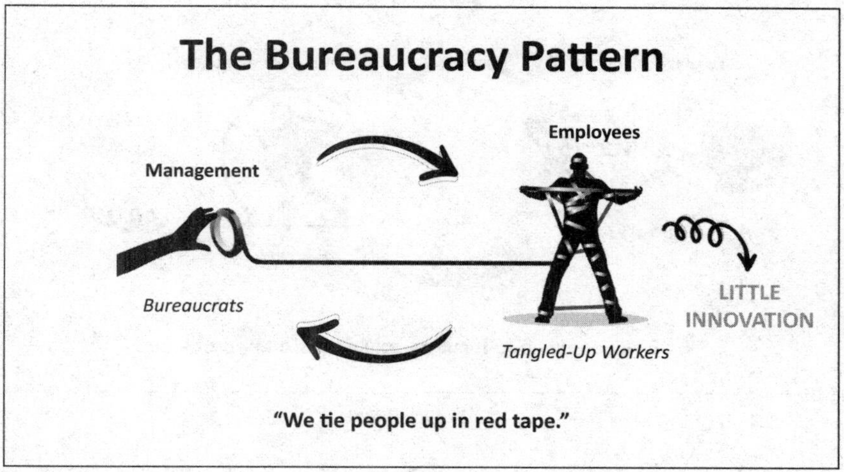

Figure 5.1

Ironically, while executives thought bureaucracy would simplify their lives, it made everything more complicated. Today's complex ecosystems cannot flourish in complicated structures. Too many management layers impede prompt decision-making; traditional silos stall the transfer of vital information from one function to another.

Grayston knew that if he could not blow up this bureaucracy and install a system that would better serve customers, TWG risked death by mummification in red tape. To avoid that fate, he partnered with the global consulting firm McKinsey in 2018 to launch 250 projects aimed at simplifying everything from store operations, pricing, and supplier negotiations to customer interactions.

These measures unwrapped the mummy, giving it the agility it needed to operate successfully in a complex business environment. As Alexandra Hall, engagement manager at McKinsey, explained, "TWG's employees were used to decisions going up and down a siloed chain of command, with leadership focused on managing and directing rather than collaborating."

On August 31, 2020, after eight months of design and preparation, TWG adopted an Agile Pattern (see figure 5.2).

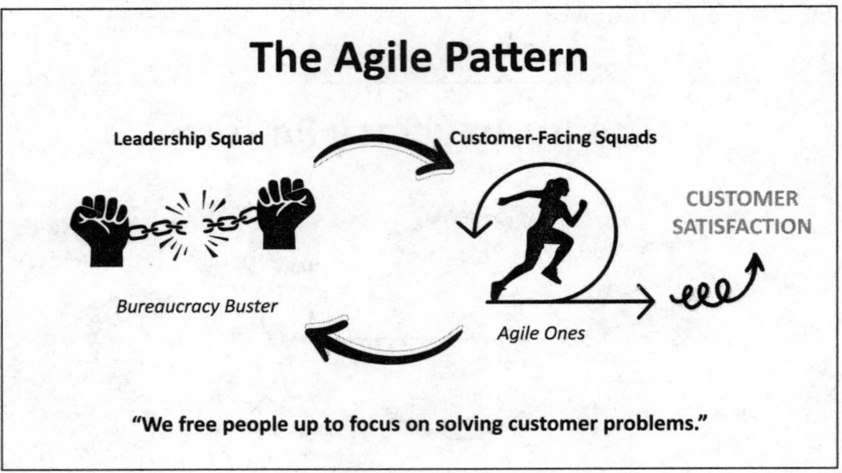

Figure 5.2

The new pattern collapsed twelve organizational layers into just three and included eighteen cross-functional teams (or squads) focused on key customer categories including:

- successful work and learning
- better ways to relax, celebrate, and get outdoors
- tools for raising good kids
- ways to look and feel better

Each squad, dedicated to solving problems for customers, consisted of people from the old functional silos who could work quickly and without hindrance to complete their mission.

At the same time, the new structure replaced the old management team with a "leadership squad" responsible for strategic planning and implementing ways for the cross-functional squads to do their jobs effectively. It also collapsed seventy job families down to forty and defined six core role types, making it easier for people to move across teams.

Employees now lived closer to their customers, collaborated more easily, innovated faster, and made business decisions that would actually "make customers' lives better every day."

For example, when Dave, a product owner in the Growth & Conversion squad, noticed that online customers were exiting the website before checkout, he decided that the website needed to be redesigned. In the old bureaucracy, his idea would have traveled through layer upon layer of managers and around and around the silos until, in the end, little or nothing happened. Now he and his squad could independently test three design variations and implement a tweak that led to a 2.5 percent improvement in conversion, adding $460,000 to annual revenue.

A countless number of similar small improvements added up to big gains at TGW. In 2021 the company announced a record result for the year with net profit after taxes up 164.6 percent over the prior year to $117.7 million.

In the first half of 2022, TWG's market share grew (despite a general decline in total retail spending across New Zealand), with an online growth rate three times that of the total retail market (at nearly 68 percent). TWG's customers also fell in love with the changes. From 2020 to 2023, satisfaction rates soared an impressive 13.5 percent.

Like TGW's Nick Grayston, Dietrich Mateschitz, founder of the global energy drinks company Red Bull, understood that it takes agility to thrive in a complex world. Vacationing in Thailand some years back, Mateschitz sampled a local drink that greatly eased his jet lag.

After tracking down the beverage's maker, Chaleo Yoovidhya, he proposed a partnership that formulated a product they called Red Bull (the soft drink "that gives you wings"). Produced in the tiny village of Fuschl in the Austrian Alps, the product spawned the new energy drink category.

Wisely, the founder did not try to control operations from the Alps but encouraged each region to bring the brand to life in a way that resonated with the local buyers. Without a top-down hierarchy, this agile global community moved quickly and effectively in the marketplace.

In the UK, for instance, Mateschitz appointed Harry Drnec, a fighter pilot and veteran of the Vietnam War, as CEO of Red Bull's operations in that country. Drnec targeted convenience stores, nightclubs, and even garage forecourts to grow Red Bull sales from six million cans in 1996 to three hundred million cans by 2006.

This decentralized approach enabled the energy drink with wings to soar successfully into 171 countries, selling 11.4 billion cans in 2022 and making its founders two of the richest people in Austria and Thailand (with a net worth of $7.1 billion and $5.4 billion, respectively). Oh, and Mateschitz was still consuming several cans of Red Bull a day.

Whatever your business, however large or small its ecosystem, you will make more honey if you award group members the freedom to act locally to meet the needs in their part of the system. The less bureaucracy you build into it, the faster you can adapt to game-changing competition and market turbulence. Given the green light to make decisions and solve problems, all of an agile organization's worker bees will buzz for change.

GENERATING A BUZZ FOR CHANGE ACROSS THE ENTIRE ECOSYSTEM

A scout returns from her inspection of a potential home on the edge of Wombat Forest and dances with gusto, making two hundred circuits along the tree branch, waggling her body violently every step of the way. Her enthusiasm commands attention and motivates others to check out her find.

As the second wave of scouts return, they persuade even more scouts to investigate the site. When the last scouts return, they rush through the crowded space, creating a vibrating, whirring sound that makes the residents excited about the impending change.

The bees know how to create a buzz for change across the entire ecosystem, something that organizers of the World Athletics Championships (WAC) in Doha, Qatar, failed to do when they brought the games to the Middle East for the first time.

When Doha made its bid for the 2019 WAC, Qatar officials assured the International Amateur Athletic Federation that every session would be sold out and that "the atmosphere surrounding the world championships will be fantastic." If only that had happened.

At the women's hundred-meter final, a centerpiece championships event, Jamaican runner Shelly-Ann Fraser-Pryce crossed the finish first not to a cheering crowd but to an eerily silent Khalifa International Stadium. Fraser-Pryce completed her victory lap, carrying her two-year-old son, Zyon, waving to a few fans and tens of thousands of empty seats in the forty-thousand-seat stadium.

The previous championships event held in London in 2017 drew 750,000 spectators and millions of television viewers. Qatar officials, embarrassed by the fiasco, blamed poor attendance on a late-night schedule to accommodate global television audiences and the enmity of neighboring countries that had boycotted the championships.

But the real culprit was their inability to generate the buzz needed to draw big crowds to the event. Hosting a major international athletic event represented a much-desired change for the Middle East. Qatar failed to fulfill its promise because, as it turned out, you can build a beautiful stadium, but you can't fill it with spectators without creating the widespread buzz that draws them to the venue.

Leaders with group intelligence create the sort of buzz that incites a fervor for change in different parts of the ecosystem. In the case of the teleconferencing service Zoom, its leaders buzzed the fact that their service is as easy as pushing a button.

We all remember when the coronavirus pandemic forced millions of us to stay home, where we could only meet with friends and colleagues on our electronic devices. The virus may have kept us in our dens, all comfy in our sweatpants and T-shirts, but it did not stop us from communicating with each other in virtual work meetings, classrooms, libraries, gyms, and restaurants.

Why did millions of people flock to Zoom's teleconferencing service? In large part, it was because Zoom's founder had created a "frictionless" tool that was hassle free and easy to use.

Eric Yuan, the son of geology engineers in China, had studied applied mathematics and computer science at Shandong University of Science and Technology before immigrating to the United States. Yuan joined Cisco to manage the firm's newly acquired WebEx engineering group but soon grew tired of hearing customer complaints about its slow and choppy videoconferencing platform.

When Cisco refused to invest in rebuilding the platform in 2011, Yuan left to start Zoom in a marketplace dominated by such giants as Microsoft (Skype), Google (Hangouts), and Cisco (WebEx). It was clearly a David versus Goliath situation.

From a run-down office with a broken elevator in Santa Clara, California, Yuan and his team of thirty engineers began building better technology for video communications. The team ironed out the bugs that plagued other tools: different versions needed for Mac and PC, viruses introduced by browser updates, the need for a super-reliable internet connection, to name a few.

Zoom's solution to the problems plaguing videoconferencing cost an unbelievably low $9.99 a month and included free videoconferencing for up to a hundred participants.

Eric Yuan was not a typical nerd who sat all day in a dark room pounding code into a keyboard; he was one very busy bee. He virtually flew around the world, he danced his message with all his might, and he insisted on holding all important meetings with potential corporate clients on a Zoom product that made life easier: easy to join, easy to set up, easy to use, and easy to customize. The tool worked just as well in a Manhattan boardroom as it did in mom's Kansas City kitchen.

The start-up became one of the rare tech unicorns to make its IPO debut with a profit, boasting fifty thousand corporate customers, including Samsung, Uber, Walmart, and Capital One. In 2022, Zoom grew 55 percent over the prior year and delivered $4 billion in revenue. Many of its seventeen hundred employees became instant multimillionaires. Buzz, buzz!

The bees specialize in "frictionless." Just watch them work smoothly to find and build a new home, to gather nectar and produce honey, and to ceaselessly buzz their way to success. Of course, they receive high satisfaction scores from their sweet-toothed customers.

A word of caution. Change teams fail to make an impact if they buzz away only in the background until it comes time to deliver the honey. Their "customers," all of the people the teams expect to climb aboard the buzz wagon, can just sit there, eyes glazed over, wondering, *What the heck? I'm supposed to do* what? Why? *Give me a break.* The change team is left thinking, *What's wrong with these people? Why don't they get it? We're doing it to benefit the whole hive.*

Advanced buzzing would have smoothed the path to change. When you build a buzz well in advance of your launch date, you will find people more eager to join the mission. Play the sales pro, who knows that you must constantly sell solutions and benefits. And you must start your pitch long before you launch the initiative.

Just as a successful product must be easy to use, a new direction must be easy to understand. To achieve that goal, you must craft a message that is clear, concise, and comprehensible. Here's the key point about messaging: when the right message moves everyone in the organization, it will probably do the same with customers.

The vodka-maker Absolut created the second bestselling vodka in the world by doing just that. The message: our vodka is absolutely pure.

In the 1970s, Absolut CEO Lars Lindmark worked with legendary marketer Gunnar Broman on a plan to convince consumers in the US to switch to his unknown brand in a fiercely competitive market, where powerhouses like Smirnoff ruled.

Broman based Absolut's bottle design on a pharmacy jar he found in an antique shop in Stockholm's Old Town, a curious link to vodka's history as medicine in the Middle Ages. The understated Absolut bottle, with its unusually shaped see-through bottle, stood out from all the competitors on store shelves. It visually drove home the message broadcast in the company's ads: "Absolut Perfection."

Absolut's marketers tailored the ad to hit specific targets: Absolut New York, Absolut London, Absolut Country, Absolut Festival, Absolut Jazz, and so on. More than fifteen hundred versions of the ad repeated the company's message over the next twenty-five years, making it the longest-running print campaign in history and propelling Absolut to a position as one of Sweden's most successful exports.

I could write a whole book about messaging. In fact, hundreds of authors have. But let me pare it down to three essentials. First, KISS it by Keeping It Short and Simple. It's a worn-out cliché, but sometimes less really *is* more.

Second, use words and language an eight-year-old child can understand. Avoid using business jargon and scientific lingo you think will make you sound smart. They just make you sound like a pompous windbag.

Third, test it on a broad range of people with different perspectives. If it works with eight-year-old Tommy, it should also work with his mother, his math teacher, and the dentist who cleans his teeth.

POINTS TO REMEMBER

- Change leaders enable solutions to emerge by activating the Hive Mind.
- Top-down decision-making creates a bottleneck where everyone looks up for direction.
- Those closest to the work make the best problem-solvers.
- Bureaucracy ties people up in red tape and paralyzes their creativity.
- Meaningful and lasting change depends on messaging that reaches all parts of the ecosystem.

6

EMERGING HIVE-WIDE LEADERSHIP

Avoid the Three Critical Mistakes Bees Never Make

During the dangerous transition to a new home, each bee takes up its specific role. While Home Inspectors scout for real estate, Security Guards cluster around the queen to keep her safe and warm.

As the sun sets, a Rainbow bee-eater approaches the colony on the exposed branch, prompting the Protectors to swoop into defense mode, stingers poised for attack.

Group survival depends on everyone taking up their change leadership roles, a fact we humans should bear in mind when we tackle any organizational change.

My consulting client "Jamal Jackson," the recently appointed CEO of "AAADoorShop," a doors and windows manufacturer headquartered in Sheffield, England, had been instructed by the board to make AAA more competitive, with the express goal of vaulting it from industry laggard to leader.

It didn't take long for Jackson to realize that he could not do it by himself.

As we will learn in this chapter, leaders tend to devote their time and energy to the daily challenges of getting products to customers. They do need to do that. But they also need to activate the Hive Mind in leading any change initiative.

It's an age-old problem. The big boss is all powerful in the social network. They can perform magic. If employees buy into that myth, they will expect their leader to ride into town on a white charger and make great things happen.

"Yay! Now that Jackson's here, he'll have all the answers. He'll tell us how to make the necessary change." That'll never happen because even the most talented and charismatic leaders cannot thrive in turbulent conditions unless they enroll each part of the ecosystem into its change role.

The bees know all about it. Rather than sitting around waiting for a queen bee to tell them what to do, they step into the individual and collective leadership roles needed to ensure hive success. In all complex ecosystems, change is never hero created. It's *cocreated* by every member of the hive.

Despite the fact that CEOs hold the most senior management position in an organization and may think they can wield that power to bring about change, they cannot make it happen all on their own. They need the leadership of everyone, from their top executives to the company's janitors and parking lot attendants.

When it comes to change, the leader of any organization or team must know how to enable everyone in their group to recognize and take up their particular change leader roles.

STEPPING INTO THE CHANGE LEADER ROLE

Eighteen months after he took the helm at AAADoorShop, Jamal Jackson leaned back in his captain's chair, gave me a weary smile, and contemplated the question I had just posed: "What does the word *leader* mean to you?" Only hours earlier he had felt as if he were facing a firing squad when the board interrogated him about the slow pace of change under his leadership.

Worried about keeping his job, Jackson had asked me for some honest advice about moving forward. We met on a foggy morning in his office next to a long, low factory building and raised our voices to hear one another over the whining screech of saw blades slicing through sheet metal.

We began with a specific issue, the snail's pace of AAA's transformation to digitized manufacturing processes. "This changeover will reduce costs and improve quality. But the transformation team is spinning its wheels."

"Let's pause a minute," I suggested. "Before we get into the nitty-gritty, tell me how you view your role as leader. What does the word mean to you?"

Jackson didn't skip a beat: "My focus has been on the big picture, improving customer delivery and generating returns for shareholders. I give the orders and leave the transformation details to the experts."

Giving the orders! Of course, he's the big boss responsible for saying, "Here's what I want you to do. Now go out and do it."

No matter how ardently Jackson believed in the change, and no matter how loudly he championed it, it would never outpace a snail if he didn't take up his own change leadership role. He needed to climb down from his perch in the C-suite and step into his change role, helping the transformation team make critical decisions, remove roadblocks, and prioritize resourcing.

"In my experience," I replied, "there are four critical leadership roles, depending on the circumstances: Delivery Leader, Business Strategist, Performance Coach, and Change Leader."

To illustrate my point, I flipped open my iPad to display the Four Leadership Roles chart I use with managers (see figure 6.1).

Leaders in successful and sustainable businesses step into four critical roles, depending on the task and the time frames. I drew Jackson's attention to the two axes: Work to Be Done and Time Horizon. "Note how the four roles depend on whether you are running the business or changing the business and on whether you are operating with a shorter or longer time horizon."

- **Delivery Lead:** Running the business on a daily basis using existing processes, skills, and knowledge.
- **Business Strategist:** Thinking about how the business will operate over a longer time horizon, leveraging existing processes, skills, and knowledge.
- **Performance Coach:** Improving how the business operates day-to-day, with a focus on helping people to adapt, improve, and learn.
- **Change Leader:** Changing the business over a longer time horizon with a focus on adapting, improving, and learning.

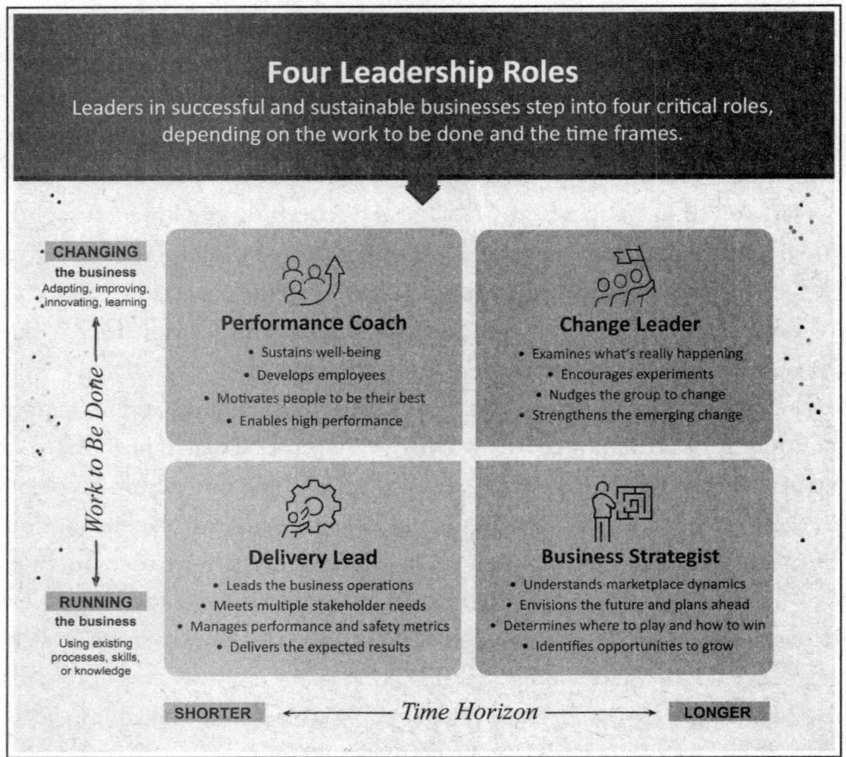

Figure 6.1

"Now here's the tricky part. You don't wake up in the morning and decide which leadership role you will step into today. You may need to step into all of these four critical roles, sometimes more than once, at various times every day."

Jackson thanked me for sharing this chart and said he would study it over the weekend before trying to apply it. "It looks simple enough," he said with a laugh. "But it's not going to be so easy to do."

"Amen, brother."

The following week, Jackson puts what he has learned into practice. On Monday morning he steps into role of Delivery Lead with Head of Operations "Ethan Cruz" to explore the recent 10 percent drop in DIFOT (Delivery In Full, On Time). Jackson shares his concerns about this downward trend. "If we don't deliver doors on time, we could lose our big new client 'BuildWell' before the ink dries on the contract."

In this case, Jackson knows he must focus on leading day-to-day business operations, meeting stakeholder needs, managing performance and safety outcomes, and delivering the expected results. Doing it well will maintain business credibility and a reputation for fulfilling promises.

With this in mind, Jackson helps Cruz systematically work through the issues and develop a high-level improvement plan before Jackson heads to the factory canteen for a coffee catch-up with Construction segment manager "Dale Ward," during which he plans to congratulate Ward on landing the important deal with BuildWell.

Now Jackson steps into the role of Performance Coach in order to help Ward capitalize on his win by gaining a greater share of the big-builder market. After the CEO asks a series of questions aimed at exploring the opportunities in this segment, Ward leaves the meeting with a clear growth plan.

The role of Performance Coach includes enabling higher performance, motivating achievement, developing employees, and sustaining well-being.

That afternoon Jackson makes his way to AAADoorShop's research lab to meet with R&D director "Dana Smit." He has prepared himself to step into the role of Business Strategist, exploring with Smit several opportunities they noted at a recent Doors Trade Show. The two spend the next hour mapping the emerging "intelligent doors" market on the whiteboard.

Jackson poses an interesting question: "Can we build a door where the reader, the door closer, and the locking mechanism communicate with each other and report an error if some component isn't working properly?" Smit nods and smiles. "I'm on it, Boss!" She's excited by the opportunity to take the company's existing processes, skills, and knowledge into the smart door future.

A spring in his step, Jackson heads to his final meeting of the day, a key update from the people involved in the manufacturing transformation project. While the CEO has let the team do its work without his direct involvement, he has decided that he needs to take up his Change Leader role. Having committed himself to stepping into all of the Four Leadership Roles, he's decided that he must personally lead the change and encourage the team to keep adapting, improving, and learning.

Jackson knows that the team has been struggling to agree on which of three dynamic scheduling tools they should adopt. Without the right tool,

AAA will make little progress toward streamlining customer deliveries. Since they've gotten stuck at this impasse, Jackson pauses the discussion to summarize the pros and cons of each option, including stating his preference, option A.

The team considers Jackson's recommendation and then agrees enthusiastically with this option, which will speed them toward their goal. They appreciate the fact that the CEO is keeping his foot on the change accelerator in the meeting by nudging the group in the right direction, removing roadblocks, helping make critical decisions, and encouraging experiments.

Far from making people nervous and reticent in the presence of an all-powerful CEO, Jackson's supportive presence energizes the team. His enthusiasm for change is infectious.

As the project progresses, the team knows their leader believes wholeheartedly in the change and will do everything he can to help the team succeed. Fifteen months later the company has completed the transformation of its manufacturing facility.

Jackson invited me to visit the plant to see the results of our discussions about leadership in a fast-changing ecosystem. "I'm chuffed," he says. "We are on track to deliver a 20 percent reduction in manufacturing costs this year. Board members couldn't be happier. When I met you, I was worried about turning in my resignation. Now I'm AAA's 'turnaround guy.'"

That comment delighted me. "Jamal, you have always been a great Delivery Lead, an excellent Business Strategist, and a superb Performance Coach. Now you can add proven Change Leader to your résumé."

When the queen senses an overcrowded hive, she sends out pheromone signals to prepare the colony for an imminent move. Each member of the hive understands and steps into its Change Leader role during the transition, something that German retailer Lidl failed to do during its 2018 systems upgrade. The lack of group intelligence led to an estimated $590 million write-down on the project. If only the "queen" had sent out the right signals.

Lidl opened its first discount store in 1973, and by 2019 it operated more than 10,800 outlets in twenty-nine countries, generating annual revenues of close to $102.4 billion. In 2011, Lidl's management decided to replace its badly outdated legacy merchandise management system with a spanking-new Systems Applications and Products (SAP) system that would more efficiently handle the company's master data.

The project (codenamed "eLWIS," pronounced Elvis) involved about one thousand employees and hundreds of consultants. The eLWIS team spent months analyzing a system that thousands of other firms across the globe had successfully implemented.

An early warning light began to blink when the project team discovered that the tried-and-true SAP system based its inventory on retail price, rather than the purchase price used by Lidl.

Nevertheless, instead of pulling the plug, management signed off on a system that did not meet the organization's needs. Bottom line: costs soared through the roof as the team configured the system to meet Lidl's needs.

Lay much of the blame at the "queen's" door. It was, sad to say, a revolving door, with three different CEOs taking the helm between 2014 and 2018. Finally, in July 2018, Danish CEO Jesper Højer pulled the plug on eLWIS and reverted to the old creaky system. Chalk it up to a failure to exercise change leadership.

In my experience, managers working toward change must devote at least 20 percent of their time to leading the charge, especially in the early days. You can't do it by yourself; and you can't do it without keeping the hive buzzing with commitment and drive. Once you step into the Change Leader role, you must keep a sharp eye out for three common mistakes the bees never make: carrying change passengers, micromanaging, and failing to live your group's values.

AVOIDING MISTAKE NUMBER ONE: CARRYING CHANGE PASSENGERS

Back in chapter 2, we saw how Kate and Bob Rowland, cofounders of San Francisco sportswear company A1ActiveWear, got mired in a Shortsighted Pattern during the COVID-19 pandemic. A year after launching their whiz-bang online shop, the Rowlands consulted me about a serious problem that was plaguing their change effort.

As Kate explained, "When our customers began complaining about delivery delays and product shipment errors, we decided to invest $20 million in new location and tracking technology for our warehouses. But the transformation is running 30 percent over budget, and our biggest investor is asking tough questions about how we will get the project back on track."

"What's causing the budget overrun?" I asked.

Bob replied, "My two cents' worth? The external consultants are techheads with no solid retail experience."

I suggested we dig a little deeper before they fired the technology consulting firm. I put on my detective's hat and trekked to a meeting room at the back of the concrete-floored warehouse, where I chatted with "Asher Slade," A1ActiveWear's chief technology officer.

Slade offered her blunt opinion. "It's a real goat rodeo. When the warehouse managers tested the new system, they were not happy with the functionality. They asked for some changes that are giving the consultants a big headache. I'm worried they can't deliver by the agreed design deadline."

Farther along the warehouse corridor in an office wallpapered with Gantt charts, I found the consulting firm's associate director, "Blanca Patel." She immediately rejected blame for the lack of progress. "A1ActiveWear's warehouse managers have been disengaged from the start. Now they want to make a raft of last-minute changes an Einstein couldn't handle. Goodbye schedule, hello costs."

The warehouse managers ridiculed Patel's explanation. A veteran manager named "Boris Peshev" showed me around the large tin-roofed warehouse facility, then summed up the managers' feelings about the situation. "We don't have a location tracking system, which means goods get lost, forgotten, or misplaced in our warehouses. The IT consultants don't have the savvy to solve that problem."

With these warring opinions in mind, I drew the pattern that lay at the bottom of the problem (see figure 6.2). The change to the new warehousing system was being "Done To" A1ActiveWear's warehouse managers. With the owners' mandate to move forward, the technology team (with all the best intentions) stepped into the role of Change Drivers, responsible for making the transformation happen.

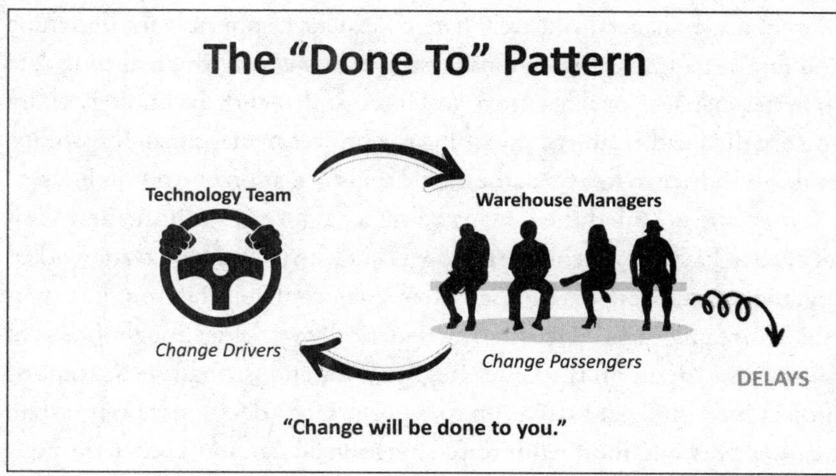

Figure 6.2

Seeing the technology team take charge, the warehouse managers assumed the role of Change Passengers, who could just sit back and watch the scenery roll by. Since someone else was responsible for bringing about the change, they skipped design meetings, tuned out of progress updates, and continued to focus on business-as-usual.

Noticing that the warehouse managers were "disengaged," the technology team ramped up efforts to get them involved with more workshops, events, and a flurry of communications, all to no avail. The technology team just pressed on, trying to design a system without the much-needed user input.

Having learned about the power of patterns, the Rowlands saw what they needed to do. Bob said, "We've been blaming delays on the consultants' incompetence. But now we see that it's a cocreated pattern. We gotta fix that."

Warning! It's always tempting to blame delays on a "skills gap" and send everyone off to a training course to "fix" the problem. This rarely works because the "retrained" people will walk back into the same dysfunctional pattern. In the case of A1ActiveWear, a lack of skills was not the real culprit. Going along for the ride was.

The next day the founders called a project meeting where Kate kicked off the discussion. "There are no passengers on this train. We're all crewmates.

Warehouse managers: you are Change Leaders, responsible for designing and implementing the warehouse system that will give you real-time data to better manage your inventory and forecast demand. Technology team: you are the Lead Enablers, providing the project management, capability, tools, and advice to fast-track the digital transformation of our warehouses."

Then she unveiled the new pattern (see figure 6.3). In the new Collaborative Pattern, warehouse managers and the technology team worked together on the new warehouse system, each contributing from its expertise. The teams joined forces and systematically worked through the list of outstanding items on the Issues Register. Warehouse managers attended project meetings, paid attention to reports, made decisions about system requirements, and thoroughly tested functionality. In short order, the project gained traction.

Figure 6.3

Eighteen months later the founders called me to share the results of the collaboration. "The new warehouse management system is up and running, and we've seen a 50 percent jump in satisfaction, with returning customers driving revenues to an all-time high. To top it off, our key investor is talking about helping us expand internationally!"

It wouldn't have happened had the Rowlands approached the problem with a mechanistic mindset of "we can fix the problem by fixing the people."

Nor would they have accomplished their goal with a social network "let's appoint champions to cheer for success" approach.

Neither method would have changed the progress-impeding "Done To" Pattern. You want to change the way things get done around here? You change the pattern, which begins with redefining roles.

A failure to clarify roles at the outset can sabotage any transformation effort, as Queensland Health found during its $6.19 million partnership with IBM Australia to replace its aging payroll system. The disastrous project ended up costing taxpayers $1.25 billion and won the dubious distinction as one of the most spectacular technology project failures in the southern hemisphere.

Queensland Health, located in northeastern Australia, provides dental, medical, hospital, and aged-care facilities to more than five million people across 1.85 million square kilometers. When IBM won the Queensland Health payroll contract in 2007, the global IT giant could hardly have guessed that eighty thousand doctors, nurses, and health professionals would end up with incorrect paychecks.

A textbook example of "how not to implement a large-scale IT change," the initiative started off with confused roles and responsibilities. Who was in charge? Governance became a juggler's ball, with numerous agencies and boards vying for authority, including the Solution Design Authority, Queensland Health Enterprise Solution Transition (Queensland HealthEST), the Executive Steering Committee, Release Steering Committee, and CorpTech (the prime contractor).

Later, the Honorable Richard N. Chesterman led a Commission of Inquiry into the project. He concluded that "it was not clear which Accountable Officer had responsibility for the overall governance and successful completion of the whole project." The vacuum left the taxpaying public with a whopping big bill.

Queensland Health's project failed so miserably it forced the resignation of the health minister, ignited industrial strike action, and prompted a flood of staff resignations. In a sense, too many hands were fighting for the steering wheel, and no one was effectively driving the bus.

Change leaders throughout the hive must understand their roles and take accountability for their contributions to a successful change initiative.

Mark Begor understood this fact of hive life when he became CEO of Equifax after the Atlanta-based credit reporting agency suffered a massive data breach in 2017.

Hackers had gained access to company files that contained the personal data of 56 percent of the American population, including their names, Social Security numbers, dates of birth, credit card numbers, and driver's license numbers.

Begor began the cleanup effort by conducting a hive-wide analysis of accountabilities. He discovered that despite warnings about its exposure just weeks before the cyberattack, IT administrators had failed to apply the correct security protocols. That left the door wide open for cyber criminals to sneak in and steal a mountain.

Although Begor eventually spent $2 billion on security infrastructure to prevent future breaches, he knew that the best security gear in the world would not keep out the burglars unless he reframed the role of the IT department from Administrators to Security Defenders.

Thinking like a true hive Change Leader, Begor required every employee in the company to take up their role as Protectors of the organization's data. Security, he insisted was everyone's job.

The upshot? As of this writing, Equifax has not incurred a major security incident since the new initiative and has exceeded the industry average on security risk as measured by the Gartner Control Maturity Benchmark. Begor didn't accomplish that feat on his own. The whole hive worked to make it happen.

That's the key to creating a culture of accountability, one where all members of all parts of the ecosystem know their role, step into it, and then hold each part accountable for results.

When you establish such hive-wide leadership, you make sure progress toward your goals. And you can only do it if you cut the strings and empower people to do their best work. Puppet Masters who micromanage their people always end up with disengaged and dispirited teams.

PREVENTING MISTAKE NUMBER TWO: PLAYING THE PUPPET MASTER

Back at AAADoorShop, customers reacted enthusiastically to the company's new line of smart doors. What safety-minded homeowner wouldn't love the security provided by the product's voice control and motion sensor features? So it came as somewhat of a surprise when CEO Jamal Jackson asked me to come to his office to discuss an unexpected problem. "One of our regional marketing and sales teams isn't hitting its sales targets. I need to figure out why."

The sound of shearing metal from next door's factory provided a constant backdrop as Jackson sketched the problem. "Every region is booming, except for Southern. They're more than 20 percent behind their goal for the year. I hate to say it, but I think we made a bad decision when we promoted 'Evander Hoffman' as the regional manager."

Jackson explained that Hoffman had been appointed to the position due to his impressive track record as a sales rep and HR's assessment that he displayed "high potential" as a leader. So why, after five months on the job, was Hoffman performing so poorly?

We agreed that I would meet with members of the Southern team to look into the matter. When I sat down with Hoffman, he was clear about the problem and insisted that it lay with the company's bonus system: "We need a better bonus program if we want to drive sales higher and succeed in this highly competitive region, Siobhán. We've lost three big building contracts because our bonus program sucks. Our competitors are hungrier and more motivated to close deals."

When I talked to members of his team, I heard a much different story, as sales rep "Cathy Oman" explained: "Evander is so obsessed with selling the new doors, he tags along on all my sales calls. He won't let me get a word in edgewise. I might as well stay home!"

Team leader "Zane Singh" added to this lament. "Evander keeps hammering home every step of the sales process, as if I don't know how to do my job. He just doesn't trust us to do our work." Further conversations with the team confirmed a pattern that I drew for Jamal Jackson when we met the following week (see figure 6.4).

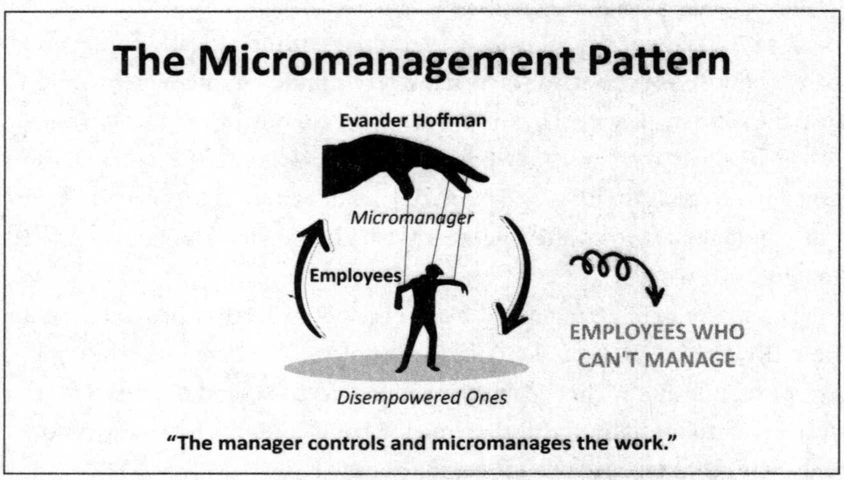

Figure 6.4

There are times when managers must manage and a time when they must lead. Great leaders know when to take up each role, just as they know when to step from one role to another in the Four Leadership Roles model we discussed earlier in this chapter.

With mounting pressure to successfully launch the new line of intelligent doors, Evander Hoffman made the mistake of taking the role of manager to a destructive extreme when he micromanaged his team. Under scrutiny, he just couldn't let go of the strings. His excessive control relegated team members to the role of Disempowered Ones who watched as the Puppet Master tried to control and do their jobs for them.

Jackson got it immediately. "So the team's performance suffers because Evander is taking up the wrong role, which pushes his people into the wrong roles. How would you rewire the pattern, Siobhán?"

I pulled up the Coaching Pattern on my laptop (see figure 6.5). I told Jackson, "Every micromanager in the world should put the Coaching Pattern on their wall."

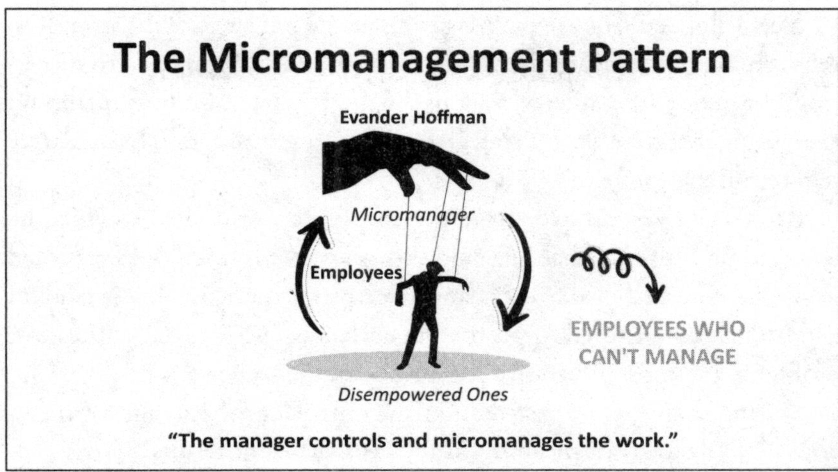

Figure 6.5

He snapped his fingers. "Bingo! I'm going to frame this image for Evander to put on his desk." He set up a meeting with Hoffman to talk about the reasons the Southern team was falling short of its goals.

Using the Micromanagement and Coaching Patterns to inform the discussion, he helped Hoffman begin to see his role differently, as an enabler who gives his people the freedom they need to sell more doors.

"I see it now," Hoffman admitted with a sigh. "Stop being a control freak and start being a supportive coach."

Jumping ahead, less than twelve months later, Southern was leading all districts in terms of sales and customer satisfaction.

Evander Hoffman came out of "micromanagement rehab" a better (and happier) manager. He went to the same "clinic" that helped Steve Jobs, the iconic leader who cofounded Apple, abandon his addiction to micromanagement when he returned to the company after leaving to start NeXT computers, where he micromanaged everything, including the landscapers.

As Randall Stross wrote in a *New York Times* article, "In this period, Mr. Jobs did not do much delegating. . . . While a delegation of visiting Businessland executives waited on the sidewalk, Mr. Jobs spent 20 minutes directing the landscaping crew on the exact placement of the sprinkler heads."

NeXT flopped. The Puppet Master just could not let go of the strings. To Jobs's credit, however, another company he founded, Pixar, sped to success from the outset. The difference? Jobs did not try to put his fingerprints on everything that went on at Pixar, giving Ed Catmull and John Lasseter free rein to run the company.

After a twelve-year exile from the corporate world, during which he reflected on his belief that he could do everything himself, Jobs returned to Apple. His rehab had been a painful learning experience, but it paid off handsomely when he led Apple to its remarkable success as one of the most profitable and most innovative companies on the planet.

During change you must relinquish control, cut the strings, and empower people to create meaningful and lasting change results.

Bees do not rely on the queen to manage every little detail. All of the bees in the colony know their roles and perform them expertly without anyone telling them where to go and what to do. Their hive mentality enables them to thrive successfully in their ecosystem. It will help you thrive in yours, assuming that you never forget that you must provide the example for the way you want your people to think and act.

SIDESTEPPING MISTAKE NUMBER THREE: FAILING TO LIVE YOUR GROUP'S VALUES

In the years leading up to 2015, German car manufacturer Volkswagen had penetrated the American market with its diesel cars. To expand further, however, VW's leaders knew they needed to improve the emissions performance of their diesel engines to meet the strict US standards mandated by the US Clean Air Act (1970).

VW engineers embarked on a crusade to find the holy grail in vehicle engineering circles: a technology that would achieve higher fuel economy and performance, while meeting the strict emissions standards in the United States.

When the engineers claimed to have found the solution, VW began a massive push into the American market, trumpeting its clean diesel cars.

But it turned out that VW had perpetrated an elaborate fraud. When scientists at West Virginia University's Center for Alternative Fuels and

Engine Emissions tested VW diesels in real-world conditions, they found that the engines failed to meet emissions standards.

How did that happen? VW had fitted the vehicles with a "defeat device" that put the cars into a low emissions mode when undergoing testing in the shop.

While VW had proudly proclaimed its undying commitment to "Taking Responsibility," a slogan featured heavily in its marketing campaigns, the company's leaders were just paying lip service to that value. Their "environmentally friendly cars" became the poster child for environmental irresponsibility.

Yes, VW was *responsible* for something, but that something was poisoning the planet with pollutant gases up to forty times the standard.

The resulting scandal, dubbed Dieselgate, seriously damaged the company's reputation. In the week after the company made the extraordinary admission that it had installed the defeat device in eleven million diesel cars worldwide, VW's stock lost nearly a third of its value, or $26.2 billion. By the end of the second quarter of 2019, the costs associated with Volkswagen's elaborate fraud had soared to $35 billion and rising.

It was a classic case of Mistake Number Three, talking a good game but failing to live the values you proclaim (see figure 6.6). When leaders play the "do as I say, not as I do" game, paying lip service to their values but ignoring them when initiating change, they create a raft of disillusioned employees and customers who may never again believe a word they say.

In a world where it's hard to earn trust but easy to lose it, leaders cannot succeed in their change efforts unless they live the values and behavior they espouse.

If world opinion had sentenced VW's leaders to the prison of lost reputations, they might have shared a cell with the leaders at Purdue Pharmaceuticals.

The company, owned by the Sackler dynasty, had claimed an admirable value when it advertised its dedication to "Integrity: We do what is right." The words flowed off their lips while in the background their behavior fueled the opioid crisis in the US that reached epidemic proportions in 2019.

Purdue Pharma makes a class of drug known as OxyContin®, an effective painkiller doctors overprescribed in large part due to the manufacturer's

Figure 6.6

insistence that the drug was safe and nonaddictive. In reality, it ended up killing hundreds of thousands of Americans.

Purdue Pharma's leaders cared less about that calamity than they did about the fortune they could make with the drug. As Andrew Kolodny, co-director of the Opioid Policy Research Collaborative at Brandeis University, wrote, "So the way you can do well with a pharmaceutical product is if doctors prescribe it for common problems like lower back pain or headaches. If you have a drug that is difficult to stop taking, you've got a pretty good recipe for financial success."

While Purdue Pharma promoted its commitment to integrity, it implemented a strategy to expand the opioid market from cancer patients to patients with acute or chronic pain, all the while downplaying the risks of addiction and abuse.

A well-intentioned doctor might prescribe the drug for a high school football player with an injured knee, unwittingly creating an addict who will lose a fortune, if not his life, buying more and more of the painkiller.

The billionaire Purdue owners continued to encourage such prescriptions despite their knowledge of the severe addictiveness of the drug.

In 2020, Purdue Pharma pleaded guilty to criminal charges and enabling the supply of drugs "without legitimate medical purpose." The company paid an $8 billion settlement for its role in the opioid epidemic, which, according to the Centers for Disease Control and Prevention, had by that point claimed the lives of more than four hundred thousand Americans over two decades.

Here's a challenge for you. You've watched me draw so many patterns in this book, I bet you can sketch one for the opposite of the Lip Service Pattern, which we might call the Walk the Talk Pattern. It will illustrate the positive effects of modeling desired values and behavior during change. It will show how an entire group can bring those values to life during their transformation efforts, day in, day out. Such consistent behavior will enhance trust, speed progress to the goal, and better serve stakeholder interests.

If you decide to travel across an uncharted mountain range, you will need a good compass. If you want to achieve meaningful and lasting change in your organization, you will need a good *moral* compass, one that guides every step of your journey from here to there.

POINTS TO REMEMBER

- Every leader must master the Four Leadership Roles: Delivery Lead, Performance Coach, Business Strategist, and Change Leader.
- A transformational leader encourages everyone to step into their Change Leader role.
- Passengers always slow progress.
- Micromanaging leads to employee disengagement.
- Failure to live the espoused values and behaviors erodes trust.

7

NUDGING THE HIVE FORWARD

Overcoming Obstacles and Objections

After a cold and dangerous night on the exposed tree branch, the bees prepare to leave for their new home. Time is ticking by, and the colony can only survive for three days on the honey the bees gorged themselves on before leaving the hive.

Without a home the bees are vulnerable, and underneath the tree branch a hungry gecko has been on the prowl all night.

As the first rays of sunlight hit the tree branch, the bees mobilize the colony by headbutting one another and emitting tiny high-pitched beeping sounds, over and over again, signaling "We've reached a decision, stop waggling, and get a move on!" Accomplishing the much-needed change requires that they nudge everyone to join the migration.

I first experienced the subtle art of nudging as a teenager when, sitting with my family at our farmhouse kitchen table in Finea, Ireland, I heard my mother muse, "Perhaps one day we will move to Australia."

Everyone fell silent except our puppy, Shack, whose tail rhythmically thumped the floor. I peered anxiously at my father, who responded, "Why would we move to the other side of the world when we love our little village here?"

My siblings and I heaved a collective sigh of relief as the conversation moved on to other topics.

But my mother, who could see few prospects for her children in 1980s recession-plagued Ireland, had planted the seed of change. One by one, my four siblings and I left the village of Finea to move to the great Down Under. We'd been nudged there.

Just like the bees, my mother understood that ecosystems, including families, contain built-in mechanisms for adaptation that often need a mere nudge to activate change. The idea of nudging toward change runs counter to what most leaders think: "We must push *hard* to get people moving in the right direction!"

Some change gurus commandeered a true story to support their contention that you must pressurize people to change.

Imagine the freezing waters 120 miles northeast of Aberdeen, Scotland. See that oil rig sitting in the middle of nowhere? Suddenly, at 11:00 p.m. on July 6, 1988, an explosion rocks the Piper Alpha rig, igniting a massive fire that ends up killing 167 men. Now picture two workers on the rig locking themselves in a room, hoping that the fire will eventually die down. When the fire only keeps raging, they decide to take drastic action and jump into the freezing waters of the North Sea in the pitch-black dark of night. Miraculously, the badly injured men survived.

The conventional change gurus twisted this harrowing tale to make the point that you need to set a blazing fire or "burning platform" that will drive people to move forward. "Jump! Or die!" In other words, scare 'em to death.

Seriously? How inhumane! You know by now that when it comes to meaningful and lasting change, fear is public enemy number one.

This brings us to the third step, the N on the Hive LENS: Nudge. In my experience pushing hard for change seldom gets the results you need. Nudging will. Let's look at the perils of pushing too hard for change.

PUSHING TOO HARD FOR CHANGE

The smell of lemon disinfectant hits me as I walk through the sliding doors at "Metro City Hospital" and make my way down a long gray corridor to my client's office.

Hospital CEO "Juliette Garnier," increasingly concerned about insufficient funds for patient care, employee wages, and maintenance, has undertaken a cost reduction initiative to keep the hospital running.

Even before I sat down, Garnier launched into a list of problems her cost-cutting measures had ignited. "We've got to run a more cost-effective organization. But when I told my heads of department that we need to reduce our running costs, all I got were weak nods around the table. Two weeks ago, I took more decisive action and proposed a cut of 10 percent from each of their budgets."

I could see it coming. She had set a fire. "How did they respond?"

"Like I'd thrown a grenade onto the table!" Garnier described how faces paled and the room went deadly silent. Later, an angry debate raged in the hospital corridors. When news of the funding cuts reached the nurses, they took swift action to protest the cost cuts.

Garnier shook a copy of the local newspaper. "Get a load of today's headline: 'Nurses Plan Strike Over Working Conditions at City Hospital.' Can you help put out this fire?"

As a first step, I conducted several workshops with employees, seeking their perspectives on the current crisis. I found hospital staff keen to express their views as we sat around a conference table in a fluorescent-lit meeting room in the hospital's basement.

Senior nurse "Carla Mendoza" spoke up first. "When there's a shortage of nurses at the bedside, that's when medical errors can happen. If management continues slashing budgets, we'll be forced to strike for our patients' welfare."

"Dan Kut," head of the Intensive Care Unit, jumped in. "How can we possibly deliver quality patient care with more cuts when we're stripped to the bone already!"

"Petra Sankar," a doctor in Cardiology, chimed in. "I can't deliver our famous cutting-edge treatments without proper funding."

Other medical staff added to the picture of an understaffed hospital, with employees working through breaks, struggling to keep up with demand for patient care, and driving home at night in tears as stress levels shot through the roof.

By the end of the week, I could see a clear pattern here. A few days later, I met with Garnier and sketched it on her office whiteboard (see figure 7.1).

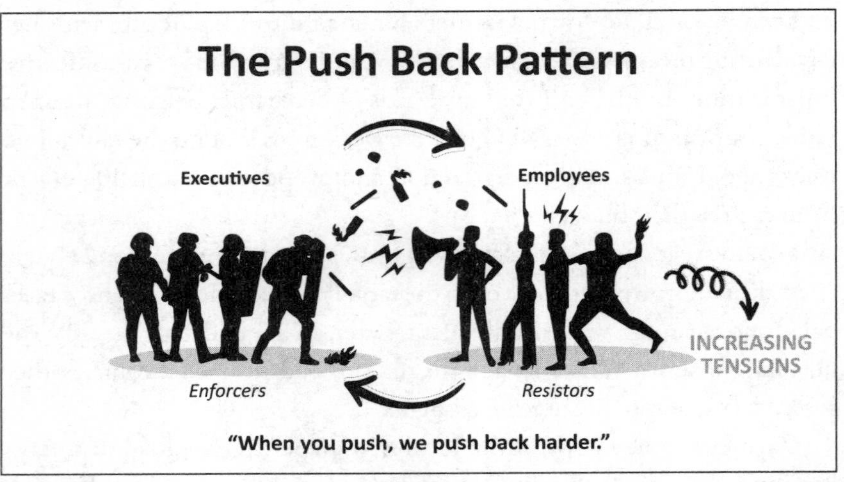

Figure 7.1

The CEO was pushing hard. Too hard? I pointed to the bottom of my drawing: "When you push, we push back harder."

Garnier could see that she and members of her executive team had stepped into the role of Enforcers, insisting rather forcefully on a 10 percent cost reduction across all departments.

On the other side, employees, fed up with ongoing staff shortages and feeling underappreciated and taken for granted, had stepped into the role of Resistors, just as forcefully blocking the cost-cutting drive. It was a classic deadlock.

Irish folklore tells how bees can so easily take offense that you must speak to them gently. Otherwise, they may rebel and cease to produce honey or even abandon the hive. Garnier needed to speak more softly. If she continued forcefully pushing the need for cost cuts, her words would fall on deaf ears. Folks might clam up and grow eerily silent.

When a group becomes quiet, you may think you're making headway, but their silence is sending a message. Underneath the silence usually lie the smoldering embers of resentment, anger, and mistrust.

Here's a good example. Back in 2020, Barclays, the UK bank, decided to install spyware on staff computers. Imagine working there, tapping away on your keyboard, when you see a flashing message on your screen: "You have not spent enough time in the zone today."

Flabbergasted that the company is spying on your work, you are about to jump out of your chair, when you receive this recommendation: "Mute the phone, disable email/chat pop-ups, avoid breaks for twenty-plus minutes, two to three times a day." What next? Spies in the bathrooms?

Barclays employees pushed back on these Big Brother tactics and leaked details of the fiasco to the English newspaper *City A.M.* "The stress this is causing is beyond belief and shows an utter disregard for employee wellbeing."

HR experts had a field day with what they saw as an abuse of employee rights. The very next day, Barclays scrapped the spyware.

Back at City Hospital, Juliette Garnier recognized the Push Back Pattern immediately. At her next meeting with the department heads, Garnier adapted her approach. "I'd like you to work together as a team to craft a savings plan that will enable our hospital to keep taking care of our patients."

Three weeks later, having consulted with all key stakeholders, the department heads presented Garnier with their collective plan to achieve a 10 percent cost reduction without compromising patient care.

Much of the savings would come from energy and water conservation, more online bookings, and an aggressive protocol for preventing hospital infections. A delighted Garnier told me about an added bonus. "The nurses are on board with the plan and have called off their threatened strike."

We will revisit City Hospital later in the book, but at this point in its saga you can file it as a classic case of how forced change invariably backfires. People don't resist change as much as they resist having a fire lit under their feet. Setting a fire and ordering people to jump off the platform will anger them and fill them with distrust and resistance.

Nudging them in the direction you want them to go is more likely to win their trust and support. Leaders with group intelligence use the gentle art of nudging to create effective and sustainable change.

MASTERING THE GENTLE ART OF NUDGING

In 2008, behavioral economists Cass Sunstein and Richard Thaler introduced the concept of nudging to the world. They used the term to describe "an intervention that maintains freedom of choice but steers people in a particular direction."

By showing respect for people's thoughts and feelings, Nudgers encourage group members to choose what will best serve the ecosystem.

The UK's prime minister David Cameron liked this idea so much, he created a Behavioral Insights Team or "nudge unit" to promote certain desired changes. An early experiment set a goal of increasing the rate of organ donation in Wales.

The nudge unit made a subtle yet consequential adjustment to the Welsh system. Instead of requiring people to opt in to organ donation, the system would now assume that people consented unless they stated otherwise (that is, deliberately chose to opt out).

Making organ donation the default option led to a surge in the consent rate from 58 percent in 2015 to 77 percent in 2019.

Welsh health minister Vaughan Gething summed up the success: "Over the last five years we have seen people's lives being transformed after receiving an organ. Not only this, but the families of donors have also taken solace in the fact their loved ones have given the gift of life to others." The success in Wales led to worldwide application of the change.

Nudges create effective transformation because they guide rather than force change. They can actually save lives. They can also fix problems as mundane as the messy urinals at Amsterdam's Schiphol Airport.

In the 1990s, Aad Kieboom, Amsterdam's airport renovations manager, and cleaning manager Jos van Bedaf came up with a novel idea to reduce cleaning costs. Hoping to encourage patrons to exercise more caution when using the toilet facilities, they sketched an extremely realistic image of a black housefly to the left of the drain in each urinal.

It turned out that men took special aim at the bug, with rather astonishing results. Precise aiming reduced spillage by 80 percent and cleaning costs by an estimated 20 percent.

The idea spread to other institutions. When Iceland's three main commercial banks collapsed in 2008, images of bankers, rather than flies, appeared in urinals.

Nudges don't try to prevent people from doing the wrong thing; they make it easier to do the right thing. Kieboom and van Bedaf did not enforce a bathroom policy, issue spillage fines, or hire attendants to police the toilets. Instead, they nudged people in a way that served everyone's best interests.

As long as you are alive and kicking, you can never *not* behave. By the same token, you can never *not* intervene in the ecosystem, whether you realize it or not.

The whole of existence is just an infinite variety of patterns that you must be able to expertly nudge in the right direction. Leaders with group intelligence decide on a few leverage points that deftly nudge the group toward change.

Take care that your interventions nudge rather than whack the group in the right direction. As my mother often told her children, "You'll catch more ants with honey than you will with vinegar." Nevertheless, even the gentlest and most persuasive nudges can meet with objections.

COUNTERING OBJECTIONS

New Jersey–based Toys "R" Us enjoyed years of growth and success in the decades following its inception in 1948 as a baby furniture store. So what explains its sorry path to financial ruin and a declaration of bankruptcy in March 2018?

Well, it just couldn't change its business model when faced with the challenges of the twenty-first century: changing customer behavior, online buying, and intense competition from mass retailers such as Walmart, Target, and Amazon.

A close look at the company's collapse reveals an abiding failure by leadership to listen to myriad suggestions that the company needed to change. They also turned a blind eye to the fact that Toys "R" Us stores aggravated shoppers with overstuffed inventory, shoddy merchandising, and poor customer service.

Employees heard and saw it, offering plenty of ideas about what needed to change to its deaf and blind leaders:

- "Let's make our stores more spacious and less crammed with stuff." Not needed!
- "Let's improve customer service." Not necessary!
- "Let's create an online store." Not us!

"No, no, no!" management insisted. "We are the center of the toy universe, customers want to shop in our stores, and an in-person experience can't be replicated online. We must stay the course!"

It was a classic Naysayer Pattern (see figure 7.2). Management, in the role of Naysayers, blocked new ideas at every turn. Employees, in the role of Stuck Ones, felt stifled and ignored.

Figure 7.2

The resultant lack of innovation inevitably led the company to its doom in a world where millennial parents, who had once flocked to the industry leader, fell in love with the convenience of ordering online. At the same time, massive retailers like Walmart and Target took huge bites out of a market once dominated by Toys "R" Us.

When you're bobbing in a sea of sharks, do you merely tread water, or do you swim with all your might in a direction that might take you to a safe shore?

The Naysayers at Toys "R" Us falsely believed the sharks were a myth or that they would magically swim away. They didn't.

The strategy of treading water while the tide shifted proved fatal for Toys "R" Us, and in March 2018, the once mighty retailer informed a US bankruptcy court that it would close hundreds of stores and liquidate its operations.

Naysayers do not just occupy the offices at the top of an organization; they can work at every level, all the way from middle management to the folks who do the day-to-day work that pays the bills. It's worth looking closely at the causes of a naysayer epidemic.

Take Aisha Sultan, the general manager of Clancy Builders, whom we met back in chapter 3. You may recall that she was working to overcome a Reactive Pattern that was blocking needed changes. She believed that if she could move people out of the Firefighter role, she could begin to create a more forward-thinking business. While Sultan was making steady progress in that direction, she was facing some resistance to going fully digital.

Sultan fervently supported the company's new Building Information Modeling (BIM) software, a tool that allowed the digital representation of assets across planning, design, and construction life cycles. Despite the fact that she had thoroughly trained employees in how to use it, many site supervisors across her division remained skeptical.

As Sultan explained over a pot of Earl Grey tea in her office overlooking Melbourne's tree-lined boulevard, "I'm having a real tough time getting our people 100 percent behind the new software and mobile technology. As a result, our competitors are stealing clients who think we are stuck in the Dark Ages."

I agreed to explore the situation with managers and supervisors to uncover the reasons for all this resistance to the BIM initiative. During my first interview, "Adam Moloney," general manager of Roads, responsible for managing construction works for highway and infrastructure projects, told me, "I think we need to play to our strengths, Siobhán, and consider the possible downsides of making a monumental change like this. If it's mismanaged, we might get change all right, but in the wrong direction. I can imagine some really poor project outcomes and some very unhappy customers."

Other managers echoed Moloney's feelings about the need for caution. Somewhat surprisingly, the supervisors voiced even stronger opinions.

After they strolled into a meeting room in a high-ceilinged steel shed near the airport, wearing hard hats and bright Day-Glo gear, their apparent spokesman, building supervisor "Toni Hurst," held nothing back. "We've always been a company where people love their pickup trucks, nail guns, cement mixers, and hydraulic excavators. It's best we stick with what we know rather than mess with this newfangled gadgetry."

Other supervisors muttered agreement. BIM technology, they believed, offered more risk than reward.

When I took my findings back to Sultan, I began by drawing the pattern (see figure 7.3). She could see it clearly. The Catastrophizing Pattern depicted the hidden agreement at Clancy Builders that "we imagine the worst-case scenario."

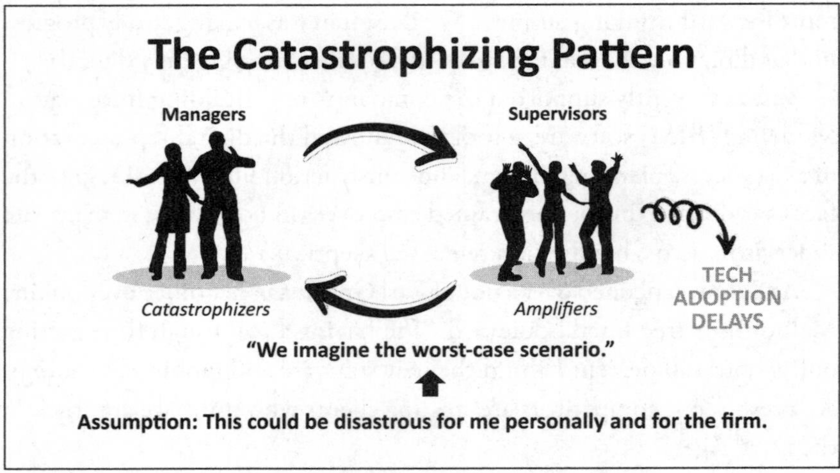

Figure 7.3

Construction managers, in the role of Catastrophizers, focused on the risks.

Supervisors, in role of Amplifiers, turned up the volume on the potential for negative outcomes.

Why were the people who had created the old ways fighting hard to keep them in place? Because they assumed that "if we get this wrong it could be disastrous for me personally and for the firm."

What does this have to do with nudging? Sultan, with all the best intentions in the world and believing so wholeheartedly in the digital revolution, had basically *told* people what to do without first uncovering their underlying assumptions.

As a first step toward busting these assumptions about technology, Sultan decided to work with construction manager "Abe Smith," a big tech fan, to launch a BIM pilot program on one of his construction jobs.

Soon, word of the benefits began to spread throughout the division, and within six months more than 80 percent of Sultan's contracts had signed up to use BIM. The benefits were obviously outweighing the risks.

Sultan had subtly introduced a new pattern at Clancy Builders (see figure 7.4). The general manager had stepped into the role of Nudger by conducting a small but successful BIM experiment that allowed employees to take up the role of Choice Makers and come onboard with the change. Remember the Hive LENS is not a linear model, so you can carry out an Experiment at any stage of change.

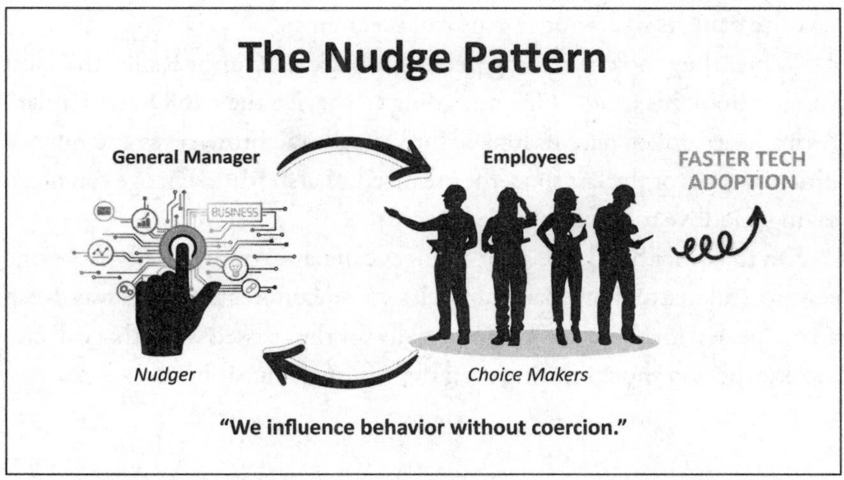

Figure 7.4

Sultan thanked me for my help as she updated me on progress. "Customers are impressed with our more efficient ways of working. We've seen a 33 percent improvement in proposal win rates. We're finally going all-out digital!"

Like Sultan, leaders with group intelligence examine the collective assumptions that fuel resistance to change. Look closely enough, and you'll see that these assumptions often hold the key to unlocking change.

Like the body of an iceberg, assumptions that feed resistance to change can often lurk far below the surface. From a helicopter, the floating ice looks like a small hill. From the viewpoint of a submarine, it looks like a massive mountain. From the point of view of the *Titanic*, it spells certain disaster if not detected soon enough.

Ecosystems usually resist shifting long-established behaviors that have served the group well in the past. Take my little family group. My father, long ensconced in his homeland, was finding it hard to leave the familiar village ways and move to Australia. One by one he watched as his children said goodbye to Finea, until my parents alone inhabited the big old farmhouse.

Eventually, my father came around to the idea of a move, and in their late fifties (Mom) and late sixties (Dad), my parents put the farm up for sale, chose treasured copy books from their children's school days, and placed favorite trinkets in a wooden trunk of belongings.

When they took our ailing pet dog, Shack, to Conor Reilly, the local vet, he shook his head. "He's not going to survive the trip Down Under." As my heartbroken parents looked into Shack's sad brown eyes and hugged him goodbye for the last time, they realized a harsh truth: change can mean saying goodbye to the things we love.

On the other hand, the right changes can pay extraordinarily satisfying rewards, no matter how many obstacles you encounter along the way. Keep an eye peeled for them, looking especially for the crossed wires that can create unexpected shocks during even the wisest change initiative.

WATCHING OUT FOR CROSSED WIRES

Timeline: 2014 at a French train station.
Announcement: "The train will not be arriving on Platform 1 anytime in the foreseeable future because it's too wide for the station."

Just as square pegs don't fit into round holes, France's new trains were not fitting into its railway stations. How could the railway have made such a preposterous mistake? Short answer: the organization got its wires crossed.

In 1997, France split its railway system in two, with Société Nationale des Chemins de fer Français (SNCF) responsible for operating the trains, and Réseau Ferré de France (RFF) responsible for the track network.

Seventeen years later, when RFF placed an order for new trains, it gave SNCF measurements for its newer, wider railway stations (less than thirty years old), when, in fact, most of France's stations were older and narrower (more than fifty years old).

When the two thousand new trains arrived, they could not fit into the old stations. This fiasco prompted French minister for transport Thierry Mariani to sum up the mess with one word: "absurd."

The mistake proved costly, with the train company shelling out over $110 million to widen thirteen hundred platforms on its regional network. As the French railway executives discovered, you'd better check for crossed wires before you plunge into an expensive venture that could end up costing you a fortune.

Of course, our friends the bees know better. Unlike the French railway officials, they travel for miles to return to the enclosed darkness of the hive in order to give accurate news flashes about the exact location of food sources.

People, on the other hand, can stumble around in the dark and come up with different conclusions. "I just stepped on a root," says one. "No," insists another, "that was a boa constrictor." The first would keep on stumbling. The second envisages getting swallowed by a hungry predator.

In a process that organizational psychologists call "sensemaking," we human beings continually try to understand what our experiences mean. For example, suppose I say the word "holiday." What do you see in your mind's eye?

Do you picture hiking in the Grand Canyon, lying on a white sandy beach in the Maldives, scuba diving the Great Barrier Reef, or visiting New York City's restaurants and museums? Me, I picture Venice's floating city built on more than a hundred islands. A thousand different people will form a thousand different pictures in their heads. That's a thousand opportunities for miscommunication.

In fact, miscommunication is the norm; perfect understanding of a situation is the exception. That's why it's so important to watch out for crossed wires.

Nathan Barry, founder of the email marketing company ConvertKit, forgot about the consequences of sensemaking when he rebranded his firm in 2018 without checking the meaning that different parts of the global ecosystem gave to the name "Seva."

The company had enjoyed great success as a marketing hub for creators that helped them grow and monetize their audience. Its twenty thousand customers received billions of marketing emails annually.

Having decided to rebrand the company, Barry and his team had spent two years researching options, finally settling on Seva. It took only a few days for bad press to emerge about the new name.

Seva, it turned out, was a sacred word to practitioners of the many religions who used it to describe the practice of giving generously to others out of love. The use of the word for marketing purposes deeply offended many Hindus, Sikhs, Buddhists, Jains, and others.

Almost immediately the CEO regretted his decision to use the word and admitted "our ignorance on the deep meaning of this sacred word." Fewer than thirty days after launch, Barry announced, "We will not be moving forward with Seva as our name. . . . The word is too sacred and too important to cultures that are not our own."

Unfortunately, the apology came after the company had wasted over half a million dollars on the rebrand. Had they only gotten their wires straight before jumping ahead with the rebranding, they would not only have saved a lot of money, they would not have suffered a lot of unwanted embarrassment.

We don't all agree on the meaning of a single word. Nor do we all see the world in the same way. It's important to make sense of words and the world around us, but the natural tendency toward sensemaking that serves us well as individuals can get us into hot water when our view runs up against the different views of others. Wires can get so easily crossed, especially in organizations.

Take the word *change*, for example. Shout it in a crowded room, and bedlam may break out. Bob thinks, *Uh-oh, this can't be good.* Juanita shivers because change has always scared her. But then Jocelyn and Ted find change exhilarating. Emotions run the gamut from fear and loathing to joyful expectation.

No wonder change initiatives can so easily fall victim to the crossed-wire syndrome. And it takes only one crossed wire to invite unintended consequences.

AVOIDING UNINTENDED CONSEQUENCES

My consulting client Jack Hammond, the CEO of the Washington, DC–based maintenance company TopChoice Maintenance (TCM) whom we met in chapter 2, had successfully broken the Nice Guy/Gal Pattern (which had cost the firm a pretty penny for favors delivered for free, which fell outside the scope of customer contracts with customers) and now needed to solve a worrisome safety issue.

He explained the situation over lattes at his favorite downtown coffee shop: "The good news is that we are back on track financially, but the bad news is workplace accidents. They've hit a ten-year high. Just last week an accident on a railway contract could have killed someone. We were lucky no one was badly injured."

On the worksite in question a TCM vehicle had collided with an approaching train. The incident spurred Hammond to instigate a review of the company's safety policies and possibly revise them to prevent this type of near miss from ever happening again. "But," he said, "I want to get it right. Any suggestions on how to make the change go smoothly without ruffling too many feathers?"

Before Hammond embarked on a policy rewrite, I offered to visit some key sites to discuss safety issues with the workers.

First, I went to the site where the recent rail accident took place. I saw large yellow utility vehicles parked trackside as I wound my way to the shed where I might find contract manager "Seth Goldstein." Handing me a yellow hard hat, he bid me a good morning. "Hope you won't need this, Siobhán. Seriously, though, we were very lucky here the other day. We were carrying out track maintenance when a freight train hit a TCM excavator. Our driver 'Terrell Williams' jumped away from the vehicle. The excavator fell over, but Williams only got a few scrapes on his knees."

Later that morning Williams added to the story. "Luckily I saw it coming. The doctor at the local medical center slapped bandages on my knees and I was back at work the next day. It's all hands on deck if we're gonna hit our project deadline."

Hmm. A bit of a rush going on here? An hour later safety officer "Hazel Bock" confirmed my suspicion. "I'm pulling my hair out with the way the guys handle safety on this site. Terrell was violating safety protocol when he moved the excavator onto the track without permission from the authorized officer. Management keeps pressing everyone to keep on schedule, no matter what. Me, I'm more worried about everyone going home to their families at night without their arms in slings, or worse!"

My visits to other TCM sites provided further evidence that the company's focus on client satisfaction and shareholder value had created a potentially dangerous pattern (see figure 7.5). I showed it to Hammond later that week. He could see how pressures to meet deadlines and stay on budget were inviting some unintended consequences. While breaking the Nice Guy/Gal Pattern had gotten everyone on the same page with respect to getting the right financial results, it had resulted in an unwritten agreement that "We break the rules to meet the deadline."

Employees, under pressure to meet deadlines, stepped into the role of Rule Breakers skirting safety regulations when they deemed it necessary

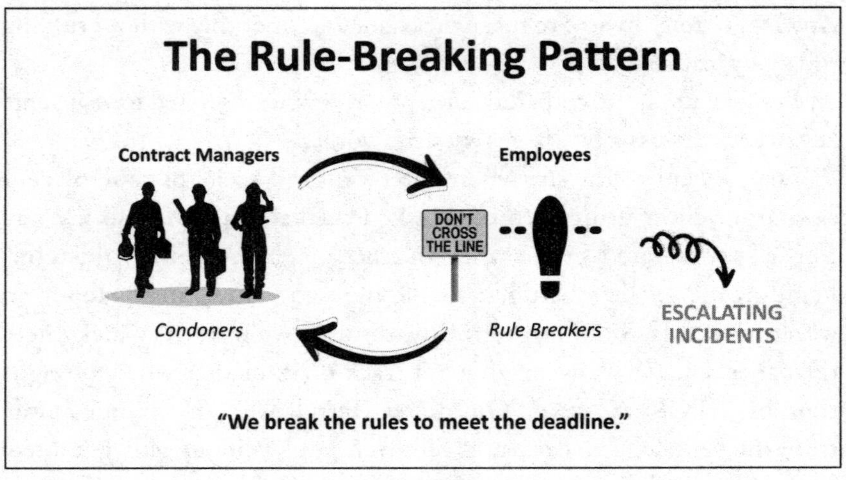

Figure 7.5

to keep on schedule. Contract managers, in the role of Condoners, turned a blind eye to the rule-breaking behavior. And round and round went the merry-go-round with the risks of a serious accident mounting every day.

Hammond shook his head. "I never intended that," he moaned. "Fix one problem and another pops up. Should we press ahead with rewriting our safety policies?"

That struck me as a classic mechanistic approach to solving a problem that required deeper thinking. "Aren't the existing policies sensible enough?"

"Aw, I guess so. New ones won't solve the problem. We just need to get everyone focused as much on safety as the bottom line."

Jack immediately called an emergency meeting with all of TCM's contracts managers to discuss the importance of managing client relationships *and* contract performance *and* the safety and well-being of all employees: "We want to make money and hit our deadlines. But listen to Hazel. We must make sure our people go home safely to their families every day."

Jack told the crew he would track safety metrics at their monthly meetings. "I want you to stick to the rules and impose consequences for anyone who breaks them." Word spread like wildfire that the boss would no longer tolerate people who bypassed the safety regulations. As a result, a new Safety Pattern began to emerge (see figure 7.6).

Figure 7.6

When we caught up six months later, Hammond proudly showed me the results. "We've had a 50 percent reduction in the number of safety incidents compared to this time last year, and it looks like we will set an all-time safety record this year."

In complex ecosystems our actions to effect change can cause an unexpected ripple effect. It's like playing with a balloon. Squish it on one side, a bubble pops up on the other. No workplace is perfect. Problems *always* pop up. You just need to think about unintended consequences every time you squish the balloon.

This brings me back to my cherished beehives. Not long ago, London residents worried so much about the existential threat to the world's bee population that they installed new hives in gardens, factory yards, and rooftops throughout the city.

Good idea, right? Not for other species of native pollinators who found themselves competing for ever-scarcer food resources. Solve a problem for one species and invite extinction for another.

According to a phenomenon called "nonlinear causality," complex systems react to simplistic responses in unexpected ways. That explains why mechanistic solutions ("Rewrite the safety rules! Hire for diversity! Restructure the organization!") so often fail. They assume that change occurs in a linear fashion. It never does.

A small change does not necessarily have a small impact. Nor does a big change necessarily have a big one. Multiple factors can affect a change outcome, as Jack Hammond discovered when a solution to one problem caused a new one.

In the world of nonlinear causality, a small change can make a huge impact, and vice versa. Edward Lorenz, the renowned mathematician, MIT meteorologist, and the founder of modern chaos theory, shed light on the topic of nonlinear causality.

Lorenz noticed, for example, that a small difference in a dynamic climate system could trigger vast and often unexpected results, a fact that made climate changes hard to predict. Lorenz called this the "butterfly effect" because a monarch butterfly flapping its wings in Brazil could create a tornado in Amarillo, Texas.

Lorenz's insights not only influenced the field of mathematics but altered the thinking in a number of fields, including the biological, physical, and social sciences. This should also influence the way we look at organizations. What Lorenz called "chaotic behavior" occurs in groups of human beings, making them much more difficult to anticipate and manage than passive, mechanical systems.

In complex, active systems, new connections and patterns constantly emerge. The Greek philosopher Heraclitus recognized this way back in 540 BCE when he said, "You never step into the same river twice." Well, you never step into the same group twice. Step out for a minute, and it's changed before you step back in.

Bees know all about the potentially dire consequences of a certain action. Roman mythology tells how sky god Jupiter was so pleased with a gift of honey that he granted the bee a wish, the ability to sting any human who stole honey from her hive. Wish granted. But what a price the bee would pay for that gift. Using its stinger to defend the hive would cost the bee its life.

Change leaders must do everything they can to avoid the stinger of unintended consequences. Whenever they embark on any change initiative, they must ponder what might happen when they intervene in the system, imagining not just the good that might come from it but the bad that might occur as well. Ask not just what will benefit the ecosystem but what might harm it as well.

In today's volatile and rapidly changing world, we need leaders who can deal with the dynamic nature of complex ecosystems. Those with group intelligence never make the mistake of thinking that their change interventions will run a smooth, linear course from here to there. They constantly check on the large and small effects of the change, making necessary adjustments along the way.

POINTS TO REMEMBER

- Smart change leaders never push too hard for change.
- A gentle nudge accomplishes more than a hard push.

- Obstacles in the form of hidden assumptions can block meaningful and lasting change.
- Crossed wires can occur because people make sense of change in different ways.
- Unintended consequences can derail the best-laid change.

8

REACHING CRITICAL MASS

Create a Powerful Swarm

As the sun begins to rise over the valley, the colony swarms from the branch, flying over meadows and around the swamp to reach the chosen tree cavity on the grassy woodland knoll.

After the swarm alights gracefully at the cavity's entrance, the queen soon arrives, slipping inside without any fanfare. By the time the sun evaporates the early morning fog, all the bees have snuggled safely inside their new home.

Smart business leaders enable people to reach critical tipping points, especially that exquisite moment when you see the group eagerly begin to take up their new roles.

Scientists confirm that a seemingly small change in one part of a complex system can mark a critical turning point, after which the change cascades throughout the whole system. We call such events "tipping points."

The concept dates back to the nineteenth century, when Henri Poincaré introduced a mathematical theory called bifurcation that demonstrated how small changes (or perturbations) in a complex dynamical system can trigger a large response.

Economists also note the importance of tipping points, citing, for example, how the global 2007–2008 financial crisis began with the collapse of the 158-year-old investment bank Lehman Brothers. That single event sent shock waves throughout the US and global economies.

The general public became aware of the importance of tipping points when Malcolm Gladwell explored their ramifications in his bestselling book on the subject.

In organizations, both large and small, tipping points occur when a change initiative begins to take on a life of its own, spreading like wildfire as it captures an increasing number of group members.

It's extremely important that leaders learn how to trigger key tipping points and harness their power. Sadly, that's not always the case. Progress can easily stall when managers trumpet the change while employees lie low, waiting for all the hoopla to pass (see figure 8.1).

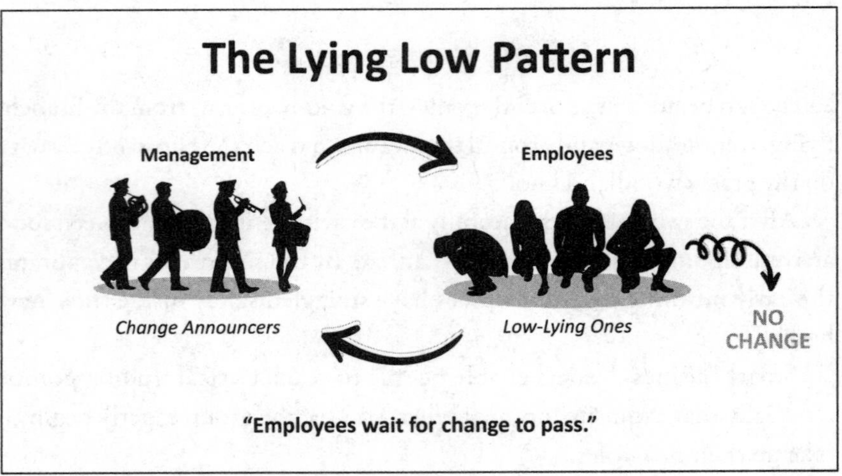

Figure 8.1

I've seen this old familiar pattern hundreds of times in workplaces where employees have come to believe that if you wait until the fanfare subsides, management will just move on to the "next big thing." Who's cocreating this sort of cynicism in the ecosystem? All the leaders who keep jumping from one bandwagon to the next. Hello inertia, goodbye tipping point.

Seasoned change leaders know that you must arrive at the key tipping point within eighteen months of embarking on change or risk confirming the group's cynicism. In order to reach this critical juncture you must, just like the bees, create a swarm where the change goes viral.

CREATING A SWARM OF VIRAL CHANGE

In 2018, Achim Steiner, newly appointed CEO, reviewed the United Nations Development Programme (UNDP) in order to gauge the organization's impact on the world's most complex problems. He hoped his findings would lead to better outcomes.

With an annual budget of $5 billion, the UNDP employed seventeen thousand people across 170 countries, all focused on sustainable development. Their mission was to eradicate poverty, reduce inequality, improve health, and provide affordable and clean energy.

After his review, Steiner decided that some well-designed changes could enable the UNDP to fulfill this mission more effectively. In January 2019 he launched one of the world's largest networks of Accelerator Labs (sixty facilities, serving seventy-eight countries) with the express aim of embedding collective intelligence principles into sustainable development work.

These labs would, Steiner believed, provide tools to explore, test, and emerge grassroots solutions for complex sustainable development problems. As he said at the time, "The labs will use collective intelligence to support partners to better understand facts and ideas, develop new solutions, promote more inclusive decision making, and provide better oversight of what is done."

The labs were not the large units you might expect at a sprawling global organization. Drawing on the expertise of ethnographers, data scientists, and social innovators, Steiner placed only three experts in each lab. Fewer experts, he reasoned, would find it necessary to forge partnerships with local agencies and other labs in order to develop the best possible solutions.

For instance, the Buenos Aires lab partnered with the open-seneca organization, a worldwide network of citizen pilots, to measure air quality. Local university students learned how to build low-cost sensors (at a cost of $150 rather than $50,000 for an "official" sensor) they could attach to their bicycles to collect data on daily air quality changes in their home city.

The massed data, uploaded to the open-seneca platform, revealed local hot spots (such as traffic junctions) that could drive decisions by the Buenos Aires Ministry of the Environment and Sustainable Development and the Buenos Aires city government to install new policies and stimulate viral community action.

In another instance, Ukraine's Accelerator Lab combined satellite and crowdsourcing data to map the open burning of waste in rural communities, a widespread practice in Ukraine, with thirty-six thousand to fifty-six thousand fires per year devastating local air quality.

Working with the Center for Innovations Development, the lab created an up-to-date dashboard of open burning and composting in rural communities that grassroots groups could use to effect important changes in affected communities.

In the Zasulska community, the data identified that most local fires occurred in cornfields. In contrast, Torchynska community residents used burning techniques in agricultural and grass fields. The lab crowdsourced the location of 367 previously unknown composting sites. All this data helped local communities identify alternatives to open burning.

The labs helped make UNDP a more agile and effective global organization that could deliver much-needed change at a local level. It was the Hive Mind at work, creating a swarm to support, share, and cocreate viral change solutions. Experimentation flourished, change accelerated, government policies evolved.

Achim Steiner summed it up: "This collective intelligence approach is founded upon the principle that an enhanced capacity to solve problems is created when people work together through the mobilization of a wider range of data, ideas, and insights."

The swarm made change go viral. In 2021, UNDP achieved 99 percent of its four-year funding target, mobilizing $20.7 billion in development finance and winning recognition as the most transparent UN agency by the International Aid Transparency Index.

Business buzzwords can easily become clichés. *Agility*, *innovation*, *transformation*, *accountability*, and *change* lose their meaning when bandied about ad nauseam. Swarms develop a shared meaning for the buzzwords. Swarms also know that when it comes to harnessing the power of group intelligence, "we" can accomplish what "I" never can. Ask not what I can do to achieve the best results for my organization, ask "How can *we* create more value together?"

Swarms capture people's imagination, as Nik Robinson, former graphic designer and entertainment executive, went on to discover in 2018 during dinner with his family. When Nik's sons, Harry (eight) and Archie (six), expressed dismay over the millions of tons of plastic waste polluting the world's oceans, their equally concerned father promised to do something to untrash the planet. Thus was born Good Citizens, a company that would make sunglasses from recycled plastic bottles.

Adopting a 100 percent recycled principle, Robinson needed to find a way to replace the conventional metal screws and hinges used in most eyeglasses. As he recalls, "We could have been lazy and done metal pins, but again, that's cheating. I want to show people that while you drink from that water bottle for thirty seconds and throw it in the bin, we're going to make something that I hope catches your imagination. That piece of trash made this good thing. It's just to inspire people." Inspiring people and capturing their imagination is the way of the swarm.

In April 2020, after 752 days and 2,500-plus failed attempts, Nik Robinson finally reached his goal of turning a plastic bottle into a pair of sunglasses. Driven by his promise to two young lads, Robinson had transformed an empty quart bottle of diet soda into a chic, beautifully designed, sustainably made pair of sunglasses.

By August 2020, Selfridges department store in London had allocated an entire window to Robinson's sunglasses, right next door to Prada, as part of its Project Earth initiative. In September 2020, Good Citizens won gold at the international Good Design Awards, and that same month Nik Robinson and his son Harry received an invitation to speak at the United Nations Global Compact Conference.

Nik Robinson would make an excellent keeper of bees because he understands how the collective mind works. The hive lets nothing go to waste, cleaning leftover pieces of honeycomb and cutting them into tiny pieces for making much-needed wax.

Like the bees' conservation-minded practices, Robinson's "no waste ever" philosophy created viral change with a swarm of followers intent on cleaning up the planet.

By capturing people's imagination, Robinson reached a tipping point, that critical juncture when the tide turns and begins to create a tsunami. Suddenly the forces for change are stronger than the forces of inertia and resistance. And you can find no better fuel for the new rising tide than the power of well-told stories.

TELLING POWERFUL STORIES TO FUEL CHANGE

In 80 percent of US households, you will find a can of WD-40, the multipurpose oil lubricant with the bright red top. Garry Ridge, who led the WD-40 company for twenty-five years before his retirement in 2022, used storytelling to turn its major product into a household name.

When Ridge took over as CEO in 1997, the company employed a mere 165 people and generated just $137.9 million in revenue, almost entirely in US business. By the time he retired, revenues had rocketed to almost half a billion dollars.

It all started with a story Ridge told employees about how WD-40 was the child of "rocket science," created by space engineers to protect the outer skin of Atlas missiles from rust and corrosion. It took the research and development team forty attempts to get the water displacement formula right; hence the name: Water Displacement-40, or WD-40 for short.

The rocket science story stuck in people's heads. Ridge didn't stop there to communicate his inclusive management philosophy, inspired by Aboriginal tribes in his native Australia.

It made a good story. "Our tribe = our success," he proclaimed. "We are a tribe, and as a tribe we're here for each other as much as we're here for the company. Our definition of tribe is a community of people with a shared purpose who help feed and defend each other."

Sounds like a swarm, doesn't it? He wanted his WD-40 swarm to support each other and the group as a whole. More stories flowed from the CEO, creating positive, lasting memories with key stakeholders. It wasn't just a lot of feel-good chatter. It was also about profits, the honey produced by the end of a long workday. "Profit is the applause of doing good work and having engaged employees, and that's what I'm most proud of. The stock price will take care of itself."

By 2021, the firm was selling WD-40 in more than 176 countries worldwide. Revenue reached $488.1 million, up 19 percent over the previous fiscal year. A nice concluding chapter to Garry's story at WD-40 came when Ridge was named as one of the World's Top Ten CEOs in 2022.

I'll bet a jar of my favorite honey that you will find it easier to remember the story of the migrating bees than an esoteric theory of systemic change. I'm hoping our busy little friends will remind you of the principles we've been discussing in this book: the power of group intelligence to create meaningful, lasting change.

I love the old proverb "Tell me the facts and I'll learn. Tell me the truth and I'll believe. But tell me a story and it will live in my heart forever."

Great stories invite people to participate in a change worth undertaking. Telling a story sweeps you into another realm and mentally transports the group to a different time and place. Scientists have found that a compelling story can make listeners' palms sweat, eyes blink faster, and hearts might flutter or skip a beat, all signs that they are engaged.

Brain scientists studying MRI scans know that many areas of the brain light up when we listen to an engaging narrative. The networks involved in language processing, emotions arising from sounds, along with areas involved in movement, become activated, especially during dramatic moments in the story.

This phenomenon also applies to our friends the bees. Their waggle dances capture attention because they deliver valuable messages related to the survival of all members of the colony.

Celtic lore also considered bees as messengers, bringing back stories from gods in the Otherworld (the supernatural realm of deities, everlasting youth, health, abundance, and joy).

Great marketers rely on stories to motivate groups both inside and outside an organization. The founders of the eyewear company Warby Parker took the market by storm with their powerful story about the time when one of the founders lost his glasses on a backpacking trip in Asia and could not believe how much it would cost to replace them.

That's not right, he thought. His frustration sparked the idea for a socially conscious company that would offer designer eyewear at unbelievably low prices. A clear, socially conscious narrative differentiated Warby Parker from its competitors:

- The eyewear material? Plant-based cellulose acetate.
- The human touch? Every pair of glasses assembled and polished by hand.
- Giving back? More than thirteen million pairs of glasses donated to those in need via Warby Parker's "Buy a Pair, Give a Pair" program.

People took the Warby Parker story to heart because they trusted it to be true. Truth and trust set the stage for powerful storytelling. You want your swarm to fly into an unknown territory, one that may be fraught with danger? First, you must earn their trust. And a true story will keep reminding them that they can trust you as they move forward.

Nike marketers relied on a memorable story in their historic 1999 advertising campaign celebrating the achievements of basketball superstar Michael Jordan. The ad's sponsor appears only at the very end when the words "Just do it" emerge alongside an old-school photo of Jordan, followed by the Nike logo.

By associating its brand with the basketball legend, Nike essentially co-opted his story to sell shoes. The athlete's association with Nike's Air Jordan model athletic shoes and related accessories continued and went on to become the subject of a popular 2023 movie.

Listeners pay less attention to self-aggrandizing stories than they do ones about people they admire. Identify the Michael Jordans in your environment or group, letting them tell their stories to explain why the change matters, how it will benefit individuals and the group, and where it connects to their values. Change leaders within your organization must step into the role of storytellers to garner the group's attention and inspire people to join the change movement.

A vivid story brings an abstract idea to life. Automaker Land Rover's marketers brilliantly incorporated a good story into the company's seventieth anniversary celebrations. They sent a film crew to the Himalayas for ten days to film *The Land of the Land Rovers*, a commercial that would unfold the story of villagers in a remote region along the Nepal/Indian border who own a fleet of forty-two old Land Rovers. That fact emphasized that the vehicle was not just a high-end luxury SUV driven by the rich and famous.

The locals use the 1957 Land Rovers to navigate the treacherous uphill mountain pass between the villages of Maneybhanjang (altitude 1,523 meters) and the snowcapped Sandakphu (altitude 3,636 meters). The commercial not only displayed this thrilling trek through spectacular scenery, but it also offered candid interviews with villagers about the importance of Land Rovers in their lives.

Toward the end of the ad, a driver gazes out onto the snowcapped Himalayas and describes the community connection to the Land Rovers as "unbreakable." Then the ad concludes with the statement "We are proud to say that we belong to the place of the Land Rovers."

The Land Rover marketers touched hearts in order to touch pocketbooks. Oh, you might drive your Land Rover only through suburban streets or on an occasional four-wheel expedition to the beach, but every mile would feel like a great adventure. The story went far beyond vehicle functionality to tap into feelings of courage, confidence, and pride that Maneybhanjang locals felt driving their own all-terrain vehicles.

Feelings drive all great movements. And good stories fuel feelings.

Indeed, you will find an evocative narrative propelling all successful changes because they bring ideas to life and move people to take action.

Leaders who grasp the power of group intelligence focus less on the mechanics and more on the vision to reach the tipping point sooner. They focus on how accomplishing the change will make people feel rather than on the step-by-step process that will get them there. Their storytelling toolbox usually includes powerful symbols that capture the imagination and help trigger the tipping point.

USING SYMBOLS TO TRIGGER THE TIPPING POINT

Symbols come in all shapes and sizes. Even everyday items can become imbued with symbolism, as *New York Times* reporter Emily Spivack found when she asked people, "What's your most prized possession?" Interviewees did not mention their Rolex watches or Mercedes sports cars but special items they held dear to their hearts.

Singer Andrea Bocelli mentioned a pair of boxing gloves signed by his friend Muhammad Ali kept in a glass case at his home; designer Scott Sternberg prized a guitar purchased in a music shop that had provided him sanctuary as an adolescent; Queens, New York, resident Mrs. Park most valued a yellow sweater given to her by a monk when, having just emigrated from South Korea, she was feeling lost in America. These fairly common objects had gained value because they symbolized something important to their owners.

People appreciate the symbolism of bees. Throughout the ages we have associated them with certain values: "making a beeline for the coffee shop" or "creating a hive of activity" or "keeping busy as a bee."

A symbol represents or stands for something else: Andrea Bocelli saw those boxing gloves as a reminder of his long friendship with an athlete who had never stopped inspiring him. During change, leaders can employ symbols to communicate such abstract concepts as values, making them concrete and memorable, thus helping people make sense of the emerging future.

One of my favorite stories about symbols dates back to 1990, when Mary Robinson became the unlikely winner of the Irish presidential election.

During her campaign, Robinson promised that if elected she would install a light in the front portico of the president's official residence, Áras an Uachtaráin (House of the President), in Phoenix Park, Dublin, to signal to the Irish diaspora around the world that their homeland would always welcome their return to the old sod.

The idea harkened back to Robinson's childhood growing up in Ballina, County Mayo, where residents put candles in their windows to welcome emigrants home for Christmas.

No other presidential candidate had ever reached out to the millions of Irish people abroad. After her unexpected victory, Robinson made good on her promise. The light in the window of the Áras became a powerful symbol of inclusiveness for people in isolated villages in the west of Ireland, in deprived inner-city slums, and emigrant communities who had suffered poverty, hardship, and depression.

When legendary US politician Tip O'Neill came to visit, he and Robinson walked down the steps of Áras an Uachtaráin together, and he turned around to gaze on the light in the upstairs window welcoming him back to his ancestral home. That symbol brought tears to the eyes of the Irish American politician.

And far away in Australia, when we got homesick, my family and I could always envision that light shining in the president's window, welcoming us home.

Robinson became one of the most consequential leaders in twentieth-century Ireland, serving as president until 1997, when she left to become the United Nations High Commissioner for Human Rights.

Learning theorist Jean Piaget argued that human minds can grasp pictures (that is, symbols) much more easily than abstract concepts. In the business world, symbols can bring abstractions to life. You can't easily picture concepts such as "distributed teams," "sustainability," and "innovation" in your mind's eye, but you can picture a virtual meeting of stay-at-home workers, a towering redwood tree, and a flashing light bulb, all of which bring what they stand for to life.

If I needed to explain the term *agile*, I might plant an image in your mind of a cheetah bounding across the Serengeti Plain. Hear *agile*, and your eyes will glaze over; hear *cheetah*, and you see a mental picture that will stick in your mind.

The explosion of data, social media distractions, and the pace of technological change can easily obscure what's really important. It can be hard to see the one gold nugget in a streambed full of sparkling gravel. The right symbol can pluck that nugget out of all the glittering confusion of the fast-flowing river. It can locate the signal in all the noise.

That's exactly what Jørgen Vig Knudstorp did at Lego. You may recall the story about the turnaround he engineered from our discussion of Fast-Forward Thinking in chapter 3.

When Knudstorp took over as CEO in 2004, the thirty-four-year-old ex-McKinsey consultant found a very troubled company desperately in need of major change. How, he wondered, could he get the message across to employees? He organized a "war room," a place where Lego's transformation team would gather to work through this crisis, assemble all pertinent facts about Lego's predicament, and forensically examine the data.

The war room created a picture in the mind's eye of every employee, reminding them that they needed to join the fight to keep their cherished company alive.

Lego's change team eventually drew up clear plans for rebuilding the company. Their war effort paid off. Four years later, Lego was back on track, with profits quadrupling between 2008 and 2010. The war room had helped Lego take its place as one of the most recognized brands around the world and the largest toy company in history.

Why do symbols like the war room work such powerful magic in our lives? Neurologists tell us that symbols live at an unconscious level in the mind, away from the parts of the brain that process data.

The neocortex, the latest part of the brain to develop, performs logical thinking. The deeper, more primitive limbic system governs our emotions, decision-making ability, and behavior. Language and logic alone cannot reach this more influential portion of the human brain. Symbols can.

When Pfizer CEO Albert Bourla wanted to mobilize his firm's massive change effort to find a vaccine for the COVID-19 virus, he called the mission Project Light Speed. That image lit up the limbic system. It conveyed the idea that "we are working against all odds to make the impossible possible." The Pfizer team went on to produce a vaccine in an extraordinary, record-breaking nine months.

Whatever symbols you choose, they must touch not just people's minds (logic) but their hearts (emotions). What images will most excite them? It might be something as simple as a project title (the "war room" and "Project Light Speed"), or it may be something as elaborate as an image of a planet-saving mission.

In 2016 the executives at Patagonia, the outdoor apparel company, embarked on a quest to become a more sustainable company, making it concrete with the words "fundraiser for the earth." The company would, it promised, donate all proceeds from their Black Friday sales to the save-the-planet mission.

The executive team, initially hoping to generate $2 million from the campaign, were staggered when it raised an astonishing $10 million.

True to their word, the following Monday the company announced that the "enormous love" that its customers had shown the planet would benefit hundreds of grassroots environmental organizations around the world who were striving to protect the earth's air, water, and soil for future generations. Patagonia's "fundraiser for the earth" symbol helped make that happen.

While symbols make abstractions concrete and memorable, they alone will not always create the tipping point during change.

In most cases, people need to put all the nice words and symbols into action, and sometimes you need to help them jump onboard with the change.

Once you capture the imagination, you must ensure that the group can adopt the new ways. To do so, change leaders employ the rituals that turn sporadic behaviors into everyday practices.

PRACTICING RITUALS THAT REINFORCE NEW HABITS

When British monarch Queen Elizabeth II died in 2022, palace beekeeper John Chapple traveled to Clarence House and Buckingham Palace to tell the bees of the monarch's passing, knocking on each of Her Majesty's seven hives to whisper, "The mistress is dead, but don't you go. Your master will be a good master to you."

For centuries the British have treated bees as important members of the family and have maintained the ritual of "telling the bees" about important family events. This sort of repeated act or custom can forge identity, revitalize meaning, and build connection during change.

During my twenty years working as a changemaker in organizations, I've observed many such practices in the workplace: Friday night drinks, birthday morning teas, toasts at send-off dinners, communal recognition of a win or a major milestone. Such workplace rituals help bind a group together, especially during a transformation journey.

I first learned about the power of rituals at the Sheffield United Football Club in the steelmaking city in northern England once famous for its cutlery.

An eager student of organizational psychology, I was delving into teamwork as part of my master's degree program at Sheffield University when newly appointed Sheffield United Club's manager Dave "Harry" Bassett invited me to the Blades (the club's affectionate nickname) to study the team's performance.

Bassett had arrived at the club at the tail end of the 1980s, just as the team was clawing its way back from its recent relegation in the English Football League. That's soccer for my American readers. After losing a crucial playoff game against Bristol City by a narrow 2–1 margin, Sheffield had fallen to the lowly Third Division.

Harry had worked hard to turn things around, bringing in famed footballer Vinnie Jones, a so-called hard man who later achieved success as a movie actor. Under Harry's firm hand the team adopted many new rituals: arduous team practices, high-pressure individual training exercises, and drills that matched anything you might see at a military training camp.

Drill, feedback, repeat. Drill, feedback, repeat.

The exhaustive repetition drew the most from Bassett's players and bound them together in a tight brotherhood. They would go through hell for one another and for the good of the team.

But Bassett was not a cruel taskmaster. He emphasized taking care of oneself, which included the importance of a nutritional diet, proper hydration, and sufficient sleep before every game. Repetition built new neural pathways and taught the athletes' bodies how to execute every skill. Trial and error, making mistakes, and correcting them became a deeply embedded ritual.

On match day, with tensions running high in the dressing room and the sound of the crowd chanting in the stadium, players went through stretching and warm-up rituals to limber up their muscles and shake off their nerves.

Once on the field, the rituals paid off. The team rose back up to the Second Division in 1988–89 and even further to the First Division in 1989–90. Steady progress finally took them to the Premier League and the semifinal game of England's Football Association Challenge Cup (more commonly known as the FA Cup).

Rituals become habits. Good habits pay big dividends; bad ones breed failure. This applies to groups as well as individuals.

Think about your own habits, both good and bad. Certainly, you might love to break a bad habit, such as smoking or overeating fatty foods. But that first cigarette with your morning coffee tastes *so* good, just before you wolf down a chocolate glazed doughnut.

Bad habits are hard to break; new habits are not so easy to make. In the case of groups, automatic behavior helps it function, but abandoning an undesired ritual and adopting a new one takes a great deal of conscious effort. It can get quite distracting and affect performance of the group's daily activities.

During change, leaders must concentrate their efforts on encouraging new rituals that support the change and promote new habits. Daily routines build confidence within the group that they can accomplish the change.

That's just what Amazon's leaders did when they inaugurated the company's "working backward" ritual, a practice designed to drive innovation by getting employees to look at their work through a customer lens.

You may have heard about one of Amazon's "working backward" rituals, its famous "6-pager," instituted by founder Jeff Bezos in 2004 when he got fed up with outline-style PowerPoint presentations peppered with bullets that failed to make a convincing argument.

To help people communicate change recommendations more clearly, Bezos asked that they present every change proposal in a six-page memo that included a one-page "press release" addressing questions such as: "How will it be different? What's the price? How will you make it happen? What resources does it need?"

The "6-pager" required clarity of thought, complete sentences, and coherent paragraphs. For instance, the development team for Amazon's Kindle would have used the format to convey a compelling case for the benefits customers would reap from the portable wireless electronic reading device.

Executives reviewing the document in a meeting would have spent the first ten minutes silently reading "The Case for the Kindle" before discussing the pros and cons of the project, perhaps sending the development team back to the drawing board to add or revise certain points.

In the end, leadership would have given the team a green light to proceed. Kindle, first released in 2007, has gone on to become the world's most popular e-reader, with Amazon's e-books capturing two-thirds of the electronic book market.

A business need becomes a ritual; a ritual becomes an ingrained habit. Amazon's "6-pagers," born from the company's "working backward" rituals, have become a lesson in good business writing taught in programs around the world.

Successful change initiatives usually depend on compelling business writing throughout the project because it's an essential element of the storytelling that can encourage people to come on board.

Successful change requires that you rewire your brain. Neuroscientists have shed light on the process. In a phenomenon called neuroplasticity, the human brain undergoes an alteration in its physical structure during transformation as it repeatedly performs new tasks.

Let's say you're learning how to ride a bicycle, a novel activity for a beginner that demands all-out concentration as your brain forms new "bike riding" connections. The more you perform this sequence of necessary actions, the stronger the neural pathway for bike riding becomes.

The nerve impulses fire faster as you keep practicing the routine until your brain stores "bike riding" as an easily recalled habit. Your brain has stored it in long-term memory. Even if you do not hop on a bike for five years, bike riding will come back to you in a flash when you take your new mountain bike for a spin.

Groups also store routines in the Hive Mind's long-term memory. During change, members of the group learn new routines they must practice repeatedly until they become easily recalled habits.

With practice, even the most challenging new ways of doing things become easier and easier, until the group grows unconsciously competent at performing them. With the new habits safely stored in long-term memory, the group can now focus its attention on solving problems and devising innovative solutions.

I urge leaders to follow the "Sixty-Six Day Rule." According to several studies, it takes an average of sixty-six days for a new routine to become automatic.

Review progress after twenty-two days. If you see good progress, urge people to keep at it for another twenty-two days.

Review progress again, then keep promoting the routine until it becomes fully embedded in the Hive Mind. Make the new routine simple and easy to perform. Then encourage group members to perform it over and over until it becomes the "way we do things around here."

Simplicity is the best antidote for complexity. If you overwhelm people with too much change all at once, their brains will freeze with information overload. Rather than joining the change movement, they will resist it, even sabotage it.

People can find even rather simple transformations difficult to navigate because change requires them to unlearn the old ways and forge new neural connections for the new ways. Patience provides the best antidote for the natural resistance to forming the new habits required for a swarm of change.

As a child I found swarms mesmerizing: schools of minnow darting in the dark pools of the river Inny, starlings swirling in the sky before flying back to northern Europe, and bees migrating from the hive in our orchard. I marveled at how these creatures moved as a single organism, and I later wondered what this collective behavior might teach us about humans embarking on a change journey.

Over the years, I've learned that swarms play a vital role in reaching the critical tipping points, where all parts of the ecosystem work in harmony to cocreate a desired change.

Smart leaders know how to nudge a group toward these critical junctures by deploying stories, symbols, and rituals that facilitate viral change. Leaders with group intelligence intervene in complex ecosystems to move the group from chaotic, milling individuals to a collective force for change.

POINTS TO REMEMBER

- The group must reach the tipping point where the change gathers momentum.

- Powerful stories help people connect to the change with their heads *and* their hearts.
- Symbols send signals that cut through the organizational noise.
- Daily rituals turn change aspirations into daily habits.

9

ALIGNING TECHNOLOGY AND PROCESSES

Install the Right Hive Infrastructure

Once the bees arrive at their destination in the tree cavity by the grassy knoll, they know they must stick to a tight timetable. With winter just around the corner, they must build a new home and gather enough nectar to survive the cold weather. If they fail, they die.

The bees step into the role of construction workers, building the hive from the top down, using nature's sturdiest pattern, the hexagon, to fashion the honeycomb.

Each cleverly planned wax cell tilts slightly backward so that the honey will not spill out and fits snugly against its neighbors on all sides.

The bees will use the mass of six-sided wax cells to store pollen, nectar, and honey in order to raise their brood. They understand the need to construct the right structures in their new home and work together on the honeycomb-building process. After all, their lives depend on it.

The leaders at Chipotle Mexican Grill, one of America's best-loved fast-food chains, realized the company needed new structures and processes back in 2020 when the government ordered Chipotle to pay $25 million to resolve criminal charges related to foodborne illness outbreaks at its restaurants.

The trouble had started in Portland, Oregon, on Friday, October 23, 2015, when a customer named Chris Collins, a thirty-two-year-old web developer and photographer, ordered his favorite chicken bowl at his local Chipotle's restaurant.

The next evening, Collins felt so sick he rushed to the emergency room, where doctors determined that he had contracted Shiga-toxin-producing E. coli O26. Could it have been caused by the twenty-one-ingredient salad he had eaten the night before?

It not only took Collins almost six weeks to recover, but several months later he was still suffering the effects of the illness. It turned out he was patient zero.

Foodborne illnesses ended up sickening another eleven hundred Chipotle customers between 2015 and 2018. When management investigated the problem, they traced the outbreaks to workers failing to follow hygiene procedures. That had to change, and it had to change fast.

The restaurant chain's leaders hired food safety expert Mansour Samadpour to alter worker and supplier behavior in order to ensure safer dining experiences for everyone who visited a Chipotle's outlet. Like the bees, Samadpour was a busy bee, working diligently to install the infrastructure that would create a massive and permanent change.

We will look more closely at the Chipotle saga in a moment. I have chosen it because it so nicely illustrates the fourth step and the S on the Hive LENS: *Strengthen*. During transformation you will need to reinforce the new ways with processes and systems that support the change.

FORMULATING POLICIES, PROCESSES, AND PROCEDURES

In her new home on the edge of Wombat Forest, the queen lays her eggs in a careful pattern, inserting each one into its own honeycomb cell. Worker bees, following her path, seal the cells with wax. The bees know the value of following the right process during change.

While documented processes and policies themselves won't make change happen, they do strengthen emerging behavior shifts. Samadpour understood that fact when he took on the daunting task of preventing further E. coli outbreaks at Chipotle's restaurants.

Knowing that E. coli can easily spread from human and animal feces, the microbiologist focused on providing strict safety standards. He employed nurses to conduct wellness checks before every shift and paid any infected workers to stay home if they felt the least bit ill.

Mansour's diligent review of every food-handling process led to numerous changes, including moving food preparation out of the restaurants and into centralized Chipotle kitchens with higher food safety standards.

The transformation was bolstered with new policies and procedures that supported much-needed wide-scale change. As I write these words, I can happily report that no further contamination outbreaks have been reported since the company implemented these changes.

Beekeepers adore a clear policy. Back in the seventh century they formulated the Bechbretha (old Irish bee laws), which forbade stealing from a hive (a capital offense), granted to anyone stung by a bee a meal of honey from the beekeeper if the victim had not retaliated, and gifted the family two hives if a member died from a bee sting. These were effective, positive policies.

A word of caution, however: policies can also become overbearing. If they strike people as unfair and burdensome, or even dangerous, they will do more harm than good.

Leaders must keep a close eye on these organizational guidelines to make sure they are positively reinforcing desired behavior. As with all communications, make sure you obey the Three Cs: Clear, Concise, and Compelling. But add a fourth C: Consistent.

When my family moved to Australia, we needed to adapt to a whole new set of processes and policies. Our banker back home had known us for decades. Our new bankers checked our identity when we opened an account, a new policy that seemed perfectly fair. Back home we had traveled on country back roads bordered by green hedgerows; here we boarded fast-moving trains that transported us though bustling city streets. The aisles of the mega supermarket were a stark contrast to the quaint shops in Finea village.

But we quickly adapted to and followed the new routines, which enabled my folks and me to adjust to a new life Down Under.

We felt especially blessed when we needed to rely on the country's excellent medical system when Mom, the visionary for the family's move to Australia, was struck down with amyotrophic lateral sclerosis (ALS), also known as motor neurone disease (MND). We will come back to what happened next a bit later, but I mention it here because it serves as a reminder that a major change can make the group more vulnerable.

Any transition takes you into unfamiliar territory. As you get established and learn the new ways, you will inevitably encounter bumps along the road. When that happens, the right processes and policies can help you to cope with them.

In organizations, clearly understood work processes help employees accommodate change. Well-written ones tell people what's required of them without needing to check in with the boss. On the other hand, weak, poorly thought-out, and badly written policies and processes can easily cause inconsistent group behavior.

At the seventy-five-year-old Toyota Motor Corporation, employees value policies, processes, and procedures because they help guarantee that the automaker delivers the highest quality vehicles. In a December 2021 live-streamed event, long-standing president Akio Toyoda announced that Toyota and premium sister brand Lexus would launch thirty new electric car models by 2030.

How could Toyoda make such a bold assertion? His confidence sprang from the firm's tried-and-true Toyota Production System (TPS), which aligns the company's policies, processes, and procedures with this historic change initiative.

TPS includes two key processes:

1. **Jidoka** (a Japanese term that roughly translates to "automation with a human touch") defines the operator as the wisdom keeper with the *chie* (accumulated wisdom) to stop work at any stage to fix an error.
2. **Just-in-time** coordinates and refines the production process to minimize manufacturing time, costs, and waste.

Developed during the second half of the twentieth century, the process continues to flourish today and has enabled Toyota to transform itself from a small division in a Japanese weaving company to a premier brand in the automobile industry, with revenues of $257 billion in 2022.

The principles of TPS (currently known as "lean manufacturing") have transformed the entire industry, with Toyota's global rivals, including Chrysler, Daimler, Ford, Honda, and General Motors, adopting versions of the system. TPS has also swept through other industries around the world, from hospitals and banks to postal services.

Whatever your industry, however large or small your organization, the digital age will have a profound effect on how you write and communicate your policies, processes, and procedures. The information age may present some daunting, even perplexing, challenges, but on the plus side, its tools may help you harness the power of group intelligence. That's a big reason why you should welcome the digital future.

EMBRACING THE DIGITAL FUTURE

Consumers and businesses alike have been swept up into a vast new universe where computers, laptops, and smartphones have transformed everything from shopping and entertainment to supply chain management and banking.

Wake up in the morning, unlock your phone, visit Amazon to order a new espresso machine, drop by the local bakery for a croissant and pay with a wallet app, arrive at the office to transmit orders and invoices for your company's supplies, stream the latest movie during lunch, then, whoa! Machines have taken over your life and your business.

To drive home that point, just consider how Shopify, Nike, and Starbucks successfully embraced digital technology to adapt and thrive during the COVID-19 pandemic.

In 2004, when Tobias Lütke, Daniel Weinand, and Scott Lake wanted to sell snowboarding equipment online, they felt so deeply frustrated by the current complicated and bulky e-commerce tools, they resolved to do something about it.

Their solution to the problem: the e-commerce engine Shopify, which allowed merchants to sell online with user-friendly software tools that were simpler, faster, and more visually appealing than those offered by competitors.

When the COVID-19 pandemic struck and people began working remotely and avoided visiting brick-and-mortar shops, Shopify helped thousands of sellers take their businesses online.

Merchants fell in love with the new tools that enabled them to build and maintain their own online stores. By 2022, more than four million business owners had flocked to the Shopify software in order to sell everything from automobiles to toothpaste on such platforms as Facebook, Instagram, Pinterest, and TikTok. This online movement soon became one of the most disruptive periods in the history of retail buying and selling.

Shopify's founders never stopped innovating, as they enhanced their digital offering with Shopify Payments (payment gateway), Shopify Email (email marketing), Shopify Markets (selling tools), Shopify Mobile (monitor and fulfill orders from the phone), tax tools, and shipping solutions. They also provided helpful tips, simple guides, FAQ pages, and analytics that helped merchants keep track of inventory and sales.

Even small businesses and mom-and-pop operations joined this digital revolution and became competitive with such behemoths as Amazon, eBay, and Walmart. In 2021, Shopify grew by 76 percent and averaged 1.16 billion unique visitors per month on the sites it powered (compared to Amazon's 1.10 billion).

That year the company's revenue increased by 57 percent to $4.6 billion. Its dramatic success earned Shopify a place on *Fast Company*'s 2022 list of the World's 50 Most Innovative Companies.

The moral of this story? In a fast and ever-changing world, companies that leverage technology can accelerate change, leapfrog the competition, and create a more connected ecosystem where data can flow freely between the parts.

Take Nike, for example. The makers of the iconic Air Jordans flourished during the pandemic despite reduced foot traffic, production problems, and shipping delays. As lockdowns forced the closure of stores on streets and malls, people flocked to Nike's digital spaces. After all, you still needed to maintain your health and fitness to combat the COVID bug.

The sportswear giant made the premium version of its Training Club app free to US consumers, giving people access to two hundred–plus workouts in such fitness activities as yoga classes, strength workouts, and bodyweight sessions, with or without equipment. A work-from-home mom, spending eight hours a day managing a remote team, could also enjoy the benefits of her own Nike personal trainer.

Nike CEO John Donahoe said, "We have gotten stronger from the pandemic and will be even stronger as we emerge from it." The company's digital initiatives drove 2020 profits up 196 percent over the prior year. Unsurprisingly, *Forbes* named Donahoe its 2021 CEO of the Year.

Nike, with its impressive online store and suite of customer-friendly apps, relied on technology to create a digital ecosystem that served as an extension of its physical stores.

Over the past few decades, digital ecosystems have not only addressed the mounting need for organizations to collect vast amounts of data but have also helped them gather the right information and make sense of it all. This has naturally led to innovation and change.

Starbucks's CEO Kevin Johnson knew exactly how to do this. In early 2021, he could see that the pandemic was forcing customers to abandon his stores. In January, visits dropped 16.1 percent compared to the previous year, followed by another 18.4 percent in February.

Johnson's team moved quickly to address the problem, adding convenient options to the traditional "coffee on the go" model. Now customers who once lingered in a shop, chatting with friends or tapping on their phones, could get their caffeine fix by ordering delivery online or picking up their orders curbside or at drive-thru or walk-up windows.

These moves, prompted by digital information–gathering and marketing techniques, turned what could have been a catastrophic problem into a win-win for both the company and its customers.

What had begun in 1971 as a single coffee-roasting shop on the cobblestoned streets of Seattle's Pike Place Market had grown into a global giant with more than thirty-two thousand retail locations by 2021. Starbucks relied on technology and the organization's retail savvy to thrive in a crisis that crippled many other retailers in the COVID era.

The future promises technological advances right out of a science fiction novel. By the time you're reading this book, artificial intelligence (AI) and robotics will be creating a world not even H. G. Wells could have imagined.

The question is, will organizations grasp and intelligently deploy these innovations, or will they let them sweep them to oblivion? If AI robots can write books, authors can either tame them to their own creative purposes or let them replace them on virtual bookstore shelves.

Here's the bad news. According to Boston Consulting Group, only 30 percent of companies navigate digital transformation successfully.

My experience and research support the fact that the problem usually stems more from the inability to shift group dynamics than from a failure to install whizbang technology.

Leaders who do not respect the Hive Mind will get steamrollered by the future; those who harness the power of group intelligence will drive the steamroller to prosperity. As much as anything else, that triumph will require fine-tuning the way we reward people for their performance.

FINE-TUNING PERFORMANCE AND REWARD SYSTEMS

If you want your change to stick, you must consider linking rewards to your change goals. This will capture people's attention and send a powerful signal to the group about what matters. PayPal's CEO Dan Schulman did just that when he developed a performance and reward system geared to a major transformation effort.

The transformation had begun in 2015 when PayPal came out from under BPAY's wing and set about reshaping the future of digital payments. It worked. Over the next few years PayPal's customer base grew from about 160 million to more than 400 million.

Then the pandemic struck in 2019, forcing yet another transformation when demand for digital payment services surged as people worked from home.

Schulman admired how conscientiously his workforce was coping with the COVID challenges, but when he investigated staff pay, he discovered that many employees were suffering from financial stress, despite the fact that PayPal's compensation exceeded the "fair market rate."

The CEO decided to make the system fairer, measuring pay in terms of net disposable income (NDI). This should, he calculated, leave employees with at least 20 percent of their wages, after taxes and household expenses, to save for emergencies, or children's education, or any nice-to-haves.

That marked a big improvement for many of PayPal's entry-level and hourly workers, whose NDI hovered below 10 percent at the time. Schulman moved swiftly to adjust salaries, grant company shares, assist with financial planning, and reduce health care costs by 60 percent for a third of PayPal employees in the US.

Little wonder, then, that PayPal won honors as a *Forbes* World's Best Employer in 2021. The new performance and reward system didn't hurt the bottom line, either. PayPal's shares surged 111 percent in 2020 and another 25 percent in the first half of 2021. *Fortune*'s 2021 list of the World's 50 Greatest Leaders ranked Schulman #3 for his efforts to improve the financial health of customers as well as the company's nearly thirty thousand employees.

In Celtic tradition a buyer never paid cash for a swarm of bees because legend had it that this would create an unproductive hive. Instead, they compensated the owner with honey and comb. During change, money talks, but so do other forms of recognition.

Research suggests that recognition can significantly increase intrinsic motivation, which spurs people to gain satisfaction from doing good work. People don't just work for a periodic paycheck. If they don't receive intangible rewards for their efforts, they may just perform the routine tasks. Boredom sets in; results decline.

But facilitate intrinsic motivation, and people will perform for the challenge, the learning, the fun, and the feeling of accomplishment that comes from going above and beyond the routine requirements of the job.

I think Jamie Dimon, chairman and CEO of New York–based lender JPMorgan Chase & Co., would appreciate that Celtic tradition. When he oversaw a major change initiative at the huge financial services firm, he was keenly aware that people are not coin-operated machines but flesh-and-blood creatures prone to all the foibles and complexities of human behavior.

Dimon, recognized as a shrewd billionaire businessman, joined the bank in 2005 with a burning desire to create a more performance-driven organization.

As a first step, he ditched the traditional half-yearly performance review and introduced a mobile app that allowed JPMorgan's 255,000 employees to give each other real-time feedback, anytime, anywhere:

- "Excellent client presentation. Well done!"
- "Impressive market analysis. The client loved it."
- "I'd like to see more case studies in the training course next time. Thank you."

A stream of constant performance feedback fostered a learning organization in one of the biggest banks in the United States. By 2022 the company had generated record revenue ($132.3 billion) for a fifth year in a row.

These days most companies focus on results. Tying rewards, both tangible and intangible, to achieving change goals motivates people to put their best efforts into getting that result. That's exactly what Jamie Dimon's feedback system did. And that's what organizations intent on transformation must do, redesigning the way they manage performance to reflect an emphasis on achieving transformation goals.

In 2012, Adobe's leaders faced a sagging share price due to lack of investor interest in what they deemed a low-growth stock. The problem stemmed mostly from the fact that after customers purchased the company's brand-name software, they seldom returned for more products.

Adobe's leaders thought that a shift from traditional software delivery to cloud-based services might solve the problem. Senior Vice President of People Resources Donna Morris knew that this change would require a radical shift in behavior for Adobe's thirteen thousand–plus workforce.

The first mountain Morris needed to scale was the company's labor-intensive, complex, and paperwork-heavy performance management system that required a staggering eighty thousand hours to administer before any performance discussions even took place.

Managers were simply buried under an avalanche of paperwork that made Mount Everest look like an anthill. It could not possibly support the shift from the traditional eighteen- to twenty-four-month product development cycles to constant, innovative, state-of-the-art cloud-based streaming.

Morris devised an ingenious yet simple solution to the problem: regular "check-in" dialogues between managers and employees. Now the company could speed forward on a level field.

In fairly short order Adobe achieved an incredibly fast transition from licensed software seller to a subscription cloud-based provider. With the paperwork mountain knocked flat, Adobe reaped a financial windfall as 2021 revenues raced to a record $15.79 billion (23 percent more than the previous year). The fine-tuned performance review system helped earn the company eighth place on *Forbes*'s list of World's Best Employers.

Feedback fuels agility, especially in turbulent times. The best companies (think Amazon, Netflix, McKinsey, and Goldman Sachs) rely on rigorous and continual performance reviews. Change demands the agility needed to stay on course in a fast-moving environment.

Of course, every organization needs more than effective feedback to emerge or cocreate change. Those who do the work at every level need the tools to get the job done. Not even the most skilled craftsman can build a fine new house without all the right tools.

EQUIPPING THE GROUP WITH THE RIGHT TOOLS

What do you do when Mother Nature blindsides you with an unexpected blizzard? How rapidly can you adjust to all that snow? In the case of Southwest Airlines, not fast enough.

In the winter of 2022, punishing winter storms spread across much of North America during one of the busiest travel periods of the year. Holiday travelers were flocking to airports from Boston to Los Angeles. Thousands of flights were delayed or canceled. Airport lobbies became jammed with angry customers. Southwest didn't have the right tools to dig its way out of the blizzard.

As other airlines bounced back from delays and cancellations, Southwest Airlines was still struggling days later from what executives and analysts describe as its biggest operational meltdown in its five-decade history.

Southwest ended up canceling more than sixteen thousand flights over the busy 2022 holiday travel season, which far exceeded any other airline and put the firm under the intense scrutiny of lawmakers and federal regulators.

The airline's chief operating officer, Andrew Watterson, blamed it all on the company's outdated scheduling software. "The process of matching up those crew members with the aircraft could not be handled by our technology." In other words, the company's workforce lacked the tools to deal effectively with Mother Nature's calamity.

Southwest CEO Bob Jordan elaborated on the problem when he admitted that the company had not integrated its route optimization program (known as "the Baker") with the crew scheduling system. The airline lacked a quick, automated way to contact crew members to reassign them to other flights.

Harried staff needed to phone or physically chase down crews to deliver information about crucial changes. The computers sat silent while Southwest schedulers reverted to pen and paper to solve complex scheduling problems, while crew members waited on hold for hours for someone to tell them what to do.

In a video statement, Bob Jordan apologized to customers and warned that it could take days to solve this "giant puzzle." Was it an unprecedented problem? Sadly, no. In 2021, Southwest had suffered another epic meltdown when it canceled more than two thousand flights over a four-day period at the cost of $75 million.

According to Captain Casey Murray, president of the Southwest Airlines Pilots Association, the problems at Southwest had been brewing for a long time: "We've been having these issues for the past twenty months," he told CNN. "We've seen these sorts of meltdowns occur on a much more regular basis and it really just has to do with outdated processes and outdated IT."

Southwest had quickly grown from a small carrier to one of the nation's largest airlines and sorely needed to install new systems that could cope with more complex business operations. In 2017, Southwest Airlines had invested $800 million in digital transformation but spent only $300 million on operations. Siloed and nonautomated systems that may have worked well when Southwest was a small regional carrier became the company's worst enemy.

Figure 9.1 depicts the essential problem. Note the hidden agreement behind the Ill-Equipped Pattern: "We don't invest in the right systems to meet our business needs."

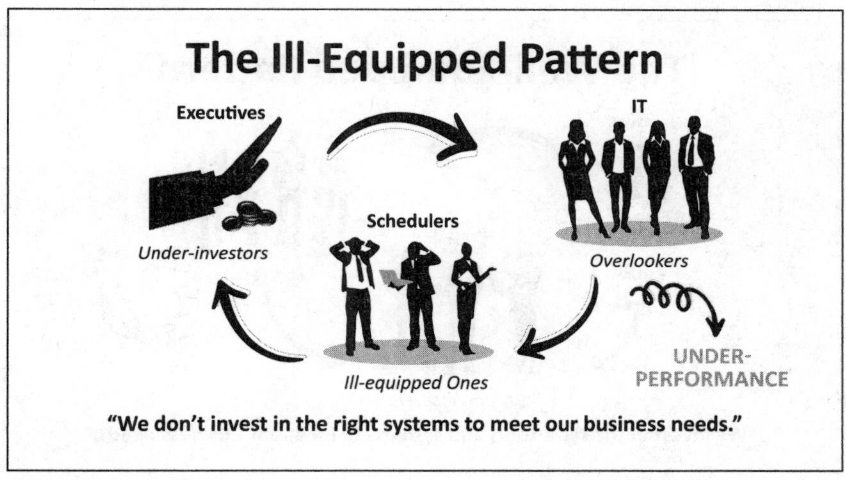

Figure 9.1

Executives, in the role of Under-investors diverted funds elsewhere, including paying out $428 million in dividends to shareholders in 2022.

Schedulers, in the role of Ill-Equipped Ones, continued to operate crew-assignment software built for a bygone era.

Meanwhile the IT team members, in the role of Overlookers, still supported outdated legacy systems and had failed to create a compelling case for new cloud-based tools.

These conditions created a perfect storm at Southwest in the winter of 2022. Just when the group most desperately needed to make lightning-quick adjustments, they looked in vain for the tools they needed to get the job done. As Bob Jordan told frustrated employees, "Part of what we're suffering is a lack of tools. . . . We've talked an awful lot about modernizing the operation and the need to do that."

Southwest's CEO could see that the organization needed to create a new pattern (see figure 9.2). This pattern would need a new agreement: "We invest in the right tools and systems to meet our business needs." It would also require that executives step into the role of Investors, schedulers into the role of System Adopters, and the IT team into the role of Enablers of scalable cloud technologies, which included equipment to better coordinate crews with aircraft.

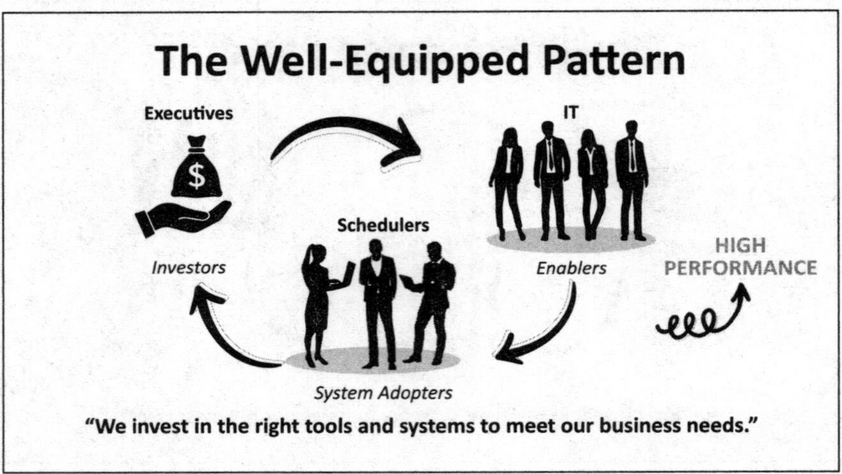

Figure 9.2

Southwest's Ill-Equipped Pattern spoiled the holiday season for perhaps a million stranded passengers and severely damaged the airline's reputation. When you lack the right business systems, you can scarcely adjust to pressing change. And your inability to do so will risk the ire of all your key stakeholders, including customers, employees, shareholders, lawmakers, and regulators.

Of course, it will also damage your bottom line. Southwest's stock price fell 16 percent in the coming months as a federal investigation got underway.

Imagine telling a mechanic to swap out that old Chevy's transmission. They nod and say, "Hand me that crescent wrench." You look puzzled and suggest, "Use your fingers." No wrench, no work, no results. Go figure.

Suppose you tell your people you want them to make a major change but expect them to work with outdated tools. No new tools, no work, no results. Go figure.

Vodafone, the British multinational telecommunications firm, also fell victim to the Ill-Equipped Pattern in 2013. Unfortunately, its attempts to address the problem only made it worse.

Vodafone's leaders, knowing full well that their company was the most unpopular provider in the UK, decided to install a new customer relationship management (CRM) system to create more customer-centric service. The system would, they assumed, reduce the time and costs of providing service and keep customers happy with speedier handling times, call transfers, incident logging, and service request processes. The change managers promised that the new CRM would free call center staff to act as Universal Agents, handling sales, service, and marketing issues.

Then reality struck as flaws began to plague the system in April 2015 when Vodafone set about migrating more than twenty-eight and a half million customer accounts onto the new platform. It was a boondoggle. Customers complained loudly about billing mistakes, mysteriously canceled debits, and problems with accessing their online accounts.

Vodafone offered "profound apologies to anyone affected by these errors," but what the company called "continued operational challenges" led to a customer exodus and a £54 million ($82.5 million) crash in sales from April to June 2015.

A 2016 review by the Telecom regulator discovered a range of issues, including 10,452 customers left out in the cold when Vodafone failed to credit their accounts after they paid to "top-up" their mobile phone credit. In October 2016, the UK watchdog slapped the telco with a £4.63 million ($6.27 million) fine for "serious and sustained" breaches of consumer protection rules.

Tools, tools everywhere, but none of them worked as advertised. Don't let it happen to you. Select the right tools for the job, bearing in mind that you can't repair a broken computer with a hammer and a can of paint. How do you know if you've picked the right tools? Smart leaders keep track of progress toward desired results by measuring milestones along the way.

TRACKING PROGRESS ALONG THE WAY

Bees use the dimensions of their bodies to measure spaces when building honeycomb in the new hive. These little mathematicians have also figured out that assembling the comb into hexagons that fit snugly together provides the most efficient use of space. When they finish the work, the hexagonal shapes will fit securely in the tree cavity at the edge of Wombat Forest.

During major transitions, you should never rely solely on your gut instincts. You should always place your trust in the cold, hard data. Like building a honeycomb, a transformation cannot succeed without sound metrics.

The yardsticks should measure progress by answering a number of critical questions, which might include: How have different parts of the group committed themselves to the mission? Are we on the right track? How far have we progressed? Are we meeting the needs of key stakeholders? Have we become more competitive? Do we need to change direction?

To appreciate the fact that accurately measuring progress can accelerate change, consider how the French successfully created a new era of gender equality. It began with the 2011 Copé-Zimmermann Law, which mandated greater gender diversity on the boards of companies listed on the French stock exchange (CAC 40).

But it did not begin without a good deal of consternation in some quarters. Vocal critics cried, "We don't have enough qualified women! The quality of our boards will suffer!"

The Naysayers fell silent, however, as they witnessed the effectiveness of the legislative hammer and positive impact on board performance. In fairly quick order the new law caused a remarkable rebalancing of the country's corporate boards, with female representation soaring from 10 percent in 2009 to 46 percent by 2021, catapulting France ahead of all others into the lead position among European countries in terms of gender equality.

Fast-forward to early 2020. Why, wondered the champions of level playing fields for all, haven't we achieved greater gender equality at the management and executive level in these companies governed by more balanced boards? They pointed to the fact that only 5 percent of CEOs across Europe were women, despite growing evidence that companies with greater gender diversity performed better.

Spurred on by the success at the board level, the French Parliament unanimously voted in 2021 to introduce gender quota tracking for executive teams and leadership pipelines for companies with more than one thousand employees, with targets of 30 percent minimum for either gender by 2027, then 40 percent by 2030.

The old adage tells carpenters that they should always "measure twice, cut once." Change leaders should heed this note of caution. Choose the right yardsticks, measure frequently, and adjust when necessary.

Michele Buck did just that when she became CEO of The Hershey Company, the 130-year-old American small-town maker of Kisses and Reese's Peanut Butter Cups. As well as diversifying the company's portfolio of brands, Buck quickly assembled the company's diversity statistics and determined that she would make sure the company set a new standard for workforce diversity, equity, and inclusion.

After Buck informed her management team that she would hold them accountable for achieving their collective goals, she began hosting a series of listening sessions across the sixteen-thousand-strong organization.

It did not take long to hear a consistent request from Hershey's employees for equal pay for equal work, regardless of gender. She got the message. The CEO knew that women working full-time in the US earned only 79 percent of men's wages for comparable work.

To address the issue, Buck established the Pathways Project, a five-year plan that included a commitment to leading the industry in paying women and people of color the same salaries as their White male colleagues in similar positions. Progress toward achieving these goals became a regular agenda item at executive meetings, with progress or lack thereof tied to executive remuneration.

According to Alicia Petross, the company's chief diversity officer, the project represented "the creation of ambitious new corporate goals around representation and equity paired with internal short-term goals to track our progress, aiming to set the bar for our industry."

The results at Hershey speak for themselves. In 2021 women represented more than 40 percent of company board members, 37 percent of the executive committee, and 48 percent of the overall workforce. And they took home the same paychecks as their male counterparts.

Note how Buck tied performance and rewards to progress. To do that she needed the right metrics that showed whether an executive was moving forward or falling behind. But it wasn't just the carrot or the stick. Most importantly, Buck intended measurement to help people adjust, in order to keep on track toward the company's goals.

On the other hand, an overabundance of metrics can boggle people's minds. Smart change leaders make the metrics visually compelling by turning them into pictures, graphs, and summary overviews. Dashboards that show change trends can convey key details in the blink of an eye, help the group make faster decisions, and reinforce accountability along the way.

The diversity, equity, and inclusion (DEI) focus at Hershey proved good for business, with company shares surging about 20 percent to $130 after Buck took over in March 2017. And the company's market cap grew from $14 billion to just over $36 billion by September 2021. That same year, *Forbes* named Hershey the World's Most Female-Friendly Company.

Buck did not rest on her laurels, however. She later stated, "By 2025, The Hershey Company aims to increase the percentage of women in its sixteen-thousand-employee workforce to 50 percent and in its leadership to 42 percent, up from the current 48 percent and 37 percent." You can bet a year's supply of honey she'll keep her yardstick handy.

We began this chapter by discussing the need for the right infrastructure to support change. Thomas Seeley, the world's leading expert on bee behavior, discovered how bees prioritize the right infrastructure when they select a new home.

As part of his PhD research at Harvard, the biologist measured hive hollows and found that all bee homes shared similar traits, with tree cavities at least ten gallons in volume and the hive perched fifteen feet (or more) off the ground. A narrow opening faced the sun.

The bees know that an overly large tree opening will inhibit their ability to fight off invaders; a too-small cavity will not allow the bees to store enough honey to survive the winter; and a hive entrance facing away from the sun will leave the hive vulnerable to winter's freezing temperatures. "It's really important to get them all right," Seeley concluded.

Heed the wisdom of the bees. Never rely on whims or leave the transition to chance, but carefully select the processes, policies, and systems that align with your transformation goals. Success will, in the end, depend on getting the infrastructure right.

POINTS TO REMEMBER

- Well-designed policies, processes, and procedures clarify expectations and strengthen the emerging change.
- Digital technology can accelerate change that leapfrogs the competition.
- Performance and reward systems should send a signal to group members that change matters.
- The right tools will help the group achieve the change goals.
- Sound measurement tracks progress, reinforces desired behavior, and allows for adjustments.

10

MAKING THE CHANGE STICK

Prepare for Distractions and Surprises

The bees forage in the wildflower meadows near Wombat Forest, gathering food supplies before winter arrives. The foragers quickly learn about their new surroundings and before their departure make looping flights over their new home in the tree cavity to memorize its location. They fly up to ten kilometers a day in twelve- to sixteen-hour shifts in order to produce a single drop of honey.

As winter approaches, their collective efforts will have produced an impressive thirty-pound stockpile. It took a lot of commitment and effort to transition to a new home, but it will take even more to make it a long-term success.

Like the bees, leaders with group intelligence continue to press the change accelerator over the longer term. In the case of Microsoft, its CEO, Satya Nadella, took over in 2014 when the company had been following a path to irrelevancy. This once-dominant, forward-looking organization had missed almost every important new technology trend since the turn of the century.

Relying on its commitment to dominating markets with the sheer force of numbers, Microsoft failed to develop innovative consumer products, such as Apple's MP3 player, the iPod. It was always coming late to the party, especially when it came to the advent of the internet.

Could Nadella turn the giant corporation in a new direction? He could. After five years of continued effort, he managed to propel Microsoft to a $1 trillion valuation, making it one of the wealthiest publicly listed companies in the world. We'll learn more about this turnaround later in this chapter.

Did Nadella take a victory lap? No, he told his employees that the trillion-dollar milestone was "not meaningful" and warned them that resting on their laurels would be "the beginning of the end." The CEO knew Microsoft could not afford to let its people slip back into the old self-satisfied patterns. Instead, he encouraged them to ensure an even better future by continuing on the path of change, reinvention, and innovation.

WATCHING OUT FOR THE OLD PATTERNS

Think of patterns as old habits, hard to break, easy to slip back into. That six-month sugar-free diet can vanish in a flash at the sight of a chocolate croissant.

I learned early in my career as a change leader at the Australian-based ANZ bank how easily groups can revert to the old ways. During the early 2000s we had worked tirelessly alongside CEO John McFarlane to address the bank's tarnished reputation as a greedy organization, interested only in profits.

After seven years of steady commitment and effort, we had achieved a remarkable turnaround: customer satisfaction had improved (by 23 percent), we'd created one of the most efficient banks in the world (with a cost-to-income ratio of 45 percent), the share price had almost tripled, profits had doubled, and we'd significantly increased employee engagement.

To top it off, ANZ had been named the number one bank globally on the Dow Jones Sustainability Index, recognized for its leadership role in addressing financial literacy in disadvantaged communities.

But in 2017, a decade after John McFarlane had left ANZ, a royal commission investigation into Australian banking skewered the big banks for pursuing profits and monetary gain at all costs.

As *Business Insider* reported, "The financial services royal commission identified dishonesty and greed as the main theme from its investigation of misconduct by the banks." At ANZ the old pattern of self-interest had snuck back in, setting back seven years of successful organizational transformation.

Leaders with group intelligence realize they must constantly keep their eyes peeled for old patterns that persist or reemerge during change. They understand the relatedness between all the ecosystem's parts; they see how all the individual trees create a forest; they see the simple patterns that enable them to make sense of complexity.

As the great systems thinker Gregory Bateson once said, it is "the pattern that connects" and makes sense of seemingly random components.

Since patterns govern group behavior, people will not easily give them up. The Hive Mind does what the Hive Mind does. Changemakers with group intelligence focus on those patterns, a skill CEO Satya Nadella displayed during his tenure at Microsoft.

When he joined Microsoft, the firm had built a reputation as a bullying, arrogant giant that ruled the tech industry with an iron fist. It dominated the market with muscle and the sheer force of numbers, always stressing quantity over quality.

Nadella knew he needed to alter that pattern by weaning the company off its addiction to the profits churned out by its Windows PC operating system. That meant, he believed, that Microsoft must move into subscription-based cloud and mobile solutions, with an emphasis on high quality consumer products.

To accomplish that mission, employees worked tirelessly to demolish the old confining silos and create "One Microsoft." Adopting a more collaborative pattern included "hackathons," where thousands of employees would work across divisions on new projects.

After five years of change, as the firm became one of the wealthiest publicly listed companies in the world, Nadella began to accelerate the company's newly forged "Partnering" Operating Model (described in chapter 4). In an interview with CRN he said, "We want to [know] from day one in any change we make—whether it's a program change or business model change—what does it mean for partners?"

Microsoft was now working hand in hand with its three hundred thousand partners globally to generate 95 percent of its revenue. In a major shift, this previously insular firm was forging collaborations with such rivals as Apple, Oracle, Red Hat, Salesforce, SAP, SAS, and Sony.

Microsoft had gone from throwing roundhouse punches with its powerful muscles to dancing with attractive partners. Before long it had created a massive cloud computing business that grew revenues from $77.8 billion in 2013 to $203 billion by 2022.

Nadella remained vigilant, championing the new pattern but always looking for signs that the old pattern might be creeping back in. Less alert leaders tend to take a mechanistic approach, believing that behavior follows a straight line, in a strict cause-and-effect fashion. Not so.

The issues we face in our workplaces are interconnected, relational, and driven by (largely invisible) patterns. Group behavior follows a circular (not a linear) path and always occurs within the context of the greater ecosystem.

To unravel complex problems, you must examine assumptions and co-create the behavior you desire in multiple parts. Otherwise some deeply embedded old patterns will persist, often hidden from view for those in the ecosystem.

After almost every corporate disaster, major accident, or serious blunder, leaders look back and wonder, "Why didn't we see that coming?"

How could Lehman Brothers fail to see the housing bubble prior to the Great Recession? How could managers at Volkswagen overlook the installation of an emission's "cheating device" in eleven million cars? How could Southwest Airlines fail to install the right scheduling systems?

An insightful analysis reveals one simple answer: the Law of Pattern Blindness. This all-too-common quirk of the human mind can cause even the brightest and most experienced leader to ignore the obvious truths about their situation.

It's not the hidden secrets that hammer us; it's what's lying right in front of our eyes. "If the old ways have worked for us in the past, they'll keep working for us now and forever."

Even when the marketplace is clamoring for change, we cling to the old, comfortable patterns. Then, failing to adopt the right new pattern, we get crushed by more agile competitors in this fast-changing world.

You must learn to view your own ecosystem like a bee. Bees notice what humans miss because their eyes are endowed with a high "flicker threshold" capable of processing information faster than humans. While a field of lavender looks like a blur to us from a moving car, a bee moving at high speed can clearly see each iridescent flower.

As you travel your change course, it may take three to five years to reach your destination, with perhaps a few reversions to old patterns along the way. Exercise patience. It takes time to embed and strengthen the new ways. But never lose heart. When you achieve important milestones, you and group members can briefly pause to celebrate your progress. Each victory reinforces the importance of staying on track.

CELEBRATING MILESTONES

Back in chapter 5 we met Patrick Houlihan, the chairman and CEO of the Melbourne-based paint company DuluxGroup who with his executive team, rapidly grew the company and took the company's much-loved brands, as well as its retail and trade capabilities, into international markets. As the mission progressed, he acknowledged each major achievement with a celebration.

At the end of each financial year, Houlihan convened an annual DuluxGroup leadership conference and awards dinner for his top two hundred executives. Outstanding individuals and teams received recognition for their accomplishments.

Houlihan singled out different company business units—the B&D garage door team for their sustainable packaging project; the Selleys' sealants team for penetrating Asian markets; the Yates garden team for moving into organic products; and the Dulux paint team for turning recycled paint pallets into roller trays, saving roughly a thousand tons of plastic from going to a landfill each year.

The CEO himself won recognition from Nippon Paint, the fourth largest paint company in the world, when it swooped in to buy DuluxGroup in 2019, offering the highest price paid for a paint company at the time.

With the support of Nippon Paint Chairman Goh Hup Jin, Houlihan forged a path into Asian and European markets, including the acquisitions of the French company Cromology and the Slovenian company JUB. Both brought new capabilities, talent, and distribution networks to the existing portfolio.

Within three years of the Nippon takeover, DuluxGroup was racking up results that many had never imagined possible.

From 2019 to 2023, DuluxGroup more than doubled in size from four thousand to nine thousand employees, while more than doubling its revenue to $4 billion. In addition to doubling the organic growth rate of the base business, DuluxGroup also enacted twenty-three acquisitions (an astonishing average of one every eight weeks). That certainly called for a huge celebration!

When you are moving as fast as you can toward your transformation goals, it's easy to keep so tightly focused on the day-to-day grind that you forget to pause, take a deep breath, and congratulate people for reaching key milestones. Doing so not only makes people happy, it deepens the bond among hardworking employees and energizes them to do even more going forward.

Marisa Thalberg, executive vice president, chief brand and marketing officer at Lowe's, came up with some creative ways to mark the North Carolina–based home improvement company's hundredth birthday. The hardware store, founded in 1921 by L. S. Lowe in Wilkesboro, North Carolina, had evolved into one of the largest retailers in the US, with more than twenty-two hundred stores.

To celebrate one hundred years of success, Thalberg created a special landing page on Lowe's website to show the company's evolution over time, complete with historical photos, milestone features, fun facts, and dynamic content. In addition, she created a series of major campaigns, including the "100 Hometowns" project, which donated $100 million to one hundred local communities across the US who had fallen on hard times.

Helping the community had always meant a lot to the company, which began life as a small-town hardware store. This principle came into play when such disasters as the COVID pandemic or extreme weather conditions plagued the country.

To underscore the company's commitment to helping those in need, Thalberg extended the concept of home, from your "own four walls" to the community at large. The 100 Hometowns campaign helped to restore and revitalize spaces that served as local hubs, including neighborhood housing, parks, and community centers.

Award-winning country music star Kane Brown, an ex-Lowe's employee, collaborated on 100 Hometowns to revitalize the local Boys and Girls Club in his hometown of Chattanooga, Tennessee. He loved Lowe's campaign. "Just being able to come full circle and partner with Lowe's for their 100 Hometowns campaign, to go back to my hometown in Chattanooga where I used to work at a Lowe's and to be able to give back to the community is just such an amazing feeling."

Pride in oneself, one's team, one's organization, one's hometown, one's country keeps people working to create a better world.

You can give someone a tangible award (an expensive dinner, a new car, or a cash bonus). But those awards often fail to gladden the heart or mean as much as a heartfelt pat on the back and a hearty, "Thank you!" A personalized note, a small, gift-wrapped present, or a morning tea to acknowledge the work can become never-to-be-forgotten gestures that cost nothing more than a little time-out from work.

Taking the time to acknowledge the efforts of group members can go a long way toward sustaining momentum during change. When the confetti has been swept from the banquet hall, the balloons safely recycled, and the tablecloths cleaned and stored away for the next celebration, it's time to get back to work, expanding the group's capability to reach its ultimate goal.

DEVELOPING THE GROUP'S CHANGE CAPABILITY

We met Juliette Garnier back in chapter 7. You may recall that City Hospital's CEO had committed her organization to becoming more efficient and patient centric. During the transformation process, I dropped into her office to hear the latest update on progress. She looked less than pleased. "The nurses are up in arms again, and the latest employee survey shows that over 60 percent of them are disengaged. I'd value your view on what's happening before we see a mass exodus!"

Of course I agreed to help and immediately scheduled a meeting with "Melissa Thomson," director of nursing. Her look of displeasure matched Garnier's, as she told me, "The latest management mantra is 'patient care.' Our nurses have *always* been passionate about providing the highest-quality care, but they require continuing education to do that. Senior management doesn't get that."

A focus group in the hospital's administration wing with early-career nurses confirmed Thomson's point. "Gabrielle Laurent," a third-year nurse, summed it up. "I was thrown in the deep end when I started work and had hoped for a lot more support. The expectation of new grads is very high, but I was given too much responsibility, too soon."

In another workshop with mid- to late-career nurses, I found much agreement on the need for ongoing education. "Roisin Farrell," a twenty-year nursing veteran, voiced the group sentiment. "I have to jump through so many hoops to get my required training done while I'm working full-time Management can trot out words like 'patient care,' but they seem to have forgotten their commitment and obligation to lifelong learning for City Hospital's nurses."

The following week I shared my findings with Garnier by sketching a pattern on her whiteboard (see figure 10.1). The pattern revealed the basic problem at City Hospital: "We don't support our people to develop, grow, and change."

Management, in the role of Unsupportive Ones, expected nurses to provide the best patient care but failed to provide the funding or time off for them to keep up with the latest approaches and techniques for providing optimum patient care.

Meanwhile, nurses, in the role of the Overlooked Ones, were on the brink of burnout, as they worked tirelessly to take care of others without sufficient time and financial support to learn more effective and efficient approaches.

Garnier nodded. "I get it! We've been funding a lot of initiatives but not investing in ongoing education. We cannot accomplish our patient care mission if our nurses do not keep up with the latest medical advancements."

At her next departmental meeting, Garnier informed her executive team that City Hospital would provide additional funds for staff training.

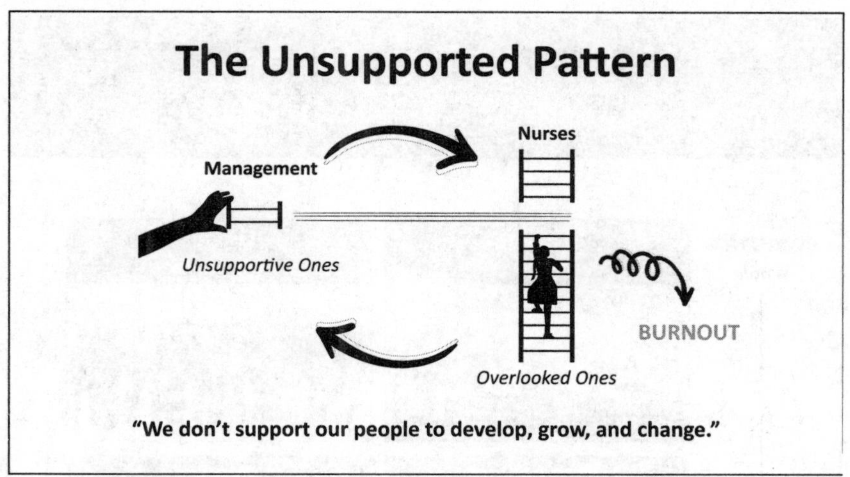

Figure 10.1

"We must become a learning organization. State-of-the-art patient care depends on it."

Surely, money would solve the problem. Well, money alone seldom does. Six months later, little had changed at City Hospital. Garnier was exasperated. "My department heads are intelligent people, Siobhán. Why are they struggling so much with this change?"

I was quite direct. "I'm not surprised. Remember, changes come in all shapes and sizes. The most difficult ones require the right sort of 'smarts.'" To illustrate my point, I brought up the Change Type Model on my laptop (see figure 10.2).

I explained the three types of intelligence required to accomplish different types of change. "On the left side, you're dealing with things, not people. With the application of IQ, you can usually figure out the necessary changes. These are relatively straightforward, cause-and-effect problems that technical experts can solve.

"On the right side, you're dealing with people. And people are a lot messier and more complicated than machines. In the bottom half, you're dealing with individual change, where you can harness emotional intelligence [EQ] to manage at an interpersonal level.

"The top half requires whole group change. And that's where you need to develop group intelligence [GQ].

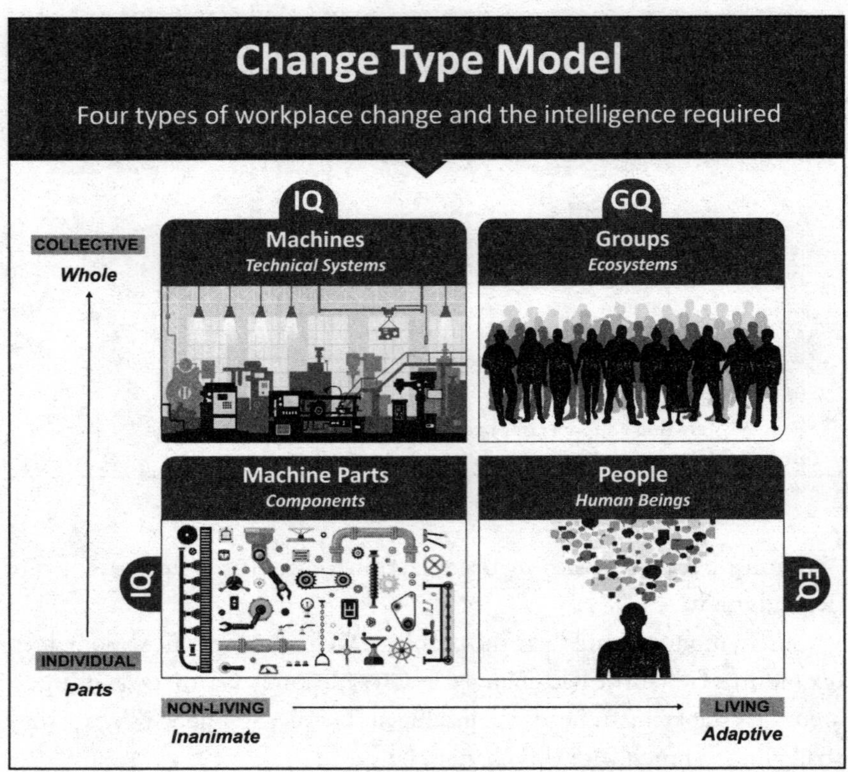

Figure 10.2

"Think of it this way. If your car starts to vibrate and pull to one side, you may be able to solve the problem by changing a flat tire (a part). On the other hand, the vibration may signal a failing suspension system, in which case you need to take it to a specialist for repair (a mechanical system).

"When it comes to people change, a supervisor with high levels of EQ can help an individual improve her performance. But an organization-wide change depends on GQ, the ability to see the deeply embedded patterns and intervene in a way that cocreates change across the whole ecosystem.

"So, what does this tell us about *your* situation, Juliette?" I had done my homework and handed Garnier a summary of progress on creating a learning organization:

1. **Parts:** The department heads at City Hospital tried to "fix" the training problem by introducing a new online training approval form for nurses. The additional paperwork only made matters worse.
2. **Machine:** The HR team jumped onboard to "fix" the training issue at City Hospital with a new learning management system that made it easier to book and track employee training. But this technical fix fell flat.
3. **People:** Next, HR introduced a "Difficult Conversations" program aimed at helping nurses negotiate time off for training with their managers. These chats just added to the nurses' annoyance and did not solve the underlying problem.

I flipped over the page. "Here's your next step, the one that harnesses the power of group intelligence."

4. **Groups:** Everyone, from the oldest serving employee to the most recent hire, composes the City Hospital ecosystem, with all of its parts and the relatedness between the parts. "Pretty overwhelming, no? Well, yes and no.

   "You face a complex problem, but you can simplify it by searching for the patterns or agreements between the parts. Rewiring these patterns is not just about fixing technical systems or working exclusively at the individual level on interpersonal issues. Effecting a major change, such as creating a learning organization, requires changing the patterns and agreements between the parts. That's where the Hive Mind and group intelligence come into play."

I watched Garnier study the front and back of the page I had handed her. When she looked up and nodded, I posed a serious question. "How have you been supporting your executive team to develop the group intelligence needed to create a learning organization?"

She shook her head and stared up at the ceiling. "I haven't been! And thanks for this insight, Siobhán. I can now see the gap and how I need to enable my leadership team to take the right steps to bring about this change."

To effectively manage this complex ecosystem change, Garnier needed to build the executive team's group intelligence. I suggested she take a lesson from our friends the bees.

"Bees know all about building capability to do an important job. In the fall the group nurtures 'winter bees,' feeding some infants a pollen-scarce diet so they will develop an extra-large body and enhanced immune system, which increases their lifespan from six weeks to six months. The 'winter bees' keep the colony alive until spring by shivering their flight muscles to generate heat."

Garnier got the message, and I helped her hire an expert to develop her executive team's group intelligence.

During monthly meetings they followed the Hive LENS approach, assessed progress, and discussed necessary adjustments.

As they did so, they began to replace old patterns, reframing the role of managers from Schedulers, who saw their jobs as filling the roster, to People Developers, who ensured that nurses got the ongoing support and training they needed to deliver top-notch patient care.

By the end of the year a new pattern was emerging at City Hospital (see figure 10.3). The executive team helped mid-level managers step into the role of Developers, ensuring that employees could fulfill the role of Continuous Learners, all in the quest of City Hospital becoming a more adaptive and patient-centric organization.

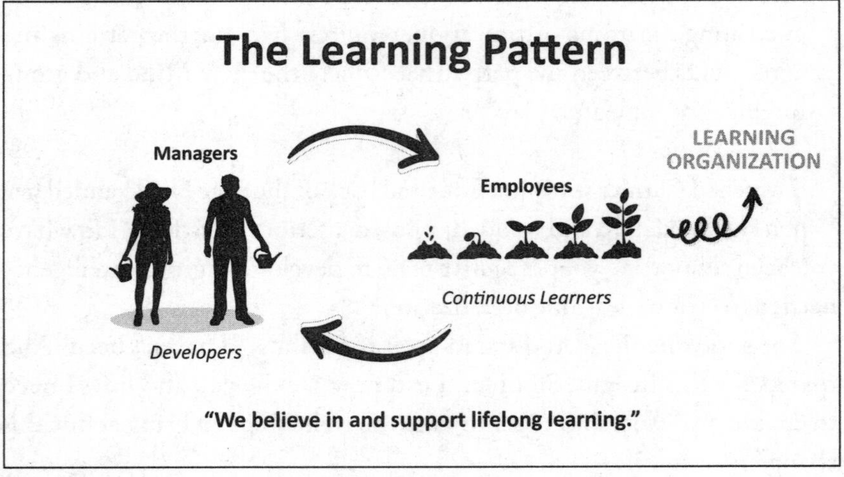

Figure 10.3

It did not unfold in a perfectly seamless fashion. Obstacles and surprises popped up along the way, but the executive team was developing the capability to manage these twists and turns on the journey.

I have found that most leaders struggle to embed change in their organization. It's tempting to rely on the conventional techniques, installing technical fixes and conducting interpersonal interventions that end up wasting a lot of time and fail to achieve desired results.

Garnier and her team avoided that pitfall. Later that year, she called me with a happy report. "The latest satisfaction scores show us in the top quartile for both patient care and employee engagement, with 80 percent of our nurses saying they are receiving the training they need to do their jobs. I feel like we are finally making progress. But we can't rest on our laurels. There's still a lot more work to do."

Garnier made an excellent point. Group intelligence works like a bicep muscle. You can't make it strong with a daily strength regimen, then stop when you think it's strong enough. If you do not continue your workouts, it will grow weak. You can no longer lift that one-hundred-pound boulder. Managing change *is* a one-hundred-pound boulder. You're not going to keep lifting it unless you maintain sufficient energy to do so.

MAINTAINING THE ENERGY FOR CHANGE

For decades, Amazon founder Jeff Bezos has maintained change momentum to create one of the strongest forces in retail, a feat that has made him one of the richest people on the planet. To understand that astonishing success, you only need to read the founder's "Day 1" philosophy, which Bezos explained in his 1997 letter to shareholders and that he has included in every annual report:

"This is Day 1 for the Internet and, if we execute well, for Amazon .com. . . . Though we are optimistic, we must remain vigilant and maintain a sense of urgency."

The Day 1 philosophy so relentlessly focused on customers that Bezos had considered naming the new company Relentless.com. If you type that into your browser, you will be whisked to the Amazon website.

Bees are equally relentless in their pursuit of nectar, visiting some one thousand flowers to make just one drop of honey. The human food supply could scarcely survive without their relentlessness, and 70 percent of our food crops could not reproduce.

Amazon's Day 1 philosophy drove the company from selling books to offering everything under the sun: CDs, electronics, accessories, housewares, hardware, computer software, and clothing, to mention but a few. Dubbed The Everything Store, it delighted customers with free shipping, cheaper prices, an infinite range of products, and timely delivery.

And that was just the beginning. Changes kept coming: One-Click purchases (1997), outdoor furniture (2004), Amazon Prime (2005), cloud computing (2006), Kindle E-Reader (2007), home goods (2008), electronic accessories (2009), Prime Now (2014), Alexa (2014), perishables such as fair-trade-certified coffee (2017), and Amazon Go's no checkout lines (2020). In 2008, Amazon bought Audible and so transformed the listening experience that by 2023 audiobooks was the fastest growing market segment for major publishers.

So why hasn't Bezos moved on to Day 2? As he acerbically asserts, "Day 2 is stasis. Followed by irrelevance. Followed by excruciating, painful decline. Followed by death. And *that* is why it is *always* Day 1."

Amazon's bottom line justifies that disdain. During the COVID pandemic that devastated many retailers, Amazon thrived. In 2021 its 1.3 million employees delivered revenues of $469 billion+, propelling the company to number two on the Fortune 500, edging ever closer to Walmart's number one position.

Successes like Amazon's and Apple's and Walmart's result from a marathon mentality. But their leaders break the long change journey into a series of sprints that take them further than the slog of an ultramarathon.

Take the Korean cosmetics giant AmorePacific, which we discussed in chapter 5. You may recall that the company created a whole new category in the cosmetics market when it launched the Cushion Compact in 2008, a marathon achievement that did not occur overnight but resulted from many short sprints.

In the 1930s, company founder Yun Dokjeong began extracting oil from camellia nut trees at her kitchen table, producing a hair treatment for Korean women. The mother of six possessed a strong work ethic, unwavering patience, and a dedication to using the highest quality raw materials, traits she passed to her son Suh Sungwhan, who took over AmorePacific in 1945.

Fast-forward to 2008, when the researchers in AmorePacific's Cushion Lab had created an all-in-one foundation, sun protection, and skin care makeup product, sold in a unique, easy-to-use container. How, wondered company strategists, can we convince customers to switch from their old tried-and-true, yet clumsy, methods?

The Cushionists spent three years promoting the product before it caught on, eventually finding success on home-shopping programs, which consumers found far more convincing than paid commercials. While sales picked up, the product continued to lose money. Borrowing the traits that the founder had instilled in the company's culture (patience, persistence, professionalism), the new product eventually transformed AmorePacific into a global powerhouse in the cosmetics industry.

Change can take years to bear fruit. When it does, people can grow weary and lose some of their energy to stay the course. How do you combat that problem? Add another P to patience, persistence, and professionalism: playfulness. Bake fun into the change process.

Scientists have shown that it takes four hundred repetitions of a new task to create a new synaptic connection in the brain unless you really enjoy the process. Then it takes between ten and twenty repetitions. The folks at AmorePacific never flagged because they deeply enjoyed the journey to success.

Change won't happen in a week. It probably won't happen in a year. That's where a fifth P comes into play: the prize. Keeping the group's eye firmly fixed on the prize helps everyone maintain the energy needed to complete a long trip.

KEEPING ALL EYES ON THE PRIZE

On a long and arduous journey, distractions can pop up at any time. A competitor's disruptive innovation, an unexpected global pandemic, or just plain weariness can interrupt or even halt progress. When that happens, leaders with group intelligence strive to keep the group's eye on the prize.

Bees bring incredible focus to their work. Their color vision and high "flicker threshold" enables them to detect a poppy flower five times faster than a human driving by a field in a car.

A bee has five eyes: three on the top of its head to see predators from above and two large compound eyes on the sides of its head with thousands of tiny individual lenses that specialize in seeing the patterns that help identify plants, flowers, and other bees. The pollinators clearly see the target even when flying at top speed.

When the entrepreneur Elon Musk formed SpaceX to launch rockets into space, he knew the journey to space would take years, even a decade, to complete. It would take tremendous concentration to keep his team's eyes on the end goal, especially when distracted by midjourney catastrophes, such as the 2016 explosion of a rocket designed to place a critical communication satellite into orbit.

It disheartened the team that Labor Day weekend when they were testing the Falcon 9 rocket just days before its launch and everyone watched in horror as the shuttle burst into flames, lighting up the sky like a spectacular aerial bomb.

The explosion destroyed onboard cargo, including the $200 million Facebook AMOS-6 communication satellite, designed to bring high speed internet to Africa. Facebook CEO Mark Zuckerberg put it mildly when he said he felt "deeply disappointed."

Musk himself described the incident as "the most difficult and complex failure we have ever had in fourteen years." It brought into question the whole mission to conquer space and place humans on Mars.

A fainthearted leader might have given up the dream. Not Musk. He urged his people to keep their eye on the prize and figure out what had gone wrong. After months of research, SpaceX engineers discovered the source of the problem: a pressure valve in the second-stage liquid oxygen tank.

Musk and SpaceX redoubled their efforts to reach their goal. In early 2017 they launched a successful flight from Kennedy Space Center launch pad 39A.

The rocket put into orbit ten satellites that would provide voice and data coverage for underserved countries around the world.

Unlike Musk, groups often set lofty change goals, eagerly pursue them with determination, then lose steam when clobbered by distractions. Bees don't do that. They never forget their mission and take some twenty-seven thousand trips to and from the meadow to make one small jar of honey.

You may not plan to send humans to a distant planet, but whatever the size and scope of your change mission, success depends on keeping a laser-like focus on the end goal. Hungarian biochemist Katalin Karikó, professor at the University of Pennsylvania School of Medicine and a senior vice president at BioNTech, the German company behind the Pfizer vaccine (see the case study in chapter 1), did what the bees do. She kept at it.

Karikó spent decades in the academic wilderness with little funding for her belief in the potential for the synthetic messenger ribonucleic acid (mRNA) to combat disease. Dedicated to reaching her goal, she continued working on mRNA with dogged determination. That dedication paid off when scientists agreed with her contention that mRNA would provide a critical ingredient in a vaccine that could save countless humans from the ravages of COVID-19.

It was a great victory for Karikó, who had left Hungary when her research program at the University of Szeged ran out of money and moved with her husband and daughter to the US.

She won a research post at Temple University in Philadelphia but ran into a wall when the school demoted her from her faculty because colleagues deemed her work "too far-fetched to attract investment." That only made her work harder to prove her theory.

Over her forty-year career, Karikó tried to convince at least thirty potential collaborators, who rebuffed her arguments extolling the benefits of mRNA, until she met Drew Weissman. Together they began working on a way to deliver mRNA into the body without triggering its immune defense system.

Eventually two biotech companies, Moderna in the US and BioNTech in Germany, noticed their work, thus paving the way for the COVID-19 vaccines. Millions of vaccinated people can thank Karikó for her untiring efforts. She never let the skeptics deter her. She kept her eye on the prize, taking one step after another until she reached her goal.

Karikó's unwavering commitment to an idea revolutionized the treatment of diseases (including cancer, heart failure, multiple sclerosis, influenza, malaria, and HIV). In 2021 she and Weissman won the Breakthrough Prize in Life Sciences for "transformative advances toward understanding living systems and extending human life," and in 2023 they went on to win the Nobel Prize in Medicine.

It's worth repeating the Five Ps: patience, persistence, professionalism, playfulness, and the prize. Successful change in complex ecosystems takes all five. My father affirmed the value of those words when my mother, his soulmate and visionary for the family's move to Australia, passed away two years after her doctors confirmed that she was suffering from amyotrophic lateral sclerosis (ALS), or motor neurone disease (MND).

Dad stepped into the role of family leader, patiently caring for Mom as her health declined, behaving like a stoic professional when dealing with doctors, and persisting with his family duties despite his sadness. When she passed away, he organized an annual fun Easter reunion with his adult children and a growing tribe of grandchildren in a rambling homestead in the foothills of Australia's Great Dividing Range in the shadow of Wombat Hill, having always valued the prize of a big, connected family.

In his ninety-first year he conquered his dyslexia in order to memorize a poem from the diaries of the great Australian writer Dorothea Mackellar, which he recited at our Easter get-together:

I love a sunburnt country,
A land of sweeping plains,
Of ragged mountain ranges,
Of drought and flooding rains.
I love her far horizons,
I love her jewel-sea,
Her beauty and her terror—
The wide brown land for me!

I bring my father's spirit and the Five Ps to my work in the business world, especially when it comes to organizational change. Change is not a journey for the fainthearted. It takes guts and a tough skin to overcome all the distractions and setbacks and surprises you encounter along the way.

Effective leaders never give up on their dream of meaningful and lasting change. They do not let the naysayers, blockers, or critics get in their way. They do not allow the obstacles, threats, noise, or turbulence to deter them. They do not crumble when confronted with setbacks, fierce resistance, or dangerous opponents. Instead, they respond to all threats with a deeper and more abiding resolution.

On your own journey you will experience many highs and lows. Celebrate the highs; never let the lows get you down. Remember, successful change comes not from those who never fail but from those who never quit.

POINTS TO REMEMBER

- Old patterns can easily reemerge and slow progress.
- Celebrations over midcourse successes boost commitment to the big win.
- Change leaders build change capability by developing their group intelligence.
- Progress depends on maintaining the energy for change.
- Ultimate success depends on keeping all eyes on the prize.

CONCLUSION

THE EVOLVING HIVE

I will arise and go now, and go to Innisfree,
And a small cabin build there, of clay and wattles made;
Nine bean-rows will I have there, a hive for the honey-bee,
And live alone in the bee-loud glade.

—William Butler Yeats

As the summer wanes and winter approaches, the honeybees remain ensconced in their new home on the edge of Wombat Forest, but they don't just sit around taking it easy; they keep buzzing around, staying warm, and eating the raw honey they have stored since their move.

Once spring arrives, the queen starts to lay a thousand to two thousand eggs per day. By early summer, when the hive has outgrown the tree cavity, half the bees prepare to swarm in search of a new home.

The continuous, never-ending cycle of adaptation continues according to the Hive LENS: Looking Beyond, Experimenting, Nudging, and Strengthening the colony.

Likewise, successful change leaders possess the group intelligence to intervene and create meaningful, lasting change with the Hive LENS. This simple but powerful model captures the essence of group intelligence practices deployed by extraordinarily successful change leaders such as Julie Sweet at Accenture, Albert Bourla at Pfizer, Satya Nadella at Microsoft, and my own mom and dad as they closed the latch on the farmhouse door in Ireland for the last time and embarked on a journey to a new life in Australia.

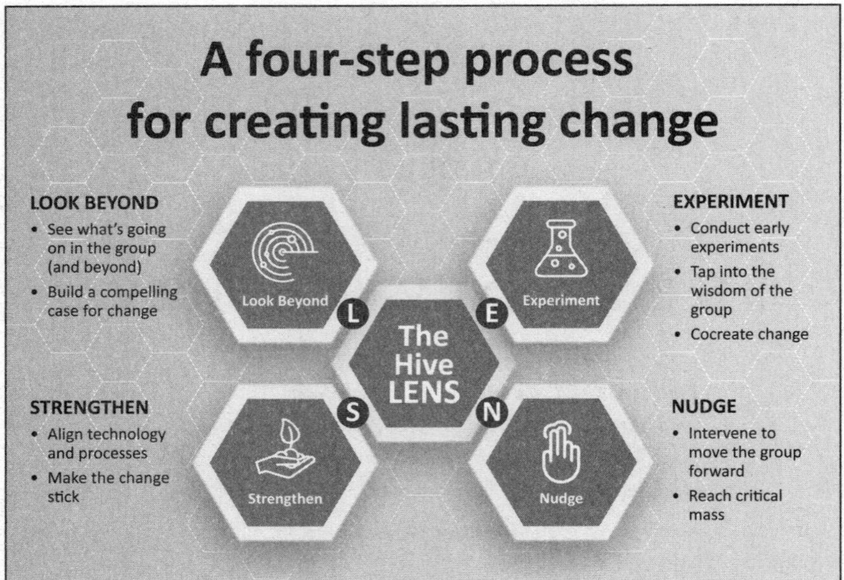
A four-step process
for creating lasting change
LOOK BEYOND
• See what's going on in the group (and beyond)
• Build a compelling case for change
EXPERIMENT
• Conduct early experiments
• Tap into the wisdom of the group
• Cocreate change
STRENGTHEN
• Align technology and processes
• Make the change stick
NUDGE
• Intervene to move the group forward
• Reach critical mass
Look Beyond
Experiment
Strengthen
Nudge
L
E
S
N
The Hive LENS

Just like the bees, these leaders understand the need for group intelligence to achieve the best possible results during potentially dangerous transitions.

The major social and organizational problems we face in the world result from the way groups of people think and behave. And people are not robots. We are living, breathing, ever-changing, often messy, unpredictable, and emotional creatures.

We may specialize in disciplines such as science, engineering, and finance, but technical skills in those areas do not make us change masters. Nor do the advanced interpersonal skills many of us develop in order to influence, manage, and control the world around us.

While today's organizations do need people with both sets of skills, those intent on change must place them within the context of the whole ecosystem. That opens our eyes to the wholeness and connectedness between the system's component parts.

When we want an organization to achieve a major transition, we cannot depend solely on champions, committees, or agents to cocreate change. We must also empower each part to fulfill its unique change role.

The old ways do not work. IQ and EQ are inadequate intelligences for the stormy seas we are navigating. The technicians and social networkers cannot move the organization into safer waters any more than a bartender or an orchestra leader can steer a *Titanic* away from an iceberg.

In today's sea of change many organizations in desperate need of a course correction are drowning. In this book I have suggested a better way forward, a way that views organizations as dynamic ecosystems governed by these Nine Laws:

1. **Law of Patterns:** Simple group rules produce complex behavior.
2. **Law of Connectedness:** All behavior ripples throughout the group.
3. **Law of Role:** Role powerfully influences behavior.
4. **Law of Multiple Perspectives:** Not everyone sees things the same way.
5. **Law of Context:** Group behavior is contextual.
6. **Law of Embeddedness:** Deeply embedded patterns resist change.
7. **Law of Pattern Blindness:** Group members can ignore the obvious.
8. **Law of Unintended Consequences:** Change efforts can produce unexpected outcomes.
9. **Law of the Tipping Point:** Even small changes can have a big impact.

The Nine Laws of Group Dynamics demand that leaders adjust their view of how they can create meaningful and lasting change in an organization. It's all about connectedness. I see it every day on Wombat Hill.

Shortly after the family reunion where my dad recited "I love a sunburnt country," my partner and I traveled back to the foothills of the Great Dividing Range and hiked over Wombat Farm for the first time, noticing an abandoned beehive at the end of the paddock near an old oak tree.

We bought the farm and the next year installed the orchard's irrigation system, planted embankments with native flowers, and built vegetable boxes for growing herbs and seasonal produce.

The following spring, when the farm blazed with colorful blossoms, the bees returned. How lovely to open the hive, listen to the murmur of bees at work, and inhale the sweet smell of the malty comb.

Nine Laws of Group Dynamics

Patterns
Simple group rules produce complex behavior

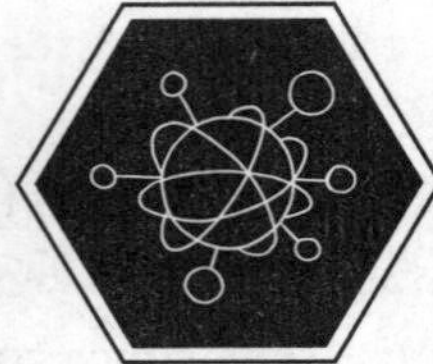

Connectedness
All behavior ripples throughout the group

Role
Role powerfully influences behavior

Multiple Perspectives
Not everyone sees things the same way

Context
Group behavior is contextual

Embeddedness
Deeply embedded patterns resist change

Pattern Blindness
Group members can ignore the obvious

Unintended Consequences
Change efforts can produce unexpected outcomes

Tipping Point
Even small changes can have a big impact

Leaders with group intelligence understand the Nine Laws of Group Dynamics

There's always honey in the farmhouse pantry. It tastes of apple blossom from the orchard and native red flowering gum trees from the nearby Wombat Forest.

But for me, bees have given me more than the product of their labor; they have gifted me with a lifelong fascination with how they work together, care for one another, and make an amazing contribution to the planet as pollinators. Look at them closely and you will see how a well-balanced ecosystem functions in a never-ending cycle of **L**ooking Beyond, **E**xperimenting, **N**udging, and **S**trengthening the colony.

Whatever your organization does, wherever it operates in the world, no matter how dominant it may be now, you cannot afford to sit back and take it easy.

In fast-changing marketplaces where organizations must change or face extinction, you will encounter enormous challenges. You cannot conquer them with a technician's tool set or a social networker's influencing skills. You can only do it by harnessing the power of group intelligence.

Admittedly, it takes time and effort to rewire your brain and stop thinking like a technician or social networker and adopt a broader view of your organization as a living, breathing ecosystem with myriad connected parts. But, trust me, it's worth it.

Polish your Hive LENS. Harness the power of group intelligence. Follow the bees to meaningful and lasting change.

Good luck!

ACKNOWLEDGMENTS

Over my thirty-year career, I've worked with many exceptional colleagues on countless change initiatives as I gained the experience and expertise to write this book. Thank you for your role in shaping my thinking.

A very special thanks to Michael Snell, a wonderful agent and fine editor. Michael and I shared the same passion for bringing this work to readers, and he even came up with the title for the book. I could not wish for a better wingman, and he walked with me every step of the writing journey, contributing greatly to the quality of the final manuscript.

A big thank-you to the team at HarperCollins Leadership for making *The Hive Mind at Work* a reality. In particular, I'd like to thank Matt Baugher (senior vice president), and Tim Burgard (senior executive editor). Thanks also go to Jeff Farr (managing editor), David McNeill (copyeditor), and Beth Metrick (production director) at Neuwirth & Associates, who expertly handled the editorial production of the book.

I wish to acknowledge my executive team colleagues at DuluxGroup, who have demonstrated the true meaning of leader-led change. They include Chairman and CEO Patrick Houlihan and my colleagues Andrew Ryan, Simon Black, Ian Rowden, Angela Anthony, Julia Myers, Helen Fitzpatrick, Brad Hordern, Pat Jones, Martin Ward, Murray Allen, Mike Kirkman, and Richard Stuckes.

A special mention goes to my talented People, Culture & Change team at DuluxGroup, who applied the change tools in this book to bring our purpose—"Imagine a better place"—to life for our customers, consumers, and employees. The team includes my accomplished leadership group of Lindy Visagie, Cassie Brain, Luke Brabender, Rebecca Cusack, Stephanie

Watt, Ella Green, Jess Rogers, and my dedicated assistant, Claudia Pernat. Thank you all.

Heartfelt gratitude goes to my partner, Trish, a fellow author, who has supported me throughout my career and while writing this book. Thank you for your love, guidance, and inspiration over the years. I could not have written this book without you.

My love and respect go to my parents, Patricia and Martin McHale, who were always courageous in the face of change and who encouraged their children to continue to adapt and grow.

During my research for this book, I encountered case studies of exceptional change leaders, intent on creating better workplaces. I have woven the stories of these change champions throughout this book, and the work is dedicated to them.

And finally, my thanks to you for spending some of your precious time reading this book. I hope its lessons can help you learn more about ecosystem change in order to create workplaces that can deliver, grow, adapt, and prosper.

NOTES

In this section I have included a detailed list of notes, references, and citations for each chapter of the book.

Prologue

xv **von Frisch found that bees performed a "waggle dance":** Karl von Frisch, *The Dance Language and Orientation of Bees* (Harvard University Press, 1967).

xvii **their team efforts can produce over three hundred pounds of honey each season:** C. L. Farrar, *The Life of The Honey Bee, Its Biology and Behavior* (American Bee Journal, 1968).

xviii **A drone's large eyes contain seven to eight thousand individual photoreceptors:** Rusty Burlew, "All the Better to See You, My Dear!" Honey Bee Suite, 2010, https://www.honeybeesuite.com/all-the-better-to-see-you-with-my-dear/.

xviii **In his color vision experiments, researcher Karl von Frisch:** Karl von Frisch, *Bees: Their Vision, Chemical Senses, and Language*, Comstock Publishing Associates, 1972.

xix **Able to detect light in wavelengths from approximately 300 to 650 nanometers:** Matt Shipman, "What Do Bees See? And How Do We Know?" *NC State University News*, July 27, 2011, https://news.ncsu.edu/2011/07/wms-what-bees-see/.

xix **Humans, able to detect wavelengths from 390 to 750 nanometers:** Dave Deriso, "The Artful Brain: Inputs and Outputs of the Neural Machine," *Scitable blog, Nature*, May 22, 2011, https://www.nature.com/scitable/blog/the-artful-brain/alternate_realities/.

xix **a 60 percent reduction in hives:** Greenpeace USA, "Save the Bees. Be the Solution to Help Protect Bees in Crisis," n.d., https://www.greenpeace.org/usa/sustainable-agriculture/save-the bees/#:~:text=U.S.%20National%20Agricultural%20Statistics%20show,critical%20metric%20of%20crop%20health.

Chapter 1

1 **"In the last eleven months, probably ten years' work has been done":** Ian Sample. "The Great Project: How Covid Changed Science Forever," *The Guardian*, December 15, 2020, https://www.theguardian.com/world/2020/dec/15/the-great-project-how-covid-changed-science-for-ever.

4 **Sir Isaac Newton.** Richard S. Westfall, "Isaac Newton, English Physicist and Mathematician," *Britannica*, updated October 2023, https://www.britannica.com/biography/Isaac-Newton.

5 **The term *social network* was coined by anthropologist J. A. Barnes:** J. A. Barnes, "Class and Committees in a Norwegian Island Parish," *Human Relations* VII (1954).

5 **Daniel Goleman stamped his mark on this movement:** Daniel Goleman, *Emotional Intelligence: Why It Can Matter More Than IQ* (Bantam Books, 1995).

6 **the idea of organizations as ecosystems:** L. von Bertalanffy, "General System Theory: A New Approach to Unity of Science," *Human Biology* 23 (December 1951), 303–61, https://pubmed.ncbi.nlm.nih.gov/14907026/.

8 **Coke selling a half liter of plain old tap water:** Matthew Beard, "The Real Thing? Coke's Water Comes Straight from the Tap with a Cool Mark-Up of 3,000 Per Cent," *The Independent*, March 2, 2004, https://www.independent.co.uk/life-style/food-and-drink/news/the-real-thing-coke-s-water-comes-straight-from-the-tap-with-a-cool-markup-of-3-000-per-cent-71689.html.

8 **Coke was extolling the virtues of its purification process:** George Wright, "Coca-Cola Withdraws Bottled Water from the UK," *The Guardian*, March 19, 2004, https://www.theguardian.com/uk/2004/mar/19/foodanddrink.

9 **a journalist at *The Grocer* magazine:** Dan Wiggins, "Only Fools and Horses: How Coca-Cola Accidentally Recreated Del Boy's 'Peckham Spring' Fiasco," My London, June 22, 2021, https://www.mylondon.news/whats-on/whats-on-news/only-fools-horses-how-coca-20874269.

9 **PR manager, poured fuel on the fire:** Felicity Lawrence, "Tap Water—It's the Real Thing," *The Guardian*, March 2, 2004, https://www.theguardian.com/uk/2004/mar/02/foodanddrink.marketingandpr.

9 **A spokesman dismissed Snyder's claim:** Matthew Beard, "The Real Thing? Coke's Water Comes Straight from the Tap with a Cool Mark-Up of 3,000 Per Cent."

11 **by 2004 Dasani had become the second-biggest selling bottled water in the US:** Alan Cowell, "Coke Recalls Bottled Water Newly Introduced to Britain," *New York Times*, March 20, 2004, https://www.nytimes.com/2004/03/20/business/international-business-coke-recalls-bottled-water-newly-introduced-to-britain.html.

11 **spent £7 million on an ad campaign:** "'Tap Water' Dasani Causes UK Storm for Coke," WARC, March 3, 2004, https://www.warc.com/newsandopinion/news/tap-water-dasani-causes-uk-storm-for-coke/en-gb/15369.

11 **We add calcium, magnesium, and sodium bicarbonate:** "Coke Pulls Water from UK Shelves," CBS News, March 3, 2004, https://www.cbsnews.com/news/coke-pulls-water-from-uk-shelves/.

12 **A massive audience of 20.1 million people:** Dan Wiggins, "Only Fools and Horses: How Coca-Cola Accidentally Recreated Del Boy's 'Peckham Spring' Fiasco."

13 **a £25 million loss from canceled production:** John Arlidge, "Don't Drink the Water," *The Guardian*, April 18, 2004, https://www.theguardian.com/lifeandstyle/2004/apr/18/foodanddrink.

15 **CEO Albert Bourla began challenging everyone in his company to "make the impossible possible":** Albert Bourla, "The CEO of Pfizer on Developing a Vaccine in Record Time," *Harvard Business Review*, May–June 2021, https://hbr.org/2021/05/the-ceo-of-pfizer-on-developing-a-vaccine-in-record-time.

15 **Bourla released a five-point plan to guide Pfizer employees:** "Pfizer Outlines Five-Point Plan to Battle COVID-19," Pfizer Press Release, March 13, 2020, https://www.pfizer.com/news/press-release/press-release-detail/pfizer-outlines-five-point-plan-battle-covid-19.

16 **Kathrin Jansen, his chief of vaccine research, spoke with the folks at BioNTech:** Matthew Herper, "In the Race for a Covid-19 Vaccine, Pfizer Turns to a Scientist with a History of Defying Skeptics—and Getting Results," Stat, August 24, 2020, https://www.statnews.com/2020/08/24/pfizer-edge-in-the-race-for-a-covid-19-vaccine-could-be-a-scientist-with-two-best-sellers-to-her-credit/.

17 **In the case of the vaccine hunt:** Jared S. Hopkins, "How Pfizer Delivered a Covid Vaccine in Record Time: Crazy Deadlines, a Pushy CEO," *Wall Street Journal*, December 11, 2020, https://www.wsj.com/articles/how-pfizer-delivered-a-covid-vaccine-in-record-time-crazy-deadlines-a-pushy-ceo-11607740483.

18 **In June, Bourla also kept pressing the manufacturing team:** "Shot of a Lifetime: How Pfizer and BioNTech Developed and Manufactured a COVID-19 Vaccine in Record Time," Pfizer website, 2021, https://www.pfizer.com/news/articles/shot_of_a_lifetime_how_pfizer_and_biontech_developed_and_manufactured_a_covid_19_vaccine_in_record_time.

19 **gearing up to produce fifty million vaccine doses in 2020 and up to 1.3 billion doses in 2021:** "Pfizer and BioNTech Announce Vaccine Candidate Against COVID-19 Achieved Success in First Interim Analysis from Phase 3 Study," Pfizer Press Release, November 9, 2020, https://www.pfizer.com/news/press-release/press-release-detail/pfizer-and-biontech-announce-vaccine-candidate-against.

19 **Pfizer vaccine became the first fully tested COVID-19 vaccine approved for emergency use:** Jocelyn Solis-Moreira, "How Did We Develop a COVID-19 Vaccine So Quickly?" Medical News Today, updated November 13, 2021, https://www.medicalnewstoday.com/articles/how-did-we-develop-a-covid-19-vaccine-so-quickly.

20 **"intercompany cooperation, liberation from bureaucracy, and most of all, hard work":** Albert Bourla, "The CEO of Pfizer on Developing a Vaccine in Record Time."

Chapter 2

21 **the queen's pheromones cannot reach the entire colony:** Thomas D. Seeley, *Honeybee Democracy* (Princeton University Press, 2011).

22 **triggering the subprime mortgage crisis that cost an estimated $10 trillion in lost economic output:** Nick Lioudis, "The Collapse of Lehman Brothers: A Case Study," Investopedia, updated March 10, 2023, https://www.investopedia.com/articles/economics/09/lehman-brothers-collapse.asp.

22 **Or you call D'Arcy Wentworth Thompson:** "Sir D'Arcy Wentworth Thompson," *Britannica*, updated June 17, 2023, https://www.britannica.com/biography/DArcy-Wentworth-Thompson.

22 **Fibonacci sequence, or "golden spiral" ratio:** Steven Rose, "Growth and Form by D'Arcy Wentworth Thompson Review—Centenary of a Darwin-Challenging Classic," *The Guardian*, July 21, 2017, https://amp.theguardian.com/books/2017/jul/21/growth-form-darcy-wentworth-thompson-review.

23 **Edward Lorenz, the American mathematician, meteorologist, and father of chaos theory:** Peter Dizikes, "When the Butterfly Effect Took Flight," *MIT Technology Review*, February 22, 2011, https://www.technologyreview.com/2011/02/22/196987/when-the-butterfly-effect-took-flight/amp/.

29 **When the New York–based investment bank Lehman Brothers came to a grinding halt:** Anne Sraders, "The Lehman Brothers Collapse and How It's Changed the Economy Today," *The Street*, September 12, 2018.

29 **"25 People to Blame for the Financial Crisis":** "25 People to Blame for the Financial Crisis: The Good Intentions, Bad Managers and Greed Behind the Meltdown," *TIME*, February 2009, https://content.time.com/time/specials/packages/article/0,28804,1877351_1877350_1877326,00.html.

29 **Harold James, a professor of history and international affairs at Princeton University:** Harold James, "Why Lehman Brother's Collapse Changed Our View of the World," *Australian Financial Review*, September 5, 2018, https://www.afr.com/opinion/why-lehman-brothers-collapse-changed-our-view-of-the-world-20180905-h14yck.

29 **The open secret on Wall Street:** Eric Dash, "What's Really Wrong with Wall Street Pay," *New York Times*, September 18, 2009, https://archive.nytimes.com/economix.blogs.nytimes.com/2009/09/18/whats-really-wrong-with-wall-street-pay/.

32 **"Back in 2012, everybody thought we were going to die":** Adi Ignatius, "Former Best Buy CEO Hubert Joly: Empowering Workers to Create 'Magic,'" *Harvard Business Review* video series *The New World of Work*, December 2, 2021, https://hbr.org/2021/12/former-best-buy-ceo-hubert-joly-empowering-workers-to-create-magic.

32 **By 2012 its share price plunged to twelve dollars:** Kindra Cooper, "How Best Buy Used CX Strategy to Rebound from a Retail Apocalypse," *Customer*

Contact Weekly, October 10, 2019, https://www.customercontactweekdigital.com/customer-experience/articles/best-buy-customer-experience.

32 **the new CEO began listening to how customers felt about Best Buy:** Marine Aubagna, "How Customer Feedback Helped Best Buy Reinvent Itself," Skeepers, December 3, 2015, https://skeepers.io/en/blog/how-customer-feedback-helped-best-buy-reinvent-itself/.

33 **the creation of "Geek Squad Lounges":** Kevin Kelleher, "How the Geek Squad Could Be Best Buy's Secret Weapon," *TIME*, July 19, 2016, https://time.com/4411333/best-buy-amazon-geek-squad-hubert-joly/.

33 **acclamation as one of the World's Best CEOs:** *Barron's* cover story (May 2018), "World's Best CEOs: 30 Leaders with Talent to Spare," *Barron's*, May 2018, https://www.barrons.com/amp/articles/worlds-best-ceos-30-leaders-with-talent-to-spare-1527300812.

33 **one of the Best-Performing CEOs in the World:** Faculty and research, Hubert Joly, Harvard Business School, 2022, https://www.hbs.edu/faculty/Pages/profile.aspx?facId=520131.

33 **They put Roger Feynman, the Nobel Prize–winning physicist, in charge of the inquiry:** Kevin Cook, "How Legendary Physicist Richard Feynman Helped Crack the Case on the Challenger Disaster," LitHub, June 9, 2021, https://lithub.com/how-legendary-physicist-richard-feynman-helped-crack-the-case-on-the-challenger-disaster/.

33 **O-ring seals on the rocket's boosters had frozen:** Rachel Feltman, "A Famous Physicist's Experiment Showed the Inevitability of the Challenger Disaster," *Washington Post*, January 27, 2016, https://www.washingtonpost.com/news/speaking-of-science/wp/2016/01/27/a-famous-physicists-simple-experiment-showed-the-inevitability-of-the-challenger-disaster/?outputType=amp.

34 **NASA officials, pressured to push ahead with the mission:** Howard Berkes, "Challenger Engineer Who Warned of Shuttle Disaster Dies," NPR News, March 21, 2016, https://www.npr.org/sections/thetwo-way/2016/03/21/470870426/challenger-engineer-who-warned-of-shuttle-disaster-dies.

34 **NASA . . . suppressed the bad news:** Jonathan Grinstein, "What the Challenger Disaster Teaches Us About Speaking Up in a New Era of Spaceflight," NeuroLeadership Institute, February 27, 2020, https://neuroleadership.com/your-brain-at-work/challenger-disaster-speaking-up/.

38 **When he joined Hasbro in 2000:** Matt Perez, "Not a Toy Story: How Brian Goldner Is Transforming Hasbro," *Forbes*, September 3, 2019, https://www.forbes.com/sites/mattperez/2019/09/03/not-a-toy-story/?sh=f491aac11a27.

39 **Hasbro's revenue hit a record $5.2 billion:** "Hasbro Reports Strong Revenue, Operating Profit and Earnings Growth for the Full-Year 2021," Hasbro Press Release, February 2022, https://investor.hasbro.com/news-releases/news-release-details/hasbro-reports-strong-revenue-operating-profit-and-earnings-0.

39 **In 2021 Brian Goldner succumbed to cancer:** R. Sandomir, "Brian Goldner, Hasbro executive with Hollywood vision, dies at 58." *New York Times*, https://

www.google.com.au/amp/s/www.nytimes.com/2021/10/15/business/brian-goldner-dead.amp.html.

39 ***Forbes* 2019 list of America's most innovative leaders:** "America's Most Innovative Leaders. Who Are the Most Creative and Successful Business Minds of Today?" *Forbes*, 2019, https://www.forbes.com/lists/innovative-leaders/#6d4a98a26aa9.

Chapter 3

41 **Apple overlooked the complexity of this market niche:** Tim Worstall, "The Number One Tech Disaster of the Year? Yup, Apple Maps," *Forbes*, December 26, 2012, https:// www.forbes.com/sites/timworstall/2012/12/26/the-number-one-tech-disaster-of-the-year-yup-apple-maps/amp/.

41 **This was not an environment:** Chris Morris, "12 Corporate Blunders That Could Have Been Avoided," CNBC, April 3, 2015, https://www.cnbc.com/2015/04/03/12-corporate-blunders-that-could-have-been-avoided.html.

42 **tarnished Apple's hard-earned reputation for reliable products.** Nicholas Fearn, "Apple Was 'Embarrassed' by Disastrous Maps Launch in 2012," Silicon UK, August 11, 2016, https://www.silicon.co.uk/mobility/mobile-apps/apple-maps-launch-embarrassment-196350.

44 **In the rush to meet the deadline:** Henrico Dolfing, "The $450 Million Software Error at Knight Capital," Henrico Dolfing website, June 2019, https://www.henricodolfing.com/2019/06/project-failure-case-study-knight-capital.html?m=1.

44 **staggering loss of $460 million:** Nathaniel Popper, "Knight Capital Says Trading Glitch Cost It $440 Million," *New York Times*, August 2, 2012, https://archive.nytimes.com/dealbook.nytimes.com/2012/08/02/knight-capital-says-trading-mishap-cost-it-440-million/.

45 **By December 2012, Knight Capital had been acquired by rival Getco:** "Getco to Buy Knight Capital in $1.4 Billion Deal," Reuters, December 19, 2012, https://www.reuters.com/article/us-knightcapital-getco-idUSBRE8BI0OF20121219.

47 **Take Frederick "Fred" Wallace Smith who created the $56 billion FedEx empire:** Stockanalysis website, May 2023, https://stockanalysis.com/stocks/fdx/statistics/.

47 **In 1971, Yale University student Smith came up with the idea:** Meg Greene, "Fred Smith 1944–," References for Business, n.d., https://www.referenceforbusiness.com/biography/S-Z/Smith-Fred-1944.html.

47 **That led him to his own motto: "People, Service, Profit":** Joel Searls, "FedEx Founder Frederick W. Smith: 'I Owe a Debt of Gratitude to the Marine Corps,'" *Leatherneck*, June 2022, https://www.mca-marines.org/wp-content/uploads/FedEx-Founder-Frederick-W.-Smith.pdf.

48 **FedEx had grown to become the biggest cargo airline in the world:** I. King, "The man who 'changed the world' Fred Smith to step down after 50 year FedEx journey." Sky News (March 29, 2022), https://news.sky.com/story/amp/the

-man-who-changed-the-world-fred-smith-to-step-down-after-50-year-fedex-journey-12577420.

49 **sales 30 percent below the prior year, losses in excess of $400 million, and a crippling debt of $800 million:** Denise H. Kenyon-Rouvinez, Anne-Catrin Glemser, and Philip Whiteley, "The Lego Group: Family Business Resilience," IMD, October 2014, https://www.imd.org/research-knowledge/strategy/case-studies/the-lego-group-family-business-resilience-a/.

49 **Lego managers had lost track of which products were actually making money:** Johnny Davis, "How Lego Clicked: The Super Brand That Reinvented Itself," *The Guardian*, June 4, 2017, https://www.theguardian.com/lifeandstyle/2017/jun/04/how-lego-clicked-the-super-brand-that-reinvented-itself.

49 **It had become a sprawling giant with too many irons in the fire:** Keith Oliver, Edouard Samakh, and Peter Heckmann, "Rebuilding Lego, Brick by Brick: How a Supply Chain Transformation Helped Put the Beloved Toymaker Back Together Again," Strategy + Business, August 29, 2007, https://www.strategy-business.com/article/07306.

49 **producing revenues of $4.5 billion and profits of $1.5 billion in 2013:** Adrian Geislinger, *A Turnaround Case Study: How Lego Rebuilt and Became the Top Toymaker in the World*, Dissertation at Universidade Católica Portuguesa, May 1, 2020, https://repositorio.ucp.pt/bitstream/10400.14/31148/1/152118010_Adrian%20Geislinger_DPDFA.pdf.

50 **she spearheaded Accenture's most ambitious brand relaunch in a decade:** "Change Powers Accenture's Biggest Brand Move in a Decade," Accenture Press Release, October 2020, https://newsroom.accenture.com/news/change-powers-accentures-biggest-brand-move-in-a-decade.htm.

50 **The firm's clients and its 720,000 employees got the message:** "Creating Value in All Directions. Accenture Annual Report, 2021," Accenture website, https://www.accenture.com/_acnmedia/PDF-165/Accenture-2021-Letter-To-Shareholders.pdf.

50 **the firm delivered a record $50.5 billion in revenue, up 14 percent over the prior year:** "Accenture Reports Very Strong Fourth-Quarter and Full-Year Fiscal 2021 Results," Business Wire, https://www.businesswire.com/news/home/20210923005360/en/Accenture-Reports-Very-Strong-Fourth-Quarter-and-Full-Year-Fiscal-2021-Results.

51 **deliver a staggering $14.6 billion worth of crop production to the US economy annually:** "Economic Value of Commercial Beekeeping," Pesticide Action Network North America, 2021, http://cues.cfans.umn.edu/old/pollinators/pdf-value/EconomicValueCommercialBeekeeping.pdf.

51 **fly the equivalent of one and a half times the circumference of the earth to make less than one teaspoonful of honey:** "Bees!" Five on Friday: Musings on Mental Health, Global Mental Health Programs, Columbia University, October 2016, https://www.cugmhp.org/five-on-friday-posts/bees/.

51 **a trap that snared Amazon during the COVID pandemic:** Annie, Palmer, "How Amazon Managed the Coronavirus Crisis and Came Out Stronger," CNBC, September 29, 2020, https://www.cnbc.com/amp/2020/09/29/how-amazon-managed-the-coronavirus-crisis-and-came-out-stronger.html.

51 **the *Guardian* newspaper described a day in the life of a frontline worker:** John Harris, "How Amazon Became a Pandemic Giant—And Why That Could Be a Threat to Us All," *The Guardian*, November 18, 2020, https://amp.theguardian.com/technology/2020/nov/18/how-amazon-became-a-pandemic-giant-and-why-that-could-be-a-threat-to-us-all.

52 **This bad press ignited intense scrutiny of the working conditions at Amazon:** Jack Kelly, "A Hard-Hitting Investigative Report into Amazon Shows That Workers' Needs Were Neglected in Favor of Getting Goods Delivered Quickly," *Forbes*, October 25, 2021, https://www.forbes.com/sites/jackkelly/2021/10/25/a-hard-hitting-investigative-report-into-amazon-shows-that-workers-needs-were-neglected-in-favor-of-getting-goods-delivered-quickly/?sh=7b6f6f3b51f5.

52 **Nestlé factory manager Omar Askar began looking for ways to use water more efficiently:** "Dairy Processing Facility Becomes First in the U.S. to Achieve Alliance for Water Stewardship Certification," Nestlé Press Release, March 2021, https://www.nestleusa.com/media/pressreleases/carnation-dairy-facility-achieves-alliance-water-stewardship.

53 **Nestlé's Carnation factory became the first dairy-processing facility in the United States to earn certification under the Alliance for Water Stewardship (AWS) standard:** Jim Cornall, "Carnation Dairy Facility First to Achieve Alliance for Water Stewardship Certification," *Daily Reporter*, March 30, 2021, https://www.dairyreporter.com/Article/2021/03/30/Carnation-dairy-facility-first-to-achieve-Alliance-for-Water-Stewardship-certification-in-US.

53 **found three-thousand-year-old edible honey in King Tutankhamun's tomb in Egypt:** Jennifer Gaeng, "Discover the Oldest Honey Ever Found (From King Tut's Tomb?)" A–Z Animals, February 28, 2023, https://a-z-animals.com/blog/discover-the-oldest-honey-ever-found-from-king-tuts-tomb/.

53 **McKinsey research reveals that 70 percent of employees define their sense of purpose from their work:** Naina Dhingra, Andrew Samo, Bill Schaninger, and Matt Schrimper, "Help Your Employees Find Purpose—Or Watch Them Leave," McKinsey Insights, April 5, 2021, https://www.mckinsey.com/capabilities/people-and-organizational-performance/our-insights/help-your-employees-find-purpose-or-watch-them-leave.

53 **the land of stratospheric costs, billions of euros over budget:** Blaine Bachelor, "Berlin's Troubled Brandenburg Airport Still in Crisis One Year After Opening," CNN Travel, updated December 13, 2021, https://edition.cnn.com/travel/amp/berlin-brandenburg-airport-one-year-on/index.html.

54 **Multiple stakeholders bickered about the airport's location**: Thomas Sedlin, Volker Beckmann, and Rong Tan, "Public Participation and Airport Development: The Case of the Site Selection for Berlin Brandenburg Airport (BER) in

Germany," *Sustainability* 12, no. 24 (December, 2020), https://doi.org/10.3390/su122410535.

54 **It took thirty years from concept to operation:** William Noah Glucroft, "Berlin's New Airport: A Story of Failure and Embarrassment," *Deutsche Welle*, October 21, 2020, https://amp.dw.com/en/berlins-new-airport-finally-opens-a-story-of-failure-and-embarrassment/a-55446329.

54 **Police Scotland and the Scottish Police Authority (SPA) awarded a ten-year, $72.1 million contract:** Jenni Davidson, J. "'No Single Reason' Why Police Scotland i6 IT Project Failed, Audit Scotland Concludes," *Holyrood*, March 9, 2017, https://www.holyrood.com/news/view,no-single-reason-why-police-scotland-i6-it-project-failed-audit-scotland-concludes_13221.htm.

55 **Audit Scotland concluded that the project "ultimately collapsed due to a damaging loss of trust . . .":** Henrico Dolfing, "How the Scottish Police Got £25 Million Back but Lost 3 Years on I6," Henrico Dolfing website, September 2021, https://www.henricodolfing.com/2021/09/case-study-scottish-police-i6-accenture.html?m=1.

55 **they began building the world's largest and most complex jetliner, which was delayed by years:** Hans Kundnani, "What's the Problem with Airbus?" *The Guardian*, October 5, 2006, https://amp.theguardian.com/business/2006/oct/05/theairlineindustry.travelnews.

55 **assigned the task of producing the 530 kilometers of copper and aluminum wiring:** "Why Do Projects Fail: Airbus—A380," Calleam Consulting, Companion website to University of British Columbia (UBC), 2020, https://calleam.com/WTPF/?p=4700.

56 **incompatible software had given the two teams quite different versions of the plane's 3D digital mock-up:** Andrew Curran, "How Computer Design Software Delayed the Airbus A380," Simple Flying, November 25, 2020, https://simpleflying.com/airbus-a380-computer-design-delay/.

56 **resulted in a massive $6 billion loss in company value:** David Gow, "EADS Shares Plummet on Airbus Fears," *The Guardian*, June 14, 2006. https://www.theguardian.com/business/2006/jun/14/theairlineindustry.money.

56 **eventually led to the resignation of EADS chief and cochief:** "Top Executives Resign After Airbus Delays," NBC News, July 2, 2006, https://www.nbcnews.com/news/amp/wbna13673239.

57 **"Mad Max on water" adventure, became one of the biggest flops in cinema history:** Alex Rodgers, "12 Major Films with So Many Development and On Set Disasters They Almost Didn't Happen," Ranker, updated September 23, 2021, https://www.ranker.com/list/films-with-huge-production-problems/alex-rodgers.

57 **reshoots extended a ninety-six-day shooting schedule to 150 days:** "Failed Projects and the Lessons Learned—2023," TrainingByteSize website, https://www.trainingbytesize.com/12-failed-projects-lessons-learned/.

57 **Revlon didn't put on their best thinking caps when they acquired Elizabeth Arden Inc., in 2018:** Bill Baumann, "4 Lessons Learned from the Revlon ERP

Failure," Panorama Consulting website, December 23 2020, https://www.panorama-consulting.com/revlon-erp-failure/.

58 **COO Christopher Peterson, noticing emerging problems with the system, reported a slowdown in his manufacturing facility:** "Cosmetic Giant Implemented the ERP System of SAP and Regretted," TAdvisor website, n.d., https://tadviser.com/index.php/Project:Revlon_(SAP_ERP).

58 **By year-end Revlon had failed to deliver $64 million worth of cosmetic orders to US customers:** Henrico Dolfing, "How REVLON Got Sued by Its Own Shareholders Because of a Failed SAP Implementation," Henrico Dolfing website, August 2019, https://www.henricodolfing.com/2019/08/case-study-revlon-sued-because-sap-implementation.html?m=1.

58 **Revlon reported a $294.2 million loss:** previous_toolbox_user, "When REVLON Changed ERP but Should Have Perhaps Settled for Simply Changing Its Lipstick," Spiceworks website, June 2, 2019, https://community.spiceworks.com/topic/2454356-when-revlon-changed-erp-but-should-have-perhaps-settled-for-simply-changing-its-lipstick.

Chapter 4

59 **Amazon spent four years (and more than $100 million) on the Fire Phone it released in 2014:** Catherine Clifford, "Jeff Bezos to Exec After Product Totally Flopped: 'You Can't, for One Minute, Feel Bad,'" CNBC, May 22, 2020, https://www.cnbc.com/amp/2020/05/22/jeff-bezos-why-you-cant-feel-bad-about-failure.html.

59 **"You can't, for one minute, feel bad about the Fire Phone. Promise me you won't lose a minute of sleep":** Jason Aten, "Jeff Bezos' Biggest Failure at Amazon Is Easily His Biggest Success," *Inc Australia*, February 2021, https://www.inc-aus.com/jason-aten/jeff-bezos-biggest-failure-at-amazon-is-easily-his-biggest-success.html.

59 **the failure spawned a dream come true: the voice recognition software that eventually resulted in Echo:** Lauren Goode, "Amazon's Smartphone Flop Was the Best Thing That Happened to Alexa / Alexa, Are You Too Good for a Smartphone?" The Verge, March 3, 2016, https://www.theverge.com/2016/3/3/11157394/amazon-alexa-fire-phone-failure-echo-success-smart-home.

61 **The queen and drones who produce up to two thousand eggs per day during a queen's two- to three-year lifespan:** "The Honey Bee Queen," Buzz About Bees, updated May 5, 2023, https://www.buzzaboutbees.net/honey-bee-queen.html.

61 **twelve-day-old bees who have developed the wax glands:** Clarence Collision, "A Closer Look: Beeswax, Wax Glands," Bee Culture, March 31, 2015, https://www.beeculture.com/a-closer-look-beeswax-wax-glands/.

61 **push the current queen to the entrance of the hive:** "The Behaviour of Honey Bees Preparing to Swarm," Arnia website, October 2021, https://www.arnia.co/post/the-behaviour-of-honey-bees-preparing-to-swarm.

61 **Several hundred bees who carry out home inspections . . . :** "Guide to bee swarming," Bees4Life, n.d., https://bees4life.org/bee-extinction/solutions/sustainable-beekeeping/swarming.

61 **Bees who keep the cluster's core temperature at 35°C/95°F:** Thomas D. Seeley, *Honeybee Democracy*, Princeton University Press, 2011.

62 **Amazon's "Two Pizza" Operating Model . . . :** Alex Hern, "The Two-Pizza Rule and the Secret of Amazon's Success," *The Guardian*, April 24, 2018, https://amp.theguardian.com/technology/2018/apr/24/the-two-pizza-rule-and-the-secret-of-amazons-success.

62 **Amazon's structure appears highly centralized, with a group of senior executives (the S Team) reporting to the CEO . . . :** Gennaro Cuofano, "Amazon Organizational Structure in a Nutshell," Four Week MBA, October 23, 2023, https://fourweekmba.com/amazon-organizational-structure/.

62 **"Customers would love a new gadget. Let's take up our role as Entrepreneurs to make it happen" . . . :** Anna Papadopoulos, "World's Most Influential and Innovative Companies, 2023," *CEO World Magazine*, March 17, 2023, https://ceoworld.biz/2023/03/17/worlds-most-influential-and-innovative-companies-2023/.

62 **Apple's "Experts Rule" Operating Model:** Joel M. Podolny and Morten T. Hansen, "How Apple Is Organized for Innovation: It's About Experts Leading Experts," *Harvard Business Review*, November–December 2020, https://www.apple.com/jobs/pdf/HBR_How_Apple_Is_Organized_For_Innovation-4.pdf.

63 **Business unit general managers competed with each other:** Jason Aten, "This Was Steve Jobs's Most Important Observation When He Returned to Apple. It Changed Everything," *Inc Australia*, May 2021, https://www.inc-aus.com/jason-aten/this-was-steve-jobs-most-important-observation-when-he-returned-to-apple-it-changed-everything.html.

63 **who began working on a string of astounding innovations that changed the shape of the industry . . . :** "The Evolution of the iPhone Camera: From 6 to 12 Pro," *GStyle Magazine*, August 9, 2021, https://gstylemag.com/2021/08/09/the-evolution-of-the-iphone-camera-from-6-to-12-pro/.

63 **No wonder Apple was voted by its peers as the Most Admired Company sixteen years in a row:** "World's Most Admired Companies," *Fortune*, February 2023, https://fortune.com/ranking/worlds-most-admired-companies/.

63 **a cartoonist had depicted Microsoft as a jumble of warring factions:** "Satya Nadella Employed a 'Growth Mindset' to Overhaul Microsoft's Cutthroat Culture and Turn It into a Trillion-Dollar Company—Here's How He Did It," *Business Insider*, March 7, 2020, https://www.businessinsider.com/microsoft-ceo-satya-nadella-company-culture-shift-growth-mindset-2020-3?amp.

63 **Four years after taking over as CEO, Nadella installed a new operating model:** Vivek Wadhwa, Ismail Amla, and Alex Salkever, "How Microsoft Made the Stunning Transformation from Evil Empire to Cool Kid," *Fortune*, December 21, 2021, https://fortune.com/2021/12/21/microsoft-cultural-transformation-book-excerpt-satya-nadella/amp/.

64 **As a result, Microsoft achieved an increase in market capitalization from roughly $300 billion in 2014:** Satya Nadella, *Hit Refresh: The Quest to Rediscover Microsoft's Soul and Imagine a Better Future for Everyone* (Harper Business, 2017).

64 **to about $2.32 trillion by 2023, becoming the second most valuable company in the world (behind Apple):** BCTA, Largest Companies by Market Cap, https://companiesmarketcap.com.

65 **In 2006, Alan Mulally, an aeronautical engineer by training:** Michael Dostefano, "Alan Mulally: The Man Who Saved Ford," Korn Ferry Insights, 2021, https://www.kornferry.com/insights/briefings-magazine/issue-20/alan-mulally-man-who-saved-ford.

65 **Ford had recently posted its biggest annual loss in its 103-year history:** "Leading in the 21st Century: An Interview with Ford's Alan Mulally," McKinsey Insights, November 1, 2013, https://www.mckinsey.com/business-functions/strategy-and-corporate-finance/our-insights/leading-in-the-21st-century-an-interview-with-fords-alan-mulally.

66 **he commenced weekly review meetings with his executive team:** Alex Taylor III, "Fixing Up Ford," CNN Money, May 12, 2009, https://money.cnn.com/2009/05/11/news/companies/mulally_ford.fortune/.

66 **In 2018, Daniel Ek and Martin Lorentzon, announced that the world's largest music streamer planned to move into podcasting:** Aakash Gupta, "How Spotify Stole Podcasts from Apple," *Gupta Blog*, December 14, 2021, https://www.aakashg.com/2021/12/14/spotify-podcasts-apple/.

67 **investing $500 million in a string of podcast companies:** Anna Nicolaou and Andrew Edgecliffe-Johnson, "Spotify Makes $500m Splurge on Podcast Start-Ups," *Financial Times*, February 6, 2019, https://www.ft.com/content/42fb0fb4-2a0c-11e9-88a4-c32129756dd8.

67 **Spotify's teams concentrated on creating new offerings across the whole ecosystem:** Howard Yu, "Two Charts That Explain How Apple Loses to Spotify in Podcasts," *Forbes*, September 30, 2021, https://www.forbes.com/sites/howardhyu/2021/09/30/two-charts-that-explain-how-apple-loses-to-spotify-in-podcasts/?sh=3957f5c5649c.

67 **By 2021 the company had surpassed $1.2 billion in yearly ad revenue:** Matthew Johnston, "How Spotify Makes Money," Investopedia, January 4, 2023, https://www.investopedia.com/articles/investing/120314/spotify-makes-internet-music-make-money.asp.

68 **"I have not failed ten thousand times":** Caroline Castrillon, "Why Failure Leads to Career Success," *Forbes*, November 20, 2019, https://www.forbes.com/sites/carolinecastrillon/2019/11/20/why-failure-leads-to-career-success/?sh=5a634fc77578.

68 **Launched in 2013 with the mission to help people get healthier:** Biz Carson, "The $700 'Keurig for Juice' Is Too Expensive to Solve a Very Real Problem," *Business Insider*, March 31, 2016, https://www.businessinsider.com/juicero-fails-to-solve-for-a-very-real-problem-2016-3.

68 **Eager investors had injected $120 million into the company:** Carl Jonson, "10 Recent Tech Fails and Disasters," List Verse, January 30, 2022, https://listverse.com/2022/01/30/10-recent-tech-fails-and-disasters/.

68 **a *Bloomberg* reporter hand squeezing a fruit packet to obtain a full glass of juice:** Sam Levin, "Squeezed Out: Widely Mocked Startup Juicero Is Shutting Down," *The Guardian*, September 1, 2017, https://amp.theguardian.com/technology/2017/sep/01/juicero-silicon-valley-shutting-down.

69 **he appeared onstage with Microsoft's Bill Gates:** Tim Stevens, "Alan Mulally: The CEO Who Mortgaged Ford's Legacy for Tech's Sake," CNET, May 1, 2014, https://www.cnet.com/roadshow/news/alan-mulally-the-ceo-who-mortgaged-fords-legacy-for-techs-sake/.

69 **"an exciting, viable Ford delivering profitable growth for all":** Michael Dostefano, "Alan Mulally: The Man Who Saved Ford."

70 **rebooting two of its most iconic cars, the Mustang and F-Series:** Tim Stevens, "Alan Mulally: The CEO Who Mortgaged Ford's Legacy for Tech's Sake."

70 **Target's new CEO, Brian Cornell, pulled the plug only two years into the retailer's disastrous foray into Canada:** Hayley Peterson, "5 Reasons Target Failed in Canada," *Business Insider*, January 15, 2015, https://www.businessinsider.com/why-target-canada-failed-2015-1?amp.

70 **Tony Fisher, was promising investors that within two years of a rapid ramp-up to one hundred–plus stores the Canadian operation would be producing huge profits:** Henrico Dolfing, "The 2.5 Billion Cross-Border Expansion Mistake by Target," Henrico Dolfing case studies, September 2019, https://www.henricodolfing.com/2019/09/case-study-target-canada-failure.html?m=1.

71 **As one former employee later said, "That was the biggest mistake we could have made":** Joe Castaldo, "The Last Days of Target: The Untold Tale of Target Canada's Difficult Birth, Tough Life and Brutal Death," Canadian Business, January 1, 2016, https://archive.canadianbusiness.com/the-last-days-of-target-canada/.

71 **Target's work on its supply chain was not keeping pace with new store openings:** Phil Wahba, "Why Target Failed in Canada," *Fortune*, January 15, 2015, https://fortune.com/2015/01/15/target-canada-fail/amp/.

71 **in January 2015, Target announced that it would exit the Canadian market:** Sid Bhandari, "Target's Failed Entry in to Canada," Harvard Business School Digital Initiative, December 8, 2015, https://digital.hbs.edu/platform-rctom/submission/targets-failed-entry-in-to-canada/.

72 **"To those who say they've seen it all, I say, buckle your seat belt . . .":** Samuel Gibbs, "Samsung's $2,000 Galaxy Fold Changes the Smartphone Game," *The Guardian*, February 21, 2019, https://amp.theguardian.com/technology/2019/feb/21/samsungs-2000-galaxy-fold-finally-changes-the-smartphone-game.

72 **Despite a price tag of $1,980:** Shona Ghosh, "The $1,980 Galaxy Fold Will Launch in 2 Months but Samsung Doesn't Seem Ready to Actually Show It to

Anyone Yet," *Business Insider*, February 21, 2019, https://www.businessinsider.com/samsung-galaxy-fold-1980-no-demo-hands-on-unpacked-2019-2?amp.

72 **he conceded that Samsung's most exciting development in years was a car wreck:** Gordon Kelly, "Samsung Confirms Sudden Galaxy Fold Smartphone Cancellation," *Forbes*, May 7, 2019, https://www.forbes.com/sites/gordonkelly/2019/05/07/samsung-galaxy-fold-upgrade-galaxy-note-10-s10-plus/?sh=283a7d352900.

72 **In its race with Chinese vendor Huawei Technologies Co.:** Deidre Richardson, "The Failed Galaxy Fold Cost AT&T Around $77 Million," Android Headlines, July 3, 2019, https://www.androidheadlines.com/2019/07/samsung-galaxy-fold-att-cost-astronomical.html/amp.

72 **As DJ Koh later admitted, "I pushed it through before it was ready":** Deidre Richardson, "Samsung CEO Admits to Rushing Galaxy Fold," Android Headlines, July 1, 2019, https://www.androidheadlines.com/2019/07/samsung-ceo-smartphones-galaxyfold.html.

72 **Tarsus Distribution, the South African IT supplier:** "How Tarsus Distribution Went from RPA Naysayers to RPA Evangelists," case study, UiPath, 2021, https://www.uipath.com/resources/automation-case-studies/tarsus-distribution.

73 **Researchers in Microsoft's Human Factors Lab:** Bruce Rogers, "Our Brains Need Breaks from Virtual Meetings," *Forbes*, April 20, 2021, https://www.forbes.com/sites/brucerogers/2021/04/20/our-brains-need-breaks-from-virtual-meetings/?sh=7649041921e9.

74 **On the morning of November 21, 1980, the Texaco team began drilling:** Ken Jennings, "How Louisiana's Lake Peigneur Became 200 Feet Deep in an Instant," Conde Nast Traveler, July 11, 2016, https://www.cntraveler.com/stories/2016-07-11/how-louisianas-lake-peigneur-became-200-feet-deep-in-an-instant#:~:text=It%20seems%20their%20drill%20had,that%20of%20a%20fire%20hydrant.

75 **When searching for a new home, a scout spends nearly an hour closely examining each potential homesite:** Thomas Seeley, *The Lives of Bees: The Untold Story of the Honey Bee in the Wild* (Princeton University Press, 2019).

75 **NASA learned this lesson the hard way when it lost the $125 million Mars Climate Orbiter (MCO):** Robin Lloyd, "Metric Mishap Caused Loss of NASA Orbiter," CNN, September 30, 1999, http://edition.cnn.com/TECH/space/9909/30/mars.metric.02/.

76 **At Amazon, Jeff Bezos measured everything:** David, Selinger, "Data Driven: What Amazon's Jeff Bezos Taught Me About Running a Company," *Entrepreneur*, September 11, 2014, https://www.entrepreneur.com/business-news/data-driven-what-amazons-jeff-bezos-taught-me-about/237326.

Chapter 5

77 **Scout bees leave the staging area to search for promising real estate:** Thomas Seeley, *The Lives of Bees: The Untold Story of the Honey Bee in the Wild.*

77 **Although the debacle happened more than twenty-five years ago it still holds a spot on *Time* magazine's list of the top ten marketing failures:** Thomas C. Frohlich, "The 10 Worst Product Fails of All Time," *Time*, March 6, 2014, https://time.com/13549/the-10-worst-product-fails-of-all-time/.

78 **Some of the bottlers in the company who tasted the new drink didn't much care for it:** D. B. Kelly, "Why Crystal Pepsi Was a Flop," Mashed, September 12, 2018, https://www.mashed.com/111261/crystal-pepsi-flop/.

78 **Crystal Pepsi launched in a splashy ad during the 1993 Super Bowl:** Kyle Murray, "Enabling Innovation: Lessons from Crystal Pepsi," The Conversation, October 17, 2017, https://theconversation.com/amp/enabling-innovation-lessons-from-crystal-pepsi-84967.

78 **"importance of letting go of my confident position momentarily so I could actively listen to the wisdom offered by those around me":** David Novak, "Learn from My Crystal Pepsi Mistake," David Novak Leadership, 2021, https://davidnovakleadership.com/blog/learn-from-my-crystal-pepsi-mistake/.

78 **James Dyson . . . decided to build a better hair dryer:** "Rethinking the Hair Dryer," Dyson website, 2023, https://www.lb.dyson.com/en-LB/haircare/supersonic/engineering-story.aspx.

79 **Four years and $71 million later:** Nick Skillicorn, "Dyson's Newest Innovation: An Ultra-Powerful $400 Hairdryer," Idea to value, April 2016, https://www.ideatovalue.com/inno/nickskillicorn/2016/04/dysons-newest-innovation-ultra-powerful-hairdryer/.

79 **By 2017 the product had become a bestseller in the UK:** Tefi Alonso, "How Dyson's Innovation Became Its Key to Success," Strategy Factory by Cascade, February 22, 2023, https://www.cascade.app/strategy-factory/studies/dyson-strategy-study.

79 **made him one of the wealthiest businessmen in Britain, with a net worth of $23 billion:** "Sir James Dyson Net Worth—Sunday Times Rich List 2022," *Sunday Times*, May 2022.

80 **an employee at the Italian carrier made one of the most expensive typos ever:** Kelly Bryant, "15 Most Expensive Mistakes Ever Made," *Readers Digest*, updated December 23, 2022, https://www.rd.com/list/most-expensive-mistakes-ever-made/.

81 **London's mayor Boris Johnson made the Garden Bridge his pet project:** Rowan Moore, "Garden Bridge Project Is a Landmark of the Post-Truth Era," *The Guardian*, April 15, 2017, https://www.theguardian.com/commentisfree/2017/apr/15/garden-bridge-project-is-a-landmark-of-the-post-truth-era.

81 **It was "utter folly":** "Failed London Garden Bridge Project Cost £53m," BBC, February 13, 2019, https://www.bbc.co.uk/news/uk-england-london-47228698.

82 **Elon Musk . . . botched the announcement that Tesla would be developing a humanoid robot dubbed Optimus:** Imogen Donovan, "Elon Musk's New Tesla Robot Is Freaking Everybody Out," Gaming Bible, August 23, 2021, https://www.gamingbible.com/news/games-technology-elon-musks-new-tesla-robot-is-freaking-everybody-out-20210823.amp.html.

82 **"Obviously that was not real . . .":** Joshua Dowling, "Tesla Mocked After Unveiling a 'Robot' That Was a Human in a Lycra Suit," Drive, August 23, 2021, https://www.drive.com.au/news/tesla-mocked-after-unveiling-a-robot-that-was-a-human-in-a-lycra-suit/.

82 **UK's 2002 National Health Service (NHS) IT project:** Alistair Maughan, "Six Reasons Why the NHS National Programme for IT Failed," *Computer Weekly*, September 13, 2010, https://www.computerweekly.com/opinion/Six-reasons-why-the-NHS-National-Programme-for-IT-failed?amp=1.

82 **"The Department could have avoided some of the pitfalls":** "The NHS IT Nightmare," editorial, *The Lancet*, August 2011, https://www.thelancet.com/journals/lancet/article/PIIS0140-6736(11)61275-0/fulltext.

83 **Finally abandoned in 2010, the NHS patient record system had frittered away:** Henrico Dolfing, "The £10 Billion IT Disaster at the NHS," Henrico Dolfing website, January 2019, https://www.henricodolfing.com/2019/01/case-study-10-billion-it-disaster.html?m=1.

83 **the Melbourne-based international paint company DuluxGroup:** My knowledge of DuluxGroup comes from my role as a member of the DuluxGroup Executive team and executive general manager of People, Culture & Change (since 2016).

83 **the fourth-biggest paint company in the world purchased DuluxGroup for $3.8 billion:** Simon Evans, "Dulux Agrees to Nippon Paints' $3.8b Takeover," *Australian Financial Review*, April 17, 2019, https://www.afr.com/companies/manufacturing/nippon-paints-lobs-3-8b-takeover-bid-for-dulux-20190417-p51ew3.

84 **Houlihan had doubled the size of DuluxGroup with two acquisitions:** "Interview: 'We Are Leveraging the High Growth Potential of the Paint Market,'" European Coatings, December 7, 2021, https://www.european-coatings.com/articles/2021/12/interview-we-leveraging-the-high-growth-potential-of-the-paint-market.

84 **Incyte, a Delaware-based global biopharmaceutical company, offers a good example of this approach:** "Incyte: A Biopharmaceutical Company with Brains and Heart," *Science*/AAAS Custom Publishing Office, February 2022, https://www.science.org/content/article/incyte-biopharmaceutical-company-brains-and-heart.

85 **winning recognition as one of the world's most innovative companies by *Forbes* magazine:** "Forbes Releases Eighth Annual List of the World's Most Innovative Companies," *Forbes*, May 2018, https://www.forbes.com/sites/forbespr/2018/05/29/forbes-releases-eighth-annual-list-of-the-worlds-most-innovative-companies/amp/.

85 **Frederick Taylor, the father of scientific management:** "Frederick Winslow Taylor," British Library, 2023, https://www.bl.uk/people/frederick-winslow-taylor.

85 **AmorePacific, the Korean beauty products company, engineered a revolution:** "Cushion: How a Stamp Made a Global Impact on Women's Beauty," AmorePacific R&D, 2023, https://www.apgroup.com/my/en/our-values/rnd/beauty-research-innovation/beauty-research-innovation-8.html.

85 **borrow a technique used by Korean parking attendants:** Tony Sekulich, "How AmorePacific Became the Hottest Name in Cosmetics Through Innovation," *Tharawat Magazine*, 2017, https://www.tharawat-magazine.com/grow/amorepacific-cosmetics-innovation/.

85 **They conducted thirty-six hundred tests on two hundred different types of sponges:** Coco Park, "Mother of All (Beauty) Invention: The Story Behind the Cushion Compact," Beauty Tap, April 9, 2018, https://beautytap.com/2018/04/cushion-compact.

86 **By 2015 a user was buying a Cushion Compact every second around the world:** Gabey Goh, "Case Study: How AmorePacific Created Space for Cushion," Campaign, March 30, 2016, https://www.campaignasia.com/article/case-study-how-amorepacific-created-space-for-cushion/406678.

86 **AmorePacific debuted at number twenty-eight on *Forbes*'s annual list of the World's Most Innovative Companies:** Art, "5 Surprising Things You Never Knew About Cushion Foundations," *Female Magazine*, December 22, 2016, https://www.femalemag.com.sg/beauty/5-surprising-things-never-knew-cushion-foundations/.

86 **At that point the firm's revenue had increased 20 percent over the previous year:** Grace Chung, "How South Korea's AmorePacific Became One of the World's Most Innovative Companies," *Forbes*, August 19, 2015, https://www.forbes.com/sites/gracechung/2015/08/19/how-south-koreas-amorepacific-became-one-of-the-worlds-most-innovative-companies/?sh=10d405002b2b.

86 **CEO Nick Grayston of The Warehouse Group (TWG) . . . :** Heather McIlvaine, "The Warehouse Group Fundamentally Changes Its Leadership Structure," Inside Retail, February 4, 2020, https://insideretail.co.nz/2020/02/04/the-warehouse-group-fundamentally-changes-its-leadership-structure/.

87 **partnered with the global consulting firm McKinsey:** "How a Major New Zealand Retailer Reinvented Itself Around Customer Satisfaction," Impact Story, McKinsey Insights, January 31, 2023, https://www.mckinsey.com/capabilities/rts/how-we-help-clients/how-a-major-new-zealand-retailer-reinvented-itself-around-customer-satisfaction.

89 **Dave, a Product Owner in the Growth & Conversion squad:** "Demonstrating Our Agile Behaviours," The Warehouse Group website, December 2020.

89 **In 2021 the company announced a record result:** "The Warehouse Group FY21 Annual Result Announcement," TWG media announcement, September 2021, https://www

.thewarehousegroup.co.nz/application/files/7616/3285/7912/3._Media_Release_The_Warehouse_Group_FY21_annual_result_announcement_FINAL.pdf.

89 **In the first half of 2022, TWG's market share grew . . . :** "How a Major New Zealand Retailer Reinvented Itself Around Customer Satisfaction," McKinsey & Company website. Jan 2023. McKinsey.com. https://www.mckinsey.com/capabilities/rts/how-we-help-clients/how-a-major-new-zealand-retailer-reinvented-itself-around-customer-satisfaction#.

89 **Vacationing in Thailand some years back, Mateschitz sampled a local drink:** "Red Bull Success Story: From Truck Driver Drink to Market Leader," Brand Riddle, May 2023, https://brandriddle.com/redbull-success-story/.

89 **Produced in the tiny village of Fuschl in the Austrian Alps:** "About Red Bull," *Forbes*, 2019, https://www.forbes.com/companies/red-bull/?sh=6056a55661ce.

89 **In the UK, for instance, Mateschitz appointed Harry Drnec . . . :** Nitin Pangarkar and Mohit Agarwal, "The Wind Behind Red Bull's Wings," *Forbes*, June 24, 2013, https://www.forbes.com/sites/forbesasia/2013/06/24/the-wind-behind-red-bulls-wings/amp/.

90 **dances with gusto, making two hundred circuits along the tree branch:** Carl Zimmer, "The Secret Life of Bees," *The Smithsonian*, March 2012, https://carlzimmer.com/the-secret-life-of-bees-271/.

90 **"the atmosphere surrounding the world championships will be fantastic":** Sean Ingle, "Dire in Doha: World Championships 'Catastrophe' Leaves Athletics Reeling," *The Guardian*, September 30, 2019, https://amp.theguardian.com/sport/2019/sep/30/doha-world-athletics-championships-crowds-iaaf.

91 **runner Shelly-Ann Fraser-Pryce crossed the finish first:** Richard Williams, "Doha's Empty Seats Tell Tale of Corruption, Warped Priorities and Vested Interests," *The Guardian*, September 30, 2019, https://amp.theguardian.com/sport/blog/2019/sep/30/doha-empty-seats-iaaf-sellout-world-athletics-championships.

91 **The previous championship event held in London:** Sean Ingle, "'London 2017 Has Given Athletics the Opportunity to Believe Again' Claim Organisers," *The Guardian*, August 14, 2017, https://amp.theguardian.com/sport/2017/aug/14/london-2017-world-athletics-championships-bolt-farah-review.

91 **Zoom's founder had created a "frictionless" tool:** "Our Mission: Make Communications Frictionless," Zoom website, December 2019, https://explore.zoom.us/docs/doc/Zoom_Platform_and_Company.pdf.

91 **Eric Yuan, the son of geology engineers in China:** Alex Konrad, "Zoom, Zoom, Zoom! The Exclusive Inside Story of the New Billionaire Behind Tech's Hottest IPO," *Forbes*, April 4, 2019, https://www.forbes.com/sites/alexkonrad/2019/04/19/zoom-zoom-zoom-the-exclusive-inside-story-of-the-new-billionaire-behind-techs-hottest-ipo/?sh=546bf0624af1.

91 **Yuan joined Cisco to manage the firm's newly acquired WebEx engineering group:** Kelly S. Murphy, "Zoom's Massive 'Overnight Success' Actually Took Nine Years," CNN Business, March 27, 2020, https://amp.cnn.com/cnn/2020/03/27/tech/zoom-app-coronavirus/index.html.

92 **In 2022, Zoom grew 55 percent over the prior year:** "Zoom Video Communications Reports Fourth Quarter and Fiscal Year 2022 Financial Results," Zoom Press Release, February 2022, https://investors.zoom.us/news-releases/news-release-details/zoom-video-communications-reports-fourth-quarter-and-fiscal-1.

93 **Absolut created the second bestselling vodka in the world:** "The 20 Best Selling Vodka Brands in the World in 2022," Vine Pair, July 2022, https://vinepair.com/articles/the-20-best-selling-vodka-brands/.

93 **In the 1970s, Absolut CEO Lars Lindmark worked with legendary marketer Gunnar Broman:** "The Story of the Absolut Bottle and Brand," Absolut website, 2021, https://www.theabsolutcompany.com/legacy/post/lo-smith-english/the-story-of-the-absolut-bottle-and-brand/.

93 **It visually drove home the message broadcast in the company's ads:** Aaron Goldfarb, "Absolut Obsessive: 30 Years After the Campaign Launched, Passion for Collecting Remains," Vine Pair, November 19, 2021, https://vinepair.com/articles/absolut-vodka-ad-collectors/.

93 **More than fifteen hundred versions of the ad repeated the company's message over the next twenty-five years**: Rebecca Greenfield, "The Evolution of Absolut Vodka's Advertising Strategy," *Fast Company*, July 9, 2014, https://www.fastcompany.com/3032598/the-evolution-of-absolut-vodkas-advertising-strategy.

Chapter 6

95 **Security Guards cluster around the queen to keep her safe and warm:** Staff at Beekeepers' Society of South Australia Inc. (October 2021). "About Bee Swarming." Bees website. https://bees.org.au/swarms#:~:text=Once%20the%20swarm%20of%20bees,for%20a%20more%20permanent%20home.

100 **When the queen senses an overcrowded hive, she sends out pheromone signals:** "Queen Pheromones," *Encyclopedia of Animal Behavior*, second edition (2010), Science Direct, https://www.sciencedirect.com/topics/agricultural-and-biological-sciences/queen-pheromones.

100 **something that German retailer Lidl failed to do during its 2018 systems upgrade:** Cliff Saran, "Lidl Dumps €500m SAP Project," *Computer Weekly*, August 16, 2018, https://www.computerweekly.com/news/252446965/Lidl-dumps-500m-SAP-project.

100 **Lidl opened its first discount store in 1973 . . . :** "Lidl to Keep Investing After Sales Rose in 2018," Reuters, May 13, 2019, https://www.reuters.com/article/us-lidl-results-idUKKCN1SJ1LW.

101 **The project (codenamed "eLWIS," pronounced Elvis) . . . :** "Lidl Cancels SAP Introduction Having Sunk €500 Million Into It," Consultancy UK, August 2018, https://www.consultancy.uk/news/amp/18243/lidl-cancels-sap-introduction-having-sunk-500-million-into-it.

101 **management signed off on a system that did not meet the organization's needs . . . :** Henrico Dolfing, "Lidl's £500 Million SAP Debacle," Henrico Dolfing

website, May 2020, https://www.henricodolfing.com/2020/05/case-study-lidl-sap-debacle.html?m=1.

105 **Queensland Health found during its $6.19 million partnership with IBM Australia:** Henrico Dolfing, "The Payroll System That Cost Queensland Health AU$1.25 Billion," Henrico Dolfing website, May 2020, Case Study 9: The Payroll System That Cost Queensland Health AU$1.25 Billion.

105 **Queensland Health's project failed so miserably:** Mark Ludlow, "IT Disasters Now Part of Modern Life," *Australian Financial Review*, December 21, 2016, https://www.afr.com/technology/it-disasters-now-part-of-modern-life-20160628-gptyw6.

106 **the Atlanta-based credit reporting agency suffered a massive data breach in 2017:** Liz Moyer, "Equifax CEO Suddenly 'Retires' Following an Epic Data Breach Affecting Up to 143 Million People," CNBC, September 26, 2017, https://www.cnbc.com/amp/2017/09/26/equifax-ceo-retires-following-an-epic-data-breach-affecting-143-million-people.html.

106 **Hackers had gained access to company files that contained the personal data of 56 percent of the American population:** Josh Fruhlinger, "Equifax Data Breach FAQ: What Happened, Who Was Affected, What Was the Impact?" CSO, February 12, 2020, https://www.google.com.au/amp/s/www.csoonline.com/article/3444488/equifax-data-breach-faq-what-happened-who-was-affected-what-was-the-impact.amp.html.

109 **Steve Jobs, the iconic leader who cofounded Apple:** Matthew Jenkin, "The Death of the Micromanager," Magazine US, 2014, https://www.regus.com/work-us/en-us/the-death-of-the-micromanager/.

109 **he micromanaged everything, including the landscapers:** Ira Kalb, "3 Ways Micromanagers Can Destroy a Company," *Business Insider*, July 7, 2014, https://www.businessinsider.com/how-micromanagers-destroy-your-business-2014-7?amp.

110 **VW's leaders knew they needed to improve the emissions performance of their diesel engines:** Russell Hotten, "Volkswagen: The Scandal Explained," BBC, December 10, 2015, https://www.google.com.au/amp/s/www.bbc.com/news/business-34324772.amp.

110 **But it turned out that VW had perpetrated an elaborate fraud:** Brian Benchoff, "Ethics in Engineering: Volkswagen's Diesel Fiasco," Hackaday, September 23, 2015, https://hackaday.com/2015/09/23/ethics-in-engineering-volkswagens-diesel-fiasco/.

111 **VW had proudly proclaimed its undying commitment to "Taking Responsibility":** Patrick Stahler, "We 'Totally Screwed Up': Values and Behaviors in Volkswagen Business Model," Business Model Innovation, September 22, 2015, https://blog.business-model-innovation.com/2015/09/values-and-behaviors-in-volkswagen-business-model/.

111 **poisoning the planet with pollutant gases up to forty times the standard:** Enrique Dans, "Volkswagen and the Failure of Corporate Social Responsibility," *Forbes*, September 27, 2015, https://www.google.com.au/amp/s/www.forbes

.com/sites/enriquedans/2015/09/27/volkswagen-and-the-failure-of-corporate-social-responsibility/amp/.

111 **VW's stock lost nearly a third of its value:** C.R./J.F., "Why Volkswagen's Share Price Has Fallen So Far: An $18 Billion Fine Is Not the Carmaker's Only Worry," *The Economist*, September 21, 2015, https://www.economist.com/news/2015/09/21/why-volkswagens-share-price-has-fallen-so-far.

111 **the costs associated with Volkswagen's elaborate fraud had soared to $35 billion:** Michael Toebe, "Critical Lessons from the Volkswagen Scandal. Ethical Failings Precipitated the Auto Giant's Reputation Crisis," Corporate Compoliance Insights (CCI), September 11, 2020, https://www.corporatecomplianceinsights.com/lessons-volkswagen-scandal-ethical-failings/.

111 **it advertised its dedication to "Integrity: We do what is right":** Will Scott, "'Compassion for Patients.' 'We Do What Is Right.' No Purdue Pharma, You Don't!" Culture Czars, 2020, https://www.cultureczars.com/company-culture-ideas-blog/perduepharma.

112 **Andrew Kolodny, codirector of the Opioid Policy Research Collaborative:** Dearbail Jordan, "Is This America's Most Hated Family?" March 22, 2019, BBC News, https://www.bbc.com/news/business-47660040.amp.

112 **In 2020, Purdue Pharma pleaded guilty to criminal charges . . .":** N. Sherman, "Purdue Pharma to Plead Guilty in $8bn Opioid Settlement," October 2020, BBC News, https://www.bbc.com/news/business-54636002.

113 **according to the Centers for Disease Control and Prevention . . . :** Jonathan H. Marks, "Lessons from Corporate Influence in the Opioid Epidemic: Toward a Norm of Separation," *Bioethical Inquiry* 17 (2020): 173–189, https://doi.org/10.1007/s11673-020-09982-x.

Chapter 7

115 **The colony can only survive for about three days:** Phyllis Styles, "It's Swarm Season: Honey Bees Are House Hunting," AppState, April 25, 2019, https://sustain.appstate.edu/news/id/swarm-season.

115 **The bees mobilize the colony by headbutting each other and emitting tiny high-pitched beeping sounds:** E. Yong, "How Headbutts and Dances Give Bees a Hive Mind," *Discover*, December 8, 2011, https://www.discovermagazine.com/planet-earth/how-headbutts-and-dances-give-bees-a-hive-mind.

116 **Suddenly, at 11:00 p.m. on July 6, 1988, an explosion rocks the Piper Alpha rig:** Terry Macalister, "Piper Alpha Disaster: How 167 Oil Rig Workers Died," *The Guardian*, July 4, 2013, https://amp.theguardian.com/business/2013/jul/04/piper-alpha-disaster-167-oil-rig.

116 **Now picture two workers on the rig locking themselves in a room:** Bernard Ross and Claire Segal, *The Strategy Workout* (Financial Times/Pearson, 2015).

118 **Irish folklore tells how bees can so easily take offense:** "The Folklore and Traditions of the Irish Hedgerow," *Irish Hedgerows Weekly*, n.d., http://irishhedgerows.weebly.com/folklore.html.

119 **Back in 2020, Barclays, the UK bank, decided to install spyware on staff computers:** Mark Murphy, "Barclays Forced to Stop 'Big Brother' Employee Tracking System After Backlash," *Forbes*, February 21, 2020, https://www.forbes.com/sites/markmurphy/2020/02/21/barclays-forced-to-stop-big-brother-employee-tracking-system-after-backlash/?sh=590c79c66ac1.

119 **leaked details of the fiasco to the English newspaper** ***City A.M.*****:** Andy Silvester, "Exclusive: Barclays Installs Big Brother–Style Spyware on Employees' Computers," *City A.M.*, February 19, 2020, https://www.cityam.com/exclusive-barclays-installs-big-brother-style-spyware-on-employees-computers/.

119 **The very next day, Barclays scrapped the spyware:** Anna Menin, "Barclays Scraps Big Brother–Style Spyware on Staff Computers," *City A.M.*, February 20, 2020, https://www.cityam.com/breaking-barclays-scraps-spyware-on-staff-computers/.

120 **In 2008, behavioral economists Cass Sunstein and Richard Thaler introduced the concept of nudging to the world:** Cass Sunstein and Richard Thaler, *Nudge: Improving Decisions About Health, Wealth, and Happiness* (Penguin Books, 2008).

120 **he created a Behavioral Insights Team or "nudge unit":** Jill Rutter, "Nudge Unit," Institute for Government UK, March 11, 2020, https://www.instituteforgovernment.org.uk/article/explainer/nudge-unit.

120 **An early experiment set a goal of increasing the rate of organ donation in Wales:** "Wales Leading the Way on Organ Donation," Press Release, Welsh Government website, July 2019, https://www.gov.wales/wales-leading-way-organ-donation.

120 **Making organ donation the default option led to a surge in the consent rate:** "'Opt-Out Organ Donation Scheme Has Transformed Lives'—Celebrates Health Minister on Fifth Anniversary of Scheme's Introduction," Press Release, Welsh Government website, July 2019, https://gov.wales/opt-out-organ-donation-scheme-has-transformed-lives-celebrates-health-minister-fifth-anniversary.

120 **They can also fix problems as mundane as the messy urinals at Amsterdam's Schiphol Airport:** Christopher Ingraham, "What's a Urinal Fly, and What Does It Have to Do with Winning a Nobel Prize?" *Washington Post*, October 9, 2017, https://www.washingtonpost.com/news/wonk/wp/2017/10/09/whats-a-urinal-fly-and-what-does-it-have-to-with-winning-a-nobel-prize/.

120 **Precise aiming reduced spillage by 80 percent and cleaning costs by an estimated 20 percent:** Blake Evans-Pritchard, "Aiming to Reduce Cleaning Costs," Works That Work, Winter 2013, https://worksthatwork.com/1/urinal-fly.

121 **When Iceland's three main commercial banks collapsed in 2008:** Blake Evans-Pritchard, "Aiming to Reduce Cleaning Costs."

121 **New Jersey–based Toys "R" Us:** Angie Basiouny, "What Went Wrong: The Demise of Toys R Us," Knowledge at Wharton, March 14, 2018, https://knowledge.wharton.upenn.edu/podcast/knowledge-at-wharton-podcast/the-demise-of-toys-r-us/.

127 **France's new trains were not fitting into its railway stations:** Peter Weber, "France's 2,000 New Trains Are Too Fat for Its Stations," *The Week*, January 8, 2015, https://theweek.com/speedreads/452986/frances-2000-new-trains-are-fat-stations.

127 **it gave SNCF measurements for its newer, wider railway stations:** Kim Willsher, "French Railway Operator SNCF Orders Hundreds of New Trains That Are Too Big," *The Guardian*, May 21, 2014, https://amp.theguardian.com/world/2014/may/21/french-railway-operator-sncf-orders-trains-too-big.

127 **French Minister for Transport Thierry Mariani to sum up the fiasco with one word:** Rod Sweet, "French Train Operator Orders Trains That Are Too Fat for Stations," Global Constriction Review, May 21, 2014, https://www.globalconstructionreview.com/french-train-operator-orders-trains-are-too-fat-st/.

127 **The mistake proved costly . . . :** "France Buys 2,000 Trains That Are Too Big for Their Platforms," *New York Post*, May 21, 2014, https://nypost.com/2014/05/21/france-buys-2000-trains-that-are-too-big-for-their-platforms/amp/.

128 **Nathan Barry, founder of the email marketing company ConvertKit . . . :** Nathan Barry, "There and Back Again: The Story of Renaming ConvertKit," Nathan Barry website, August 2020, https://nathanbarry.com/rename/.

128 **the apology came:** Nathan Barry, "We Listened. We Learned. We Have a New Appreciation for the Word Seva and We Won't Be Changing Our Name After All. We're Sorry for Our Mistake," ConvertKit, 2020, https://convertkit.com/staying-convertkit.

128 **the company had wasted over half a million dollars on the rebrand:** Disha Gupta, "5 Change Management Strategy Failures to Learn From," WhatFix, August 28, 2020, https://whatfix.com/blog/5-change-management-strategy-failures-to-learn-from/.

132 **they installed new hives in gardens, factory yards, and rooftops:** Alexander Turner, "'Honeybees Are Voracious': Is It Time to Put the Brakes on the Boom in Beekeeping?" *The Guardian*, July 24, 2021, https://amp.theguardian.com/environment/2021/jul/24/this-only-saves-honeybees-the-trouble-with-britains-beekeeping-boom-aoe.

132 **Lorenz called this the "butterfly effect":** James Gleick, *Chaos: Making a New Science* (Viking Penguin, 1987).

133 **Roman mythology tells how sky god Jupiter was so pleased with a gift of honey:** "Roman Myths: Jupiter and the Bee," Mythologian, 2023, https://mythologian.net/roman-myths-jupiter-and-the-bee/.

Chapter 8

135 **Henri Poincaré introduced a mathematical theory called bifurcation:** Richard Blaustein, "Henri Poincare's Legacy for Tipping Points," SAO/NASA Astrophysics Data System, April 2021, https://ui.adsabs.harvard.edu/abs/2021EGUGA..2316427B/abstract.

136 **the collapse of the 158-year-old investment bank Lehman Brothers:** Laura Rodini "What Happened to Lehman Brothers? Why Did It Fail?" *The Street*, updated July 2023, https://www.thestreet.com/markets/lehman-brothers-collapse-14703153.

136 **Malcolm Gladwell . . . bestselling book:** Malcolm Gladwell, *The Tipping Point: How Little Things Can Make a Big Difference* (Little, Brown, 2006).

137 **In January 2019 he launched one of the world's largest networks of Accelerator Labs:** "Accelerator Labs: We Celebrate Grassroots Innovations That Move Us Towards a More Sustainable Planet," UNDP, 2023, https://www.undp.org/acceleratorlabs.

138 **For instance, the Buenos Aires Lab:** Aleks Berditchwvskaia, Kathy Peach, Gina Lucarelli, and Mirko Ebelshaeuser, "Collective Intelligence for Sustainable Development: 13 Stories from the UNDP Accelerator Labs," UNDP, May 13, 2021, https://www.undp.org/acceleratorlabs/publications/collective-intelligence-sustainable-development-13-stories-undp-accelerator-labs.

138 **In 2021, UNDP achieved 99 percent of its four-year funding target . . . :** "Development Never Stops," UNDP Annual Report, 2021, https://annualreport.undp.org/2021/.

139 **as Nik Robinson . . . in 2018 . . . :** Afdhel Aziz, "How This Dad and His Sons Are Creating Good Citizens: A 100% Sustainable Australian Sunglass Range Made from Recycled Plastic Bottles," *Forbes*, June 17, 2020, https://www.forbes.com/sites/afdhelaziz/2020/06/17/how-this-dad-and-his-sons-are-creating-good-citizens-a-100-sustainable-australian-sunglass-range-made-from-recycled-plastic-bottles/.

139 **Robinson needed to find a way to replace . . . metal screws and hinges:** Glynis Traill-Nash, "Turning Recycled Plastic Bottles into Chic Sunnies," *The Australian*, August 21, 2020, https://www.theaustralian.com.au/business/companies/turning-recycled-plastic-bottles-into-chic-sunnies/news-story/.

139 **By August 2020, Selfridges department store in London had allocated an entire window to Robinson's sunglasses:** "Selfridges Exclusive Window Display," Good Citizens, March 2022, https://www.goodcitizens.com.au/blogs/news/selfridges-exclusive-launch-with-good-citizens.

140 **In 80 percent of US households, you will find a can of WD-40:** Douglas Martin, "John S. Barry, Main Force Behind WD-40, Dies at 84," *New York Times*, July 22, 2009, https://www.nytimes.com/2009/07/22/business/22barry1.html.

140 **Garry Ridge, who led the WD-40 company for twenty-five years before his retirement in 2022:** Matthew Cranston, "The Little-Known Aussie Behind One of the World's Top Brands," *Australian Financial Review*, August 12, 2022, https://www.afr.com/world/north-america/the-aussie-stepping-down-as-ceo-of-a-brand-everyone-knows-20220725-p5b46g.

140 **how WD-40 was the child of "rocket science":** "Fascinating Facts You Never Learned in School," WD-40 website, 2023, https://www.wd40.com/history/.

140 **Our tribe = our success. We are a tribe, and as a tribe we're here for each other as much as we're here for the company:** "2021 Annual Report," WD-40 website,

2021, https://s201.q4cdn.com/722056013/files/doc_financials/2021/AR/2021-Annual-Report.pdf.

141 **"Profit is the applause":** James F. Peltz, "Q&A: WD-40 CEO Garry Ridge Explains Company's Slick Success," *Los Angeles Times*, July 30, 2015, https://www.latimes.com/business/la-fi-qa-wd-40-20150730-story.html.

141 **By 2021, the firm was selling WD-40 in more than 176 countries worldwide. Revenue reached $488.1 million, up 19 percent over the previous fiscal year:** "2021 Annual Report," WD-40 website, 2021, https://s201.q4cdn.com/722056013/files/doc_financials/2021/AR/2021-Annual-Report.pdf.

141 **Ridge was named as one of the World's Top 10 CEOs in 2022:** Marcel Schwantes, "The World's 10 Top CEOs (They Lead in a Totally Unique Way)," *Inc. Australia*, March 29, 2017, https://www.inc-aus.com/marcel-schwantes/heres-a-top-10-list-of-the-worlds-best-ceos-but-they-lead-in-a-totally-unique-wa.html.

141 **Scientists have found that, a compelling story . . . :** Max Frenzel, "How Stories Can Influence Our Physiology," Medium, December 8, 2021, https://medium.com/yudemon/how-stories-can-influence-our-physiology-564c895973ec.

141 **Brain scientists studying MRI scans . . . :** Paul J. Zak, "Why Inspiring Stories Make Us React: The Neuroscience of Narrative," *Cerebrum* 2015 (February 2, 2015):2, https://www.ncbi.nlm.nih.gov/pmc/articles/PMC4445577/.

142 **one of the founders lost his glasses on a backpacking trip in Asia:** "How a Lost Pair of Glasses and a Friendship Disrupted the Eyewear Industry," CNBC.com, December 12, 2019, https://www.cnbc.com/amp/2019/12/12/warby-parker-how-a-lost-pair-of-glasses-disrupted-the-eyewear-industry.html.

142 **A clear, socially conscious narrative differentiated Warby Parker from its competitors:** "History," Warby Parker website, 2023, https://www.warbyparker.com/history.

142 **advertising campaign celebrating the achievements of basketball superstar Michael Jordan:** "Air Michael Jordan Nike Commercial retirement 1999," Nike ad, YouTube, https://m.youtube.com/watch?v=FZSYD5OYSqc.

143 **villagers in a remote region along the Nepal/Indian border:** Amy Corr, "For Generations, These Himalayan Villagers Have Been Land Rover's Most Loyal Fans," *Adweek*, August 9, 2018, https://www.adweek.com/creativity/for-generations-these-himalayan-villagers-have-been-land-rovers-most-loyal-fans/.

144 **she asked people "What's your most prized possession?":** Emily Spivak, "Series: The Story of a Thing," *New York Times Magazine*, 2019, https://www.nytimes.com/2019/06/19/t-magazine/andrea-bocelli-muhammad-ali-boxing-gloves.html.

144 **Robinson promised that if elected she would install a light in the front portico:** John McManus, "Taoiseach Blows Out Mary Robinson's Light," *Irish Times*, March 18, 2017, https://www.irishtimes.com/opinion/john-mcmanus-taoiseach-blows-out-mary-robinson-s-light-1.3014719.

144 **Robinson became one of the most consequential leaders in twentieth-century Ireland:** Niall O'Dowd, "President Mary Robinson: The Woman Who Changed

Ireland," Irish Central, March 10, 2023, https://www.google.com.au/amp/s/www.irishcentral.com/opinion/niallodowd/mary-robinson-woman-changed-ireland.amp.

145 **Learning theorist Jean Piaget argued that human minds can grasp pictures:** Rebecca Joy, "Abstract Thinking: What It Is, Why We Need It, and When to Rein It In," Healthline, September 5, 2019, https://www.healthline.com/health/abstract-thinking.

146 **Lego's change team eventually drew up clear plans:** Johnny Davis, "How Lego Clicked: The Super Brand That Reinvented Itself," *The Guardian*, June 4, 2017, https://amp.theguardian.com/lifeandstyle/2017/jun/04/how-lego-clicked-the-super-brand-that-reinvented-itself.

146 **symbols live at an unconscious level in the mind:** Hayley Langsdorf, "Symbols Are Short Cuts for Our Brain," Thoughts Drawn Out, June 11, 2017, https://thoughtsdrawnout.com.au/symbols-are-short-cuts-for-our-brains/.

146 **Albert Bourla . . . called the mission Project Light Speed:** "Shot of a Lifetime: How Pfizer and BioNTech Developed and Manufactured a COVID-19 Vaccine in Record Time," Pfizer website, 2023, https://www.pfizer.com/news/articles/shot_of_a_lifetime_how_pfizer_and_biontech_developed_and_manufactured_a_covid_19_vaccine_in_record_time.

146 **the executives at Patagonia, the outdoor apparel company, embarked on a quest:** Chris D'Angelo, "Patagonia Had $10 Million in Sales on Black Friday and Is Donating Every Cent to Save the Planet," *HuffPost*, November 28, 2016, https://www.huffpost.com/entry/patagonia-black-friday-record-sale.

147 **palace beekeeper John Chapple traveled to Clarence House . . . :** Josh Salisbury, "Royal Beekeeper Informs the Buckingham Palace Bees of Queen's Passing in Traditional Ritual," *Evening Standard*, September 10, 2022, https://www.standard.co.uk/news/uk/royal-beekeeper-informs-the-buckingham-palace-bees-that-the-queen-has-died-b1024779.html.

149 **One of Amazon's "working backward" rituals, its famous "6-pager":** Tim Carmody, "Working Backwards: Dave Limp on Amazon's Six Page Memo," Amazon Chronicles, October 12, 2021, https://amazonchronicles.substack.com/p/working-backwards-dave-limp-on-amazons.

150 **Amazon's e-books capturing two-thirds of the electronic book market:** Derek Haines, "Why Does the Amazon Book Market Share Dominate the Market?" Just Publishing Advice, updated April 4, 2023, https://justpublishingadvice.com/why-do-amazon-sell-more-ebooks-than-other-retailers/.

150 **it takes an average of sixty-six days for a new routine to become automatic:** James Clear, *Atomic Habits: An Easy & Proven Way to Build Good Habits & Break Bad Ones* (Avery, 2005).

Chapter 9

153 **using nature's sturdiest pattern, the hexagon, to fashion the honeycomb:** "The Hexagon," *Berkeley Economic Review*, March 8, 2022, https://econreview.berkeley.edu/the-hexagon/.

153 **ordered Chipotle to pay $25 million:** Chris Heasman, "Scandals Chipotle Can Never Live Down," Mashed, September 22, 2020, https://www.mashed.com/250704/scandals-chipotle-can-never-live-down/.

154 **hired food safety expert Mansour Samadpour:** Susan Berfield, "Inside Chipotle's Contamination Crisis," *Bloomberg Business Week*, December 22, 2015, https://www.bloomberg.com/features/2015-chipotle-food-safety-crisis/.

154 **Samadpour was a busy bee:** Aaron Schnoor, "How Chipotle Overcame a 3-Year Scandal to Become a Restaurant Empire," Better Marketing, March 1, 2021, https://bettermarketing.pub/how-chipotle-overcame-a-3-year-scandal-to-become-a-restaurant-empire-ea4e4d271f3b.

155 **Bechbretha (old Irish bee laws):** Thomas Charles-Edwards and Fergus Kelly, *Bechbretha: An Old Irish Law-Tract on Bee-Keeping* (Dublin Institute for Advanced Studies, 1983).

156 **In a December 2021 live-streamed event:** "Toyota Motor Corporation unveils full global battery electric line-up," Toyota Press Release, December 2021.

156 **Toyota Production System (TPS):** "Toyota Production System," Global Toyota, 2023, https://global.toyota/en/company/vision-and-philosophy/production-system/.

157 **with revenues of $257 billion in 2022:** "Toyota's net revenue 2012–2022," Statista, September 2022, https://www.statista.com/statistics/262752/total-net-revenues-of-toyota/.

158 **By 2022, more than four million business owners had flocked to the Shopify software:** "2021 Was Shopify's Biggest Year Ever. 2022: Let's Go!" Shopify website, February 2021.

158 **In 2021, Shopify grew by 76 percent:** Vipal Monga, "Shopify's Secret Weapon Is Thousands of New Business Owners," *Wall Street Journal*, February 16, 2021, https://www.google.com.au/amp/s/www.wsj.com/amp/articles/shopifys-secret-weapon-is-thousands-of-new-business-owners-11613484000.

158 **earned Shopify a place on *Fast Company*'s 2022 list of the World's 50 Most Innovative Companies:** "The World's Most Innovative Companies of 2022," *Fast Company*, 2022, https://www.fastcompany.com/most-innovative-companies/2022.

159 **Nike's digital spaces:** Ian Stonebrook, "At Nike, the Virtual Is Reality," Boardroom, December 2021, https://boardroom.tv/nike-2021-year-in-review/.

159 **The company's digital initiatives drove 2020 profits up 196 percent:** Shelley Kohan, "Nike Annual Profits Soar 196%, Best in Company History," *Forbes*, June 2021, https://www.forbes.com/sites/shelleykohan/?sh=3ed1a5c426b4.

159 ***Forbes* named Donahoe its 2021 CEO of the Year:** Chris Walton, "Retail Awards - Amazon, Kroger, Nike, & More 'Just Walk Out' with This Year's Hardware,"

Forbes, December 2021, https://www.forbes.com/sites/christopherwalton/2021/12/27/2021-retail-awardsamazon-kroger-nike--more-just-walk-out-with-this-years-hardware/.

159 **Starbucks . . . visits dropped 16/1 percent . . . followed by another 18.4 percent in February:** Ethan Chernofsky, "Starbucks - 2021 Recap," Placer, January 31, 2022, https://www.placer.ai/blog/starbucks-2021-recap.

159 **more than thirty-two thousand retail locations:** "Starbucks to Transform U.S. Store Portfolio by Building on the Strength of Digital Customer Relationships and the Convenience of the Starbucks App," Starbucks Stories and News, n.d., https://stories.starbucks.com/press/2020/starbucks-to-transform-us-store-portfolio-by-building-on-the-strength-of-digital-customer-relationships/.

160 **According to Boston Consulting Group:** "Digital Transformation," Boston Consulting Group website, 2023, https://www.bcg.com/capabilities/digital-technology-data/digital-transformation/overview.

160 **PayPal's customer base grew from about 160 million to more than 400 million:** Rachel Armstrong, "PayPal Says 'Buy Now, Pay Later' Volumes Surged 400% on Black Friday," Reuters, December 3, 2021, https://www.reuters.com/markets/us/paypal-says-buy-now-pay-later-volumes-surged-400-black-friday-2021-12-03/.

161 **employees were experiencing from financial stress:** David Gelles, "How One CEO Improved Results by Investing in His Workers," *Time*, June 30, 2022, https://time.com/6192213/paypal-daniel-schulman-capitalism/.

161 **PayPal won honors as a *Forbes* World's Best Employer:** Samantha Todd-Ryan, "Meet the World's Best Employers 2021," *Forbes*, October 12, 2021, https://www.forbes.com/sites/samanthatodd/2021/10/12/meet-the-worlds-best-employers-2021/?sh=1ce535d23b37.

161 **PayPal's shares surged 111 percent in 2020**: Sergei Klebnikov, "PayPal Stock Crash Wipes Out Over $50 Billion in Market Value After Company Lowers Profit Outlook," *Forbes*, February 2, 2022, https://www.forbes.com/sites/sergeiklebnikov/2022/02/02/paypal-stock-crash-wipes-out-over-50-billion-in-market-value-after-company-lowers-profit-outlook/amp/.

161 ***Fortune*'s 2021 list of the World's 50 Greatest Leaders ranked Schulman:** "The World's 50 Greatest Leaders," *Fortune*, 2021, https://fortune.com/worlds-greatest-leaders/2021/dan-schulman/.

161 **In Celtic tradition a buyer never paid for a swarm of bees:** James Slaven, "The Celtic Lore of the Honey Bee," Owlcation, August 2022, https://owlcation.com/humanities/Celtic-Lore-of-the-Honey-Bee.

162 **recognized as a shrewd billionaire businessman:** Peter Lee, "The Bankers That Define the Decades: Jamie Dimon, JP Morgan Chase," Euromoney, June 10, 2019, https://www.euromoney.com/article/b1fq6yftgm9nrv/the-bankers-that-define-the-decades-jamie-dimon-jpmorgan-chase.

162 **introduced a mobile app:** Hugh Son, "At JPMorgan, Your Performance Review Is Now. And Now. And Now . . . ," *Bloomberg*, March 9, 2017, https://www

.bloomberg.com/news/articles/2017-03-09/at-jpmorgan-your-performance-review-is-now-and-now-and-now.

162 **by 2022 the company had generated record revenue . . . for a fifth year in a row:** Jamie Dimon, "Chairman & CEO Letter to Shareholders," JP Morgan Annual Report, 2022, https://reports.jpmorganchase.com/investor-relations/2022/ar-ceo-letters.htm.

162 **change would require a radical shift in behavior:** Peter Cohen, "Adobe's Stock Up 68% Since It Dumped Stack Ranking, Will Microsoft's Follow?" *Forbes*, November 29, 2013, https://www.forbes.com/sites/petercohan/2013/11/29/adobes-stock-up-68-since-it-dumped-stack-ranking-will-microsofts-follow/amp/.

163 **Adobe reaped a financial windfall as 2021 revenues raced to a record $15.79 billion:** Sabrina Escobar, "Adobe Stock Sinks as Fiscal 2022 Forecast Falls Short of Estimates," *Barron's*, December 16, 2021, https://www.google.com.au/amp/s/www.barrons.com/amp/articles/adobe-adbe-stock-earnings-guidance-51639662909.

163 **earn the company eighth place on *Forbes*'s list of World's Best Employers:** Elisabeth Brier, "World's Best Employers," *Forbes*, October 2022, https://www.forbes.com/lists/worlds-best-employers/?sh=388b14f91e0c.

164 **Southwest . . . biggest operational meltdown in its five-decade history:** Ian Duncan and Justin George, "Southwest Didn't Heed Calls to Upgrade Tech Before Meltdown, Unions Say," *Washington Post*, December 28, 2022, https://www.washingtonpost.com/transportation/2022/12/28/southwest-airlines-flight-cancellations/.

164 **The airline's chief operating officer, Andrew Watterson, blamed . . . :** Neil Raden, "What Just Happened to Southwest Airlines? A Cautionary Tale About Underfunding Key IT Technology," Diginomica, January 3, 2023, https://diginomica.com/what-just-happened-southwest-airlines-cautionary-tale-about-underfunding-key-it-technology?amp.

164 **Bob Jordan apologized to customers:** Douglas B. Laney, "20 Ways to Avert Your Company's Own Southwest Meltdown," *Forbes*, January 5, 2023, https://www-forbes-com.cdn.ampproject.org/c/s/www.forbes.com/sites/douglaslaney/2023/01/05/20-ways-to-avert-your-companys-own-southwest-meltdown/amp/.

164 **According to Captain Casey Murray . . . :** David Goldman, "Why Southwest Is Melting Down," CNN Business, December 28, 2022, https://amp.cnn.com/cnn/2022/12/27/business/southwest-airlines-service-meltdown/index.html.

165 **Southwest Airlines had invested $800 million in digital transformation:** Isaac Sacolick, "5 Questions CIOs Must Ask After Southwest Airlines' Failure," CIO, January 4, 2023, https://www.cio.com/article/418756/5-questions-cios-must-ask-after-southwest-airlines-failure.html/amp/.

165 **Bob Jordan told frustrated employees . . . "Part of what we're suffering is a lack of tools":** Forrest Brown, "Massive Southwest Airlines Disruption Leaves Customers Stranded and Call Centers Swamped," CBS News, December 26,

2022, https://www.cbsnews.com/amp/sacramento/news/massive-southwest-airlines-disruption-leaves-customers-stranded-and-call-centers-swamped/.

167 **Vodafone's leaders, knowing full well that their company was the most unpopular provider in the UK:** "Vodafone Worst Mobile Provider for Customer Satisfaction for Seventh Year Running," Which Press Release, April 2018, https://press.which.co.uk/whichpressreleases/vodafone-worst-mobile-provider-for-customer-satisfaction-for-seventh-year-running/.

167 **Vodafone offered "profound apologies to anyone affected by these errors":** Julia Kollewe, "Vodafone Fined £4.6m for Serious Breaches of Consumer Protection Rules," *The Guardian*, October 26, 2016, https://amp.theguardian.com/business/2016/oct/26/vodafone-fined-46m-for-serious-breaches-of-consumer-protection-rules.

167 **A 2016 review by the Telecom regulator discovered a range of issues:** Steve McCaskill, "Vodafone Is Fined £4.6m for Billing and Complaints Failures," Silicon, October 2016, https://www.silicon.co.uk/networks/carriers/vodafone-ofcom-fine-billing-complaints-199549/amp.

167 **In October 2016, the UK watchdog slapped the telco with a £4.63 million ($6.27 million) fine:** Henrico Dolfing, "Vodaphone's $59 Million Customer Relationship Disaster," Henrico Dolfing website, May 2020, https://www.henricodolfing.com/2020/05/case-study-vodafone-crm-disaster.html?m=1.

168 **Bees use the dimensions of their bodies to measure spaces:** "How do honeybees construct their hive?" Herstat, n.d., https://herstat.com/propolis-information/how-do-bees-make-honeycomb-for-their-hive.html.

168 **Copé-Zimmermann Law, which mandated greater gender diversity:** Avivah Wittenberg-Cox, "France Unanimously Votes Gender Quotas for Executive Leadership," *Forbes*, May 15, 2021, https://www.forbes.com/sites/avivahwittenbergcox/2021/05/15/france-unanimously-votes-gender-quotas-for-executive-leadership/?sh=20f6fa0d2b8e.

168 **caused a remarkable rebalancing of the country's corporate boards:** Madeline Hislop, "French Parliament Unanimously Votes in Favour of Gender Quotas for Executive Leadership," Women's Agenda, May 17, 2021, https://womensagenda.com.au/latest/french-parliament-unanimously-votes-in-favour-of-gender-quotas-for-executive-leadership/.

169 **only 5 percent of CEOs across Europe were women:** Chloe Taylor, "Under 5% of Europe's Top Companies Have a Female CEO, Study Finds," CNBC, January 16, 2020, https://www.cnbc.com/amp/2020/01/16/under-5percent-of-europes-top-companies-have-a-female-ceo.html.

169 **women working full-time in the US earned only 79 percent of men's wages:** Glenn Kessler, "Here Are the Facts Behind That '79 Cent' Pay Gap Factoid," *Washington Post*, April 14, 2016, https://www.washingtonpost.com/news/fact-checker/wp/2016/04/14/here-are-the-facts-behind-that-79-cent-pay-gap-factoid/.

169 **Buck established the Pathways Project:** Alicia Petross, "How We're Holding Ourselves Accountable and Being Transparent in Our Diversity, Equity and Inclusion Goals," Hershey's website, 2020, https://www.thehersheycompany.com/en_us/home/newsroom/blog/how-were-holding-ourselves-accountable-and-being-transparent-in-our-diversity-equity-and-inclusion-goals.html.

169 **According to Alicia Petross:** Alicia Petross, "Empowered by Pathways: Embarking on an Equitable Future Together," Hershey's website, 2020, https://www.thehersheycompany.com/en_us/home/newsroom/blog/empowered-by-pathways-embarking-on-an-equitable-future-together.html.

170 **The diversity, equity, and inclusion (DEI) focus at Hershey proved good for business . . . :** Paul A. Argenti, Jenifer Berman, Ryan Calsbeak, and Andrew Whitehouse, "The Secret Behind Successful Corporate Transformations," *Harvard Business Review*, September 14, 2021, https://hbr.org/2021/09/the-secret-behind-successful-corporate-transformations.

170 **That same year, *Forbes* named Hershey the World's Most Female-Friendly Company:** Samantha Todd-Ryan, "Meet the World's Top Female-Friendly Companies 2021," *Forbes*, November 2, 2021, https://www.forbes.com/sites/samanthatodd/2021/11/02/meet-the-worlds-top-female-friendly-companies-2021/?sh=4c7edc241007.

170 **Buck did not rest on her laurels, however:** Sean Adams, "The Hershey Co. Is the World's Most Female-Friendly, *Forbes* Says," Pennlive, November 4, 2021, https://www.google.com.au/amp/s/www.pennlive.com/life/2021/11/the-hershey-company-is-the-worlds-most-female-friendly-according-to-forbes.html.

170 **Thomas Seeley, the world's leading expert on bee behavior, discovered how bees prioritize the right infrastructure:** Carl Zimmer, "The Secret Life of Bees."

Chapter 10

173 **make looping flights over . . . the tree cavity:** Dean Haley, "Moving Native Bees," Australian Native Bee, 2016, https://www.australiannativebee.com/2015/09/03/moving-native-bees/.

173 **They fly up to ten kilometers a day:** "Bees Behaviour During Foraging," Apiculture factsheet, Minister of Agriculture, Food and Forestry, British Columbia, https://www2.gov.bc.ca/assets/gov/farming-natural-resources-and-industry/agriculture-and-seafood/animal-and-crops/animal-production/bee-assets/api_fs111.pdf.

173 **in twelve- to sixteen-hour shifts in order to produce a single drop of honey:** "Short but Mighty: The Stages of Life," Bee Pods website, January 2022, https://www.beepods.com/short-but-mighty-the-stages-of-life/.

174 **managed to propel Microsoft to a $1 trillion valuation:** Stephen Grocer, "Microsoft Touches $1 Trillion Value, Signaling Big Tech's Stockmarket Comeback," *New York Times*, April 25, 2019, https://www.nytimes.com/2019/04/25/business/dealbook/microsoft-1-trillion.html.

174 **the trillion-dollar milestone was "not meaningful":** Roma Christian, "Microsoft CEO 'Disgusted' by Staff Celebrating Trillion Dollar Milestone," Channel News, May 3, 2019, https://www.channelnews.com.au/microsoft-ceo-disgusted-by-staff-celebrating-trillion-dollar-milestone/.

175 ***Business Insider* reported . . . :** Paulina Duran, "Australia Bank NAB's CEO to Take Long Holiday Around Inquiry Report Release," *Business Insider*, December 17, 2018, https://www.businessinsider.com/r-australia-bank-nabs-ceo-to-take-long-holiday-around-inquiry-report-release-2018-12?amp.

175 **In an interview with CRN . . . :** Donna Goodson, "Microsoft CEO Satya Nadella's Plan to Unlock 'Trillions of Dollars' in Partner Opportunity," CRN, April 12, 2021, https://www.crn.com/news/cloud/microsoft-ceo-satya-nadella-s-plan-to-unlock-trillions-of-dollars-in-partner-opportunity.

176 **grew revenues from $77.8 billion in 2013 to $203 billion by 2022:** Microsoft market cap, 2023, https://companiesmarketcap.com/microsoft/revenue/.

177 **Bees . . . with a high "flicker threshold":** Sharla Riddle, "How Bees See and Why It Matters," Bee Culture, May 20, 2016, https://www.beeculture.com/bees-see-matters/.

178 **Marisa Thalberg, executive vice president, . . . :** Vicki Salemi, "Here's How One Essential Retailer Is Celebrating Their 100-Year Anniversary," *Forbes*, March 9, 2021, https://www.forbes.com/sites/vickisalemi/2021/03/09/heres-how-one-essential-retailer-is-celebrating-their-100-year-anniversary/.

178 **founded in 1921 by L. S. Lowe . . . :** "Our History," Lowe's website, 2023, https://corporate.lowes.com/who-we-are/our-history.

179 **Award-winning country music star Kane Brown:** "Lowe's Extending Plan to Give $100M to Help Communities Across the U.S.," Outsider, March 7, 2022, https://outsider.com/news/lowes-extending-plan-give-100m-help-communities-across-us.

185 **"Day 1" philosophy:** Justin Bariso, "This Original Letter from Jeff Bezos to Amazon Shareholders Teaches Some Extraordinary Lessons in Leadership," *Inc. Australia*, April 20, 2017, https://www.inc-aus.com/justin-bariso/20-years-ago-amazons-jeff-bezos-sent-an-extraordinary-letter-to-shareholders.html.

186 **delivered revenues of $469 billion+:** Amazon revenue, July 2023, Macro trends website, https://www.macrotrends.net/stocks/charts/AMZN/amazon/revenue#:~:text=Amazon%20annual%20revenue%20for%202021,a%2037.62%25%20increase%20from%202019.

186 **In the 1930s, company founder Yun Dokjeong . . . :** "Our Story," AmorePacific website, n.d., https://www.apgroup.com/int/en/about-us/amorepacific/our-story/our-story.html.

187 **eventually finding success on home-shopping programs.** Gabey Goh, "Case Study: How AmorePacific Created Space for Cushion," Campaign website, March 30, 2016, https://www.campaignasia.com/article/case-study-how-amorepacific-created-space-for-cushion/406678.

189 **Dr. Karikó tried to convince at least thirty potential collaborators:** Kate Guest, "Meet the Women Behind the Vaccines, Helping to Find a Path Out of the Coronavirus Pandemic," ABC News, March 7, 2021, https://amp.abc.net.au/article/13219120.

190 **she and Weissman won the Breakthrough Prize in Life Sciences:** Alex Knapp, "2022 Breakthrough Prizes Announced: mRNA Vaccine Pioneers Awarded $3 Million," *Forbes*, September 9, 2021, https://www.forbes.com/sites/alexknapp/2021/09/09/2022-breakthrough-prizes-announced-mrna-vaccine-pioneers-awarded-3-million/.

INDEX

AAADoorShop (pseudonym), 95–100, 107
A1ActiveWear (pseudonym), 35–37, 64–65, 101–4
Aberdeen, Scotland, 116
Absolut, 93
Accelerator Labs, 137–38
Accenture, 50, 54–55, 193
accountability, 105, 106, 169
Adobe, 162–63
Agile Pattern, 88–89
agility, 88–89, 145, 163
Airbus A380, 55–56
Akira, Noah (pseudonym), 42, 45
Alexa, 186
Ali, Muhammad, 144
alignment, on vision, 53–56
Alitalia Airlines, 80
Alliance for Water Stewardship (AWS), 53
Amazon, 32, 51–52, 59, 62, 64, 76, 149–50, 157, 158, 185–86
ambition, 82
AmorePacific, 85–86, 186–87
AMOS-6 communication satellite, 188
Amsterdam, Netherlands, 120–21
Andover, Mass., 19
"And" Pattern, 26–28
ANZ (Australia and New Zealand Banking Group), xiv, 174–75
Apple, 62–64, 66, 67, 109, 110, 174, 186
Apple Maps, 41–42
Aquafina, 11
Architects' Journal, 81
artificial intelligence (AI), 160
Askar, Omar, 52–53
assumptions, 70–73, 126
Atlas missiles, 140
Audible, 186
Australia and New Zealand Banking Group (ANZ), xiv, 174–75
AWS (Alliance for Water Stewardship), 53

bad habits, breaking, 149
Bad News Pattern, 33–34
Barclays, 119
Barnes, J. A., 5
Barron's magazine, 33
Barry, Nathan, 128
Bassett, Dave "Harry," 148
Bateson, Gregory, 175
Beaumont, Mike (pseudonym), 43, 44
Bechbretha (bee laws), 155
bee colonies
- capabilities of, 184
- collective decisions in, 31, 77, 78
- compensation for, 155, 161
- continuous adaptation for, 193
- ecosystem of, xiii, 177
- excitement for change in, 90, 92
- experimentation by, 59, 60, 75, 76
- focus on target for, 188, 189
- Hive LENS process in, 197
- infrastructure for, 153, 170–71
- long-term success for, 173
- looking beyond by, 21
- measurements in, 168
- mobilization for change in, 115
- Nine Laws of Group Dynamics for, xv–xx
- nonlinear causality for, 132
- operating models of, 60–61

bee colonies (*cont'd*)
patterns of behavior in, 23
planning for change in, 41, 46, 56
processes in, 154
and ritual of "telling the bees," 147
roles in, 95, 96, 100
story telling about, 141
tipping point for, 135
welfare of ecosystem and, 51, 53
Begor, Mark, 106
Behavioral Insights Team, 120
Berlin, Germany, 53–54
Bertalanffy, Ludwig von, 6
Best Buy, 32–33
Bezos, Jeff, 59, 62, 76, 149, 185–86
bifurcation, 135
BIM (Building Information Modeling) software, 123–25
BioNTech, 16, 17, 19, 189–90
Bloomberg News, 68
Bocelli, Andrea, 144
Bock, Hazel (pseudonym), 130, 131
Boeing, 65
Boston Consulting Group, 160
Bourla, Albert, 15–20, 146, 193
BPAY, 160
brain, narratives/symbols and, 141, 146
Brandenburg airport, 53–54
Breakthrough Prize in Life Sciences, 190
Broman, Gunnar, 93
bromate, 12–13
Brown, Kane, 179
Buck, Michele, 169–70
Buenos Aires, Argentina, 138
Building Information Modeling (BIM) software, 123–25
bureaucracies, 86–90
Bureaucracy Pattern, 87, 89
Business Insider, 175
Businessland, 109
Business Strategist role, 97–99
butterfly effect, 23, 132–33

CAC 40 stock exchange, 168
Cameron, David, 120
Canada, 70–71
case for change, 41–58
with alignment around vision, 53–56
and avoiding reactive response, 42–46
best action for ecosystem in, 51–53
envisioning future in, 47–48
with fast-forward thinking, 48–51
and high-level change plan, 56–58
Catastrophizing Pattern, 124–25
Catmull, Ed, 110
Celtic lore and traditions, 141, 161
Center for Alternative Fuels and Engine Emissions, 110–11
Center for Innovations Development, 138
Centers for Disease Control and Prevention, 113
Challenger catastrophe, 33–35
change
complexity and, 2–4
developing capability for, 179–85
failed attempts at, 2–5, 7–13
Five Ps for, 187, 190, 191
generating buzz for, 90–94
Hive LENS process for lasting, 13–20
intelligence for types of, 181–82
long-term, 173–91
mindsets about, 4–7
multiple perspectives about, 31–35
pushing too hard for, 116–19
sensemaking about, 126–29
viral, 137–40
see also case for change
Change Leader role, 96–101, 104, 106
Change Operating Model, 60–61
Change Passengers, 101–6
Change Type Model, 181–82
chaos theory, 132, 133
Chapple, John, 147
Chattanooga, Tenn., 179
Chesterman, Richard N., 105
Chipotle Mexican Grill, 153–55
choice, freedom of, 120–21
circular group behavior, 176
Cisco, 91–92
Clancy Builders (pseudonym), 42–46, 123–26
Clear-Sighted Pattern, 36–37
CNN network, 164
Coaching Pattern, 108–10
Coca-Cola, 7–12
Collaborative Pattern, 104
collective decisions, 31–32, 151
Collins, Chris, 154, 155
Colony Collapse Disorder, xix–xx
command-and-control organizations, 4

communication, 55–56, 126–29, 155
competence, assumption of, 71
complexity, 2–4, 50
connectedness, 29, 31. *see also* Law of Connectedness (2)
context. *see* Law of Context (5)
continuous adaptation, 193–94
ConvertKit, 128
Copé-Zimmermann Law, 168
Cornell, Tony, 70, 71
CorpTech, 105
Costner, Kevin, 57
cost-plus contracts, 26
COVID-19 pandemic
  digital technology in, 91, 157–61, 186
  ecosystem welfare in, 51–52
  group intelligence in, 1
  new work habits during, 73–74
  reality for businesses in, 35–37
  vaccine program, 15–20, 146, 189
crisis management, 64–65
critical change decisions, 77–94
  in bureaucracies, 86–90
  front-line problem-solving for, 83–86
  generating buzz for change, 90–94
  solutions from Hive Mind, 78–81
  top-down, 81–83
critical mass. *see* tipping point
CRM (customer relationship management) system, 167
CRN magazine, 175
Cromology, 84, 178
crossed wires. *see* miscommunication
Cruz, Ethan (pseudonym), 98–99
Crystal Pepsi, 77–78
culture, 23–24, 187
Cushion Compact, 85–86, 186–87
customer relationship management (CRM) system, 167

Dasani, 7–12
Dash, Eric, 29
dashboards, 170
Day 1 philosophy, 185–86
decision-making, 45, 81–83, 89–90. *see also* critical change decisions
DEI (diversity, equity, and inclusion) efforts, 169–70
Delivery Lead role, 97–99
Detroit, Mich., 11
Diamond Crystal Salt, 74
Dieselgate, 110–11
digital technology, 91, 157–61, 186
Dimon, Jamie, 161–62
diversity, equity, and inclusion (DEI) efforts, 169–70
Doha, Qatar, 90–91
Donahoe, John, 159
"Done To" Pattern, 102–3, 105
Dow Jones Sustainability Index, xiv, 174
Drnec, Harry, 89–90
DuluxGroup, 83–84, 177–78
Dyson, James, 78–79
Dyson Group, 78–79

EADS, 56
Echo, 59
E.coli outbreaks, at Chipotle, 153–55
ecosystem model of change, 2, 5–7, 62, 182, 194–95
ecosystem(s)
  adaptation in, 116
  bee's view of, 177
  cocreation of, 96
  considering welfare of, 51–53
  emergence in, 79
  group intelligence in, xiii
  mapping, 29–31
  Nine Laws of Group Dynamics in, 195
  seeing patterns in, 22–23
  tipping points in, 151
  unintended consequences in, 132, 133
Edison, Thomas, 68
Ek, Daniel, 66–68
Elizabeth Arden Inc., 57–58
Elizabeth II, Queen, 147
eLWIS project, 101
embeddedness. *see* Law of Embeddedness (6)
emergence, 79
emotional quotient (EQ), 2, 5, 6, 14, 181, 195
English Football League, 148
Equifax, 106
Evans, Doug, 68
Experiment (Hive LENS process)
  avoiding leadership mistakes, 95–113
  carrying change passengers, 101–6
  change leader role, 96–101
  conducting research experiments, 65–70

Experiment (Hive LENS process) (*cont'd*)
debunking false assumptions, 70–73
defined, 14
dismantling bureaucracies, 86–90
emerging Hive Mind solutions, 78–81
failing to live group values, 110–13
front-line problem-solving, 83–86
generating buzz for change, 90–94
making critical change decisions, 77–94
measuring impacts, 73–76
and micromanaging, 107–10
with operating model, 60–65
in Pfizer's vaccine program, 17
testing new patterns, 59–76
and top-down decision-making, 81–83
Experimental Pattern, 69
Experts Rule Operating Model, 62–63

Facebook, 188
FA Cup (Football Association Challenge Cup), 148
Falcon 9 rocket, 188
Farrell, Roisin (pseudonym), 180
Fast Company, 158
Fast-Forward Thinking, 48–51
Federal Reserve System, 31
FedEx, 47–48
feedback, 77–78, 163
Feynman, Roger, 33–35
Fields, Mark, 66
Finea, Ireland, xiii, 115–16, 126
Fire Phone, 59
Fisher, Tony, 70–71
Five Ps for change, 187, 190, 191
Fleming, Alexander, 3
focus, maintaining, 187–91
Football Association Challenge Cup (FA Cup), 148
Forbes magazine, 39, 85, 86, 161, 163, 170
Ford Edge, 66
Ford F-Series trucks, 70
Ford Motor Company, 65–66, 69–70
Ford Mustang, 70
Ford Taurus, 70
Forward-Thinking Pattern, 45–46
fractals, 22
France, 55–56, 126–27, 168–69
Fraser-Pryce, Shelly-Ann, 91
frictionless interactions, 91–92
front-line employees, 83–86
Fuld, Richard, Jr., 22, 29
fundraiser for the earth, 146–47
Fuschl, Austria, 89
future, envisioning, 47–48

Galaxy Fold, 72
Garden Bridge, 81
Garnier, Juliette (pseudonym), 117–19, 179–85
Gates, Bill, 69
Geek Squad, 32–33
gender equality, 168–70
Germany, 17, 53–56, 189
Getco, 45
Gething, Vaughan, 120
Gladwell, Malcolm, 136
Goh, Hup Jin, 83, 177, 178
Goldner, Brian, 38–39
Goldstein, Seth (pseudonym), 129
Goleman, Daniel, 5
Gonzalez, Diego (pseudonym), 25
Good Citizens, 139
Google, 41, 92
GQ. *see* group intelligence quotient
Grayston, Nick, 86–87, 89
Great Dividing Range, xx, 190, 195
Great Recession, 29, 136, 176
Grocer magazine, 9
group intelligence (Hive Mind), xiii
ambition without, 82
case for change to harness, 42
for collective decisions, 31–32
in COVID-19 pandemic, 1
in dangerous transitions, 194
effectively managing, 23
emerging solutions from, 78–81
failure to respect, 160
for front-line problem solving, 85
generating a buzz about change, 91
Hive LENS and, 14–20
for innovation, 64, 67
leader's activation of, 96
in Learning Pattern, 183
for long-term change, 173–74
for looking beyond, 21, 39
measurements that foster, 76
missions that capture, 50–51
nudging to harness, 119
old habits and, 175
purpose and, 53

routines in, 150–51
to see patterns, 26–28
to shift mental maps, 65
on stakeholder needs, 51–52
strengthening, 185
tools to harness, 157
for viral change, 137–40
and vision for change, 46
whole vs. sum of parts in, 80
group intelligence quotient (GQ), 2, 6, 14, 181
Guardia Civil police service, 54–55
Guardian, 51–52

habits, 147–51, 174–77
Hall, Alexandra, 87
Hammond, Jack (pseudonym), 24–27, 129–32
Hangouts, Google, 92
hard contracts, 26
Harvard Business Review, 32, 33
Harvard University, 170
Hasbro, 38–39
Heraclitus, 133
Hershey Company, 169–70
high-level change plans, 56–58
Himalayas, 143
Hive LENS process
about, 13–15
in bee colonies, 197
continuous adaptation with, 193–94
in COVID vaccine program, 15–20
in meetings, 184
see also specific steps
Hive Mind. *see* group intelligence
Hoffman, Evander (pseudonym), 107–9
Højer, Jesper, 101
Honda, 65
Houlihan, Patrick, 83–84, 177–78
Huawei Technologies Co., 72
Human Factors Lab, 73–74
humility, 80–81
Hurst, Toni (pseudonym), 124

IBG YBG issue, 29
IBM Australia, 105
Iceland, 121
Ill-Equipped Pattern, 165–66
Incyte, 84–85
influencers, 5
infrastructure, 153–71, 170–71
digital technology, 157–60
performance/reward systems, 160–63
policies and processes, 154–57
progress tracking, 168–71
tools for well-equipped groups, 163–67
integrity, 111–12
intelligence quotient (IQ), 2, 4, 6, 14, 181, 195
International Aid Transparency Index, 139
International Amateur Athletic Federation, 90–91
iPhone, 63
iPod, 174
IQ. *see* intelligence quotient
Ireland, xiii, 115–16, 126, 144–45, 155

Jackson, Jamal (pseudonym), 95–100, 107–8
James, Harold, 29
Jansen, Kathrin, 16–18
Jet Propulsion Laboratory, 75
jidoka, 156
Jobs, Steve, 62–63, 109–10
Johnson, Boris, 81
Johnson, Kevin, 159–60
Joly, Hubert, 32–33
Jones, Vinnie, 148
Jordan, Bob, 164–66
Jordan, Michael, 142
Joyce, Thomas, 44–45
JPMorgan Chase & Co., 161–62
JUB, 84, 178
Juicero, 68
Jupiter (god), 133
just-in-time process, 156

Kangaroo Island, Australia, xviii
Karikó, Katalin, 189–90
Kennedy Space Center, 188
Khalifa International Stadium, 91
Kieboom, Aad, 120, 121
Kindle, 149–50, 186
KISS principle, for messaging, 93
Knight Capital Group, 44–45
Knudstorp, Jørgen Vig, 49–50, 145–46
Koh, DJ, 72
Kolodny, Andrew, 112
Konzi, Akin, 79
Kotter, John, xiv

Kut, Dan (pseudonym), 117

Lake, Scott, 157
Lake Peigneur sinkhole, 74–75
Land Rover, 143
Lasseter, John, 110
Laurent, Gabrielle (pseudonym), 180
Law of Connectedness (2), xvi–xvii, 9, 52–53, 195
Law of Context (5), xviii, 10–11, 195
Law of Embeddedness (6), xviii–xix, 11, 195
Law of Multiple Perspectives (4), xvii–xviii, 10, 195
Law of Pattern Blindness, xix, 12, 176, 195
Law of Patterns (1), xv–xvi, 8–9, 23, 195
Law of Role (3), xvii, 9–10, 65, 195
Law of Tipping Point (9), xx, 13, 195
Law of Unintended Consequences (8), xix–xx, 12–13, 195
leaders, 95–113
  carrying of change passengers by, 101–6
  case for change by, 41–42
  change leader role for, 96–101
  changing of patterns by, 28–29
  experimentation by, 70
  failure to live group values for, 110–13
  foresight of, 38–39
  high-level change plans of, 56–58
  humility for, 80–81
  micromanaging vs. coaching by, 107–10
  milestones for, 167
  policy creation by, 155
  tipping point for, 135–36, 137
  vision of future for, 46
lean manufacturing, 157
Learning Patterns, 182–84
Lego, 49–50, 145–46
Lehman Brothers, 22, 29–31, 136, 176
Lexus, 156
Lidl, 100–101
Lindmark, Lars, 93
Lip Service Pattern, 112, 113
Lockheed Martin, 75
London, England, 3, 91, 132, 139
long-term change, 173–91
  avoiding old patterns for, 174–77
  celebrating milestones for, 177–79
  focus for, 187–91
  group's capability for, 179–85
  momentum for, 185–87
Look Beyond (Hive LENS process)
  and alignment around vision, 53–56
  avoiding reactive responses, 42–46
  for bees, 21
  in COVID vaccine program, 15–16
  creating case for change, 41–58
  defined, 14
  and ecosystem welfare, 51–53
  envisioning better future, 47–48
  fast-forward thinking, 48–51
  high-level change plan, 56–58
  identifying threats to survival, 21–22
  learning to see patterns, 22–29
  listening to multiple perspectives, 31–35
  mapping key patterns, 29–31
  for patterns that govern behavior, 21–40
  seeing reality of situation, 35–39
Lorentzon, Martin, 66–67
Lorenz, Edward, 23, 132–33
Lou Gehrig's disease, 156, 190
Lowe, L. S., 178
Lowe's, 178–79
Lütke, Tobias, 157
Lying Low Pattern, 136

Mackellar, Dorothea, 190
Macworld Expo, 63
Maine, xviii
Malmesbury, England, 79
Maneybhanjang, India, 143
Maps, Google, 41
Mariani, Thierry, 127
Mars Climate Orbiter (MCO), 75
Mateschitz, Dietrich, 89–90
Mate X, 72
McDermott, Mark, 18, 19
McFarlane, John, 174
McKinsey, 53, 87, 146
MCO (Mars Climate Orbiter), 75
McQueen, Emma (pseudonym), 25
measuring impact, of new pattern, 73–76
mechanistic approach to change
  in Change Type Model, 182
  described, 2
  development of, 4
  and "Done To" Pattern, 104
  operating models in, 61
  other models of change vs., 6
  at Top Choice Maintenance, 26

Mendoza, Carla (pseudonym), 117
mental maps, shifting, 65
messaging, 92–94
Metro City Hospital (pseudonym), 116–19, 179–85
micromanagement, 107–10
Micromanagement Pattern, 107–9
Microsoft, 63–64, 73–74, 92, 173–76, 193
milestones, 173–74, 177–79
miscommunication, 55–56, 126–29
mission statements, 49–51
Moderna, 189
Modesto, Calif., 52–53
Moloney, Adam (pseudonym), 123–24
momentum, 50, 185–87
moral hazard problem, 29
Morris, Donna, 162–63
Morton Thiokol, 34
motor neurone disease, 156, 190
Mulally, Alan, 65–66, 68–70
multiple perspectives, 31–35, 80. *see also* Law of Multiple Perspectives (4)
Murray, Casey, 164
Musk, Elon, 82, 188–89

Nadella, Satya, 63–64, 173–76, 193
Nagano, Japan, xviii
NASA, 8, 10, 11, 33–35, 75
National Health Service (NHS), 82–83
Naysayer Pattern, 122–23
Nestlé Carnation, 52–53
net disposable income (NDI), 161
neuroplasticity, 150
Newton, Isaac, 4
NeXT computers, 109–10
NHS (National Health Service), 82–83
Nice Guy/Gal Pattern, 25–27, 129, 130
Nike, 142, 157–59
Nine Laws of Group Dynamics
  about, xiv–xv, 7, 196
  behavior of bees and, xv–xx
  Coke's failure to obey, 7–13
  in dynamic ecosystems, 195
  see also specific laws by name
Nippon Paint, 83–84, 177–78
Nobel Prize in Medicine, 190
nonlinear causality, 132–33
North American International Auto Show, 69
Novak, David, 77–78

Nudge (Hive LENS process)
  avoiding miscommunication, 126–29
  countering objections, 121–26
  in COVID vaccine program, 18
  creating viral change, 137–40
  defined, 15
  mastering art of gentle, 120–21
  overcoming obstacles, 115–34
  pushing too hard for change, 116–19
  reaching tipping point, 135–52
  reinforcing habits with rituals, 147–51
  telling stories, 140–44
  and unintended consequences, 129–33
  using symbols, 144–47
Nudge Pattern, 125–26

objections, countering, 121–26
obstacles, overcoming, 115–34
  with gentle nudging, 120–21
  miscommunication, 126–29
  by pushing too hard for change, 116–19
  unintended consequences of, 129–33
Oman, Cathy (pseudonym), 107
100 Hometowns project, 178–79
O'Neill, Tip, 145
One Microsoft initiative, 175
One Team Operating Model, 70
Only Fools and Horses (TV series), 12
operating models, 60–65, 175
opioid epidemic, 111–13
Opioid Policy Research Collaborative, 112
Optimus, 82
Order-Taker Pattern, 8–10, 83
organ donation, 120
OxyContin, 111–13

Partnering Operating Model, 63–64, 175
Patagonia, 146–47
Patel, Blanca (pseudonym), 102
Pathways Project, 169
pattern blindness. *see* Law of Pattern Blindness
patterns, 21–40
  learning to see, 22–29
  and listening to multiple perspectives, 31–35
  looking beyond for, 21–22
  mapping, 29–31
  seeing reality of current situation, 35–39

patterns (*cont'd*)
testing new, *see* testing new patterns
watching out for old, 174–77
see also Law of Patterns (1); *specific patterns by name*
PayPal, 160–61
People, Service, Profit motto, 47–48
Pepsi, 11, 77–78
Performance Coach role, 97–99
performance management, 162–63
Peshev, Boris (pseudonym), 102
Peterson, Christopher, 58
Petross, Alicia, 169
Pfizer, 15–20, 146, 189, 193
Piaget, Jean, 145
Pidgeon, Caroline, 81
Piper Alpha oil rig explosion, 116
Pixar, 110
Poincaré, Henri, 135
Pokémon, 38
Police Scotland, 54–55
policies, 3, 155–56
Premier League, 148
Prime Now, 186
problem solving, 78–81, 83–86
processes, 4, 154–57. *see also* infrastructure
Production Operating Model, 60–61
profit, 48, 49, 141
progress tracking, 168–71
Project Earth initiative, 139
Project Light Speed, 146
Proome, Tim, 73
Punishment Pattern, 66, 67
Puppet Masters, 106–10
Purdue Pharmaceuticals, 111–13
purpose, 53
Push Back Pattern, 118
pushing too hard for change, 116–19

Queensland Health, 105
Queensland Health Enterprise Solution Transition, 105

Reactive Pattern, 43–44, 123
reactive response, 42–46
reality, of current situation, 35–39
Red Bull, 89–90
Reilly, Conor, 126
Réseau Ferré de France (RFF), 127
Revlon, 57–58
rewards, 160–62
RFF (Réseau Ferré de France), 127
Ridge, Garry, 140–41
rituals, 147–51
Robinson, Archie, 139
Robinson, Harry, 139
Robinson, Mary, 144–45
Robinson, Nik, 139–40
robotics, 72–73, 82, 160
roles
Change Leader, 96–101, 104, 106
clarifying, at outset, 105
redefining, 105, 106
see also Law of Role (3); *specific patterns by name*
Roman mythology, 133
Rowland, Bob (pseudonym), 35–36, 101–3
Rowland, Kate (pseudonym), 35–36, 64–65, 101–4
Rule-Breaking Pattern, 130–31

Sackler family, 111
safety issues, 129–32
Safety Pattern, 131
Saint Louis, Mo., 19
Saint Mary's hospital, 3
Salk, Jonas, 3
Samadpour, Mansour, 154, 155
Samsung Electronics, 72
Sandakphu, Nepal, 143
Sankar, Petra (pseudonym), 117
SAP. *see* systems applications and products
Schiphol Airport, 120–21
Schmidt, Adam (pseudonym), 43
Schulman, Dan, 160–61
Scotland, 54–55, 116
Scottish Police Authority (SPA), 54–55
Seeley, Thomas, 170–71
Selfridges, 139
Selleys adhesive products, 84, 177
sensemaking, 126–29
Seva, 128
Shakespeare, William, xiii
Sheffield United Football Club, 148
Sheffield University, xiii, 148
Shopify, 157, 158
Shortsighted Pattern, 36, 37, 101
Short-Termism Pattern, 30–31
silence, in groups, 118–19
Siloed Pattern, 15–16

silos, 15–16, 86–87
Singh, Zane (pseudonym), 107
6-pagers, 149–50
Sixty-Six Day Rule, 150–51
skills gaps, 103
Skype, 92
Slade, Asher (pseudonym), 102
Smit, Dana (pseudonym), 99
Smith, Abe (pseudonym), 125
Smith, Frederick "Fred" Wallace, 47–48
SNCF (Société Nationale des Chemins de Fer Français), 127
Snyder, Judith, 9
social network model of change
  described, 2
  development of, 5
  and "Done To" Pattern, 105
  operating models in, 62
  other models of change vs., 6
  at Top Choice Management, 26
Société Nationale des Chemins de Fer Français (SNCF), 127
Solution Design Authority, 105
Southwest Airlines, 163–66, 176
Southwest Airlines Pilots Association, 164
SPA (Scottish Police Authority), 54–55
SpaceX, 188–89
Spataro, Jared, 73–74
specialization, 4
Spielberg, Steven, 38–39
Spivack, Emily, 144
Spotify, 66–67
stakeholder misalignment, 54–55
stakeholder needs, 51–52
Starbucks, 157, 159–60
Steiner, Achim, 137–38
Sternberg, Scott, 144
storytelling, 140–44
Strengthen (Hive LENS process)
  celebrating milestones, 177–79
  defined, 15
  developing change capability, 179–85
  embracing digital technology, 157–60
  equipping group with tools, 163–67
  with infrastructure, 153–71
  for long-term change, 173–91
  maintaining focus, 187–91
  maintaining momentum, 185–87
  with performance/reward systems, 160–63
  in Pfizer's vaccine program, 18–20
  with policies and processes, 154–57
  tracking progress, 168–71
  watching out for old patterns, 174–77
Stross, Randall, 109
Suh Sungwhan, 187
Sultan, Aisha (pseudonym), 42–45, 123–26
Sunstein, Cass, 120
Super Bowl, 78
Supersonic, Dyson, 79
survival, threats to, xx, 21–22, 95, 115, 153, 171
Swain, Paula, 84
Sweet, Julie, 50, 193
symbols, 144–47
SYNC, 69
systems applications and products (SAP), 58, 100–101, 176

Target, 70–71
Tarsus Distribution, 72–73
Taylor, Frederick, 85
TCM (Top Choice Maintenance) (pseudonym), 24–27, 129–31
technology, 91, 157–61, 186. *see also* infrastructure
Temple University, 189
Tesla, 82
testing new patterns, 59–76
  conducting experiments, 65–70
  debunking assumptions, 70–73
  measuring impact during, 73–76
  redesigning operating model, 60–65
Texaco, 74–75
TfL (Transport for London), 81
Thalberg, Marisa, 178–79
Thaler, Richard, 120
Thames Water, 9
Thompson, D'Arcy Wentworth, 22
Thomson, Melissa (pseudonym), 180
Three Cs of communication, 155
Time magazine, 29
tipping point, 135–52
  reinforcing habits with rituals, 147–51
  storytelling to reach, 140–44
  symbols and, 144–47
  for viral change, 137–40
  see also Law of Tipping Point (9)
Tollens, 84

Top Choice Maintenance (TCM) (pseudonym), 24–27, 129–31
top-down decision-making, 81–83, 89
Torchynska, Ukraine, 138
Toyoda, Akio, 156
Toyota Motor Corporation, 65, 156–57
Toyota Production System (TPS), 156–57
Toys "R" Us, 39, 121–23
TPS (Toyota Production System), 156–57
Training Club app, 159
Transformers (film), 38–39
Transformers toy brand, 38–39
Transport for London (TfL), 81
trial-and-error experiments, 68
tribes, organizational, 140–41
Truth-Telling Pattern, 35
TWG (The Warehouse Group), 86–89
Two Pizza Operating Model, 62

UK. *see* United Kingdom
Ukraine, 138
UNDP (United Nations Development Programme), 137–39
unintended consequences, 129–33. *see also* Law of Unintended Consequences (8)
United Kingdom (UK), 7–12, 82–83, 89–90, 147, 167
United Nations Development Programme (UNDP), 137–39
United Nations Global Compact Conference, 139
United Nations High Commissioner for Human Rights, 145
United States, Dasani launch in UK vs., 10–11
University of Pennsylvania School of Medicine, 189
University of Szeged, 189
Unpacked event, 72
Unsupported Pattern, 180–81
US Clean Air Act, 110
US Food and Drug Administration, 17

values, living group's, 110–13
van Bedaf, Jos, 120, 121
viral change, 137–40
vision (sight), xviii, xix, 177
vision for change, 53–56
Vodafone, 167
Volkswagen (VW), 110–11, 176
von Frisch, Karl, xv, xvi, xviii, 16, 22, 29
vulnerability, 156

WAC (World Athletics Championships), 90–91
waggle dance, xv, 23, 46
Wales, 120
Walk the Talk Pattern, 113
Walmart, 186
Warby Parker, 142
Ward, Dale (pseudonym), 99
The Warehouse Group (TWG), 86–89
war rooms, 146
waste reduction, 139–40
Waterworld (film), 57, 58
Watterson, Andrew, 164
WD-40, 140–41
WebEx, 91, 92
Weinand, Daniel, 157
Weissman, Drew, 189, 190
well-equipped groups, 163–67
Well-Equipped Pattern, 166
West Virginia University, 110–11
Wilkesboro, N.C., 178
William, Terrel (pseudonym), 129–30
Windows, 63–64, 175
wisdom of the group. *see* critical change decisions
Wombat Farm, 195
Wombat Forest, 77, 90, 154, 168, 173, 193, 196
Wombat Hill, xx, 190, 195
working backward ritual, 149, 150
World Athletics Championships (WAC), 90–91

Yeats, William Butler, 193
Yoovidhya, Chaleo, 89
Yuan, Eric, 91–92
Yun Dokjeong, 186

Zasulska, Ukraine, 138
Zoom, 91–92
Zuckerberg, Mark, 188

ABOUT THE AUTHOR

SIOBHÁN MCHALE grew up in the southern Irish village of Finea, where, as an eight-year-old, she became fascinated with the bees as they swarmed in the orchard on her family's farm. Her childhood experience watching the bees launched a lifetime of research into group intelligence in human ecosystems.

Siobhán attended Sheffield University, gaining her master's degree in organizational psychology, and went on to spend the next three decades studying groups in the workplace, first as a management consultant, then as a hands-on change leader in organizations.

As an executive in charge of change in a series of international firms, she rolled up her sleeves and set to work, helping leaders at all levels make change happen. This experience taught her about the power of harnessing the Hive Mind and the group intelligence needed to create meaningful and lasting change.

One of her most successful transformational change programs took place at the Melbourne-based Australia and New Zealand Banking group (commonly known as ANZ). After seven years of hard work, ANZ went from the lowest-performing financial institution in the country to the number one bank globally on the Dow Jones Sustainability Index.

Siobhán's groundbreaking approaches drew international attention when John Kotter, Harvard's renowned Professor of Leadership and the acknowledged expert on change, assembled a case study based on her work.

Unlike the consultants, academics, and journalists writing on the topic, Siobhán has worked inside organizations as a change leader. Much of her thinking goes against the theories that have dominated the change management discipline for decades, and her ideas often shatter some prevailing myths about transformation.

McHale fervently believes that organizational leaders need a new approach to change in this era of relentless innovation, global crises, ferocious competition, and unstoppable disruption. Her real-life case studies come from groups she's worked with and approaches she's developed over the years as the executive in charge of transformation—drawing on her knowledge of how we can harness group intelligence in our human organizations to create meaningful and lasting change.

Siobhán has been recognized by Thinkers50 as someone whose ideas are "most likely to shape the future," and her first book, *The Insider's Guide to Culture Change*, won accolades as a Best Business Book of 2021 by Soundview.

Siobhán's fascination with bees continues today on her 7.5-acre farm in the foothills of Australia's Great Dividing Range, where she hosts an abundance of bees who feed on embankments of native flowers. Nothing delights her more than a spoonful of honey gathered from one of their hives.